D0085449

ART THERAPY:
An Introduction

Judith Aron Rubin

Figure 2.1 – Copyright ©Fred Babb, Torrance CA. Reprinted by permission. **Figure 4.4** –From Mr. Rogers' Neighborhood. © Family Communications, Inc. Used with permission. **Figure 10.2** – Frida Kahlo, La Columna Rota (The Broken Column). Reprinted by permission of the Instituto Nacional de Bellas Artes y Literatura, Mexico and Banco de Mexico. **Figure 10.5, 10.6** – Reprinted from *Arts in Psychotherapy*, Vol. 11, pp. 165ff, J. Wald, 1984, with permission from Elsevier Science. **Figure 10.7** – Reprinted from *Arts in Psychotherapy*, Vol. 7,No. 3, G.D. Becker, G. Cividalli, and N. Cividalli, "Psychological Considerations in the Management of Patients with Thalassaemia Major" 1980, with permission from Elsevier Science. **Figure 10.18** – Copyright © Charlotte Salomon Foundation. Reprinted by permission **Figure 10.20**– From Unforgettable Fire by the Japanese Broadcasting Association, editor. Copyright © 1977 by Nippon Hososhuppan Kyokai. Reprinted by permission of Pantheon Books, a division of Random House, Inc. **Figure 10.21** – Copyright © 1968 Education Development Center. Reprinted by permission.

The Publisher has tried in good faith to secure all permissions for copyrighted material present in this book. If material for which you or your organization own the copyright appears in this book without permission or proper credit, please contact the Publisher at Brunner/Mazel, Permissions Department, 325 Chestnut Street, Philadelphia, PA 19106.

ART THERAPY:

An Introduction

by Judith Aron Rubin

"It Is Only in Being Creative

That the Individual

Discovers the Self."

D. W. WINNICOTT

USA	Publishing Office:	BRUNNER/MAZEL *A member of the Taylor & Francis Group* 325 Chestnut Street Philadelphia, PA 19106 Tel: (215) 625-8900 Fax: (215) 625-2940
	Distribution Center:	BRUNNER/MAZEL *A member of the Taylor & Francis Group* 47 Runway Road Levittown, PA 19057 Tel: (215) 629-0400 Fax: (215) 629-0363
UK		BRUNNER/MAZEL *A member of the Taylor & Francis Group* 1 Gunpowder Square London EC4A 3DE Tel: +44 171 583 0490 Fax: +44 171 583 0581

ART THERAPY: An Introduction

Copyright © 1999 Taylor & Francis. All rights reserved. Printed in the United States of America. Except as permitted under the United States Copyright Act of 1976, no part of this publication may be reproduced or distributed in any form or by any means, or stored in a database or retrieval system, without prior written permission of the publisher.

1 2 3 4 5 6 7 8 9 0

Printed by Edwards Brothers, Lillington, NC, 1998

A CIP catalog record for this book is available from the British Library.
 ⊗ The paper in this publication meets the requirements of the ANSI Standard Z39.48-1984 (Permanence of Paper).

Library of Congress Cataloging-in-Publication Data

Rubin, Judith Aron.
    Art therapy : an introduction / by Judith Aron Rubin.
       p.   cm. — (Basic principles into practice series)
    Includes bibliographical references and index.
    ISBN 0-87630-897-3 (case : alk. paper)
    1. Art therapy.   2. Art therapy—Moral and ethical aspects.
  I. Title.   II. Series.
RC489.A7R834   1998
615.8'5156—dc21   98-35409
                                                                    CIP

ISBN 0-87630-897-3

Contents

Acknowledgements

Many people have helped in the work on this book; I can express my gratitude to only a few. My thanks to Kathryn Stern of Stern's Book Service and Magnolia Street Publishers for her assistance in helping me find my way through the recent literature on art therapy, and for the book she contributed. My gratitude to Janice Palmer of the Cultural Services Program, Duke University Medical Center, who donated a copy of *The Hospital Arts Handbook*; to Norman Goldberg of MMB Music for issues of the *International Journal of Arts Medicine*; and to those members of that group who responded to my requests for information—Dr. John Graham-Pole and Cynthia Perlis. I also want to thank the following publishers for their generosity in making recent books on art therapy available to me: Jessica Kingsley, Charles C. Thomas, Routledge, W. W. Norton, North Star Press, Thorsons, Brunner/Mazel, Taylor & Francis, and the Child Welfare Association of America.

There are many individuals to whom I am grateful for their work on the photographs which illustrate this book. Most of the illustrations are from my own files, and were shot by Norman Rabinovitz of Children's Hospital, or the Media Services of Western Psychiatric Institute & Clinic. Recent pictures were done by Jim Burke and Len Gendry of Photographic Services, Center for Instructional Development, University of Pittsburgh. In addition, some of the photographs were taken by freelance artists, such as the picture of Edith Kramer with Eleanor Roosevelt by Herschel Stroyer, and the photo of Bruce Moon by George Pugh. Several images were taken by the late Jacob Malezi, a number were photographed by Richard Hurst, and some were donated by Lynn Johnson.

Pictures of pioneers were generously provided by art therapists from their own records or the archives of others. My thanks to: Gladys Agell, Frances Anderson, Robert Ault, Sandra Graves, David Henley, Don Jones, Cliff Joseph, Edith Kramer, Mildred Lachman-Chapin, Myra Levick, Bruce Moon, Aina Nucho, Arthur Robbins, Mary Cane Robinson, Rawley Silver, Patricia St. John, Christine Turner, Harriet Wadeson, Christine Wang, and Diane Waller of Goldsmith's College in London.

Thanks to the Van Pelt Memorial Library of the University of Pennsylvania for photographs from the Margaret Naumburg archives, and to Tom and Kate Frank for a picture of Ms. Naumburg, who was Dr. Frank's mother. Thanks also to the Archives of the Pennsylvania State University, and to John Michael and Alice Schwartz Mattil for pictures of Viktor Lowenfeld. Thanks as well to Nancy Knapp, Emporia State University, and the AATA archives at the Menninger Foundation, for photographs of Florence Cane and Mary Huntoon.

Thanks to Monika Smith of the Zierer Archives at the College of New Rochelle for a picture of Edith Zierer. Thanks to Mr. Harold Dorwin of the Anacostia Museum (Smithsonian Institute) for a photograph of Georgette Powell. Thanks, too, to Dr. Janet Simon of the Western Pennsylvania School for Blind Children, for a photograph of Susan Aach, and to Edna Nyberg of the Pittsburgh Center for the Arts for pictures of women from Sojourner House in activities sponsored by the Arts Education Network.

As for the written part, I thank Natalie Gilman, my first editor on this project, for talking me into it, and my colleague Laurie Wilson, who helped me to outline the book, and who contributed a previously unpublished case study. I am grateful, too, to Suzi Tucker, who took over as editor in midstream, and whose responses helped me to improve the manuscript. Finally, I thank Lansing Hays, Toby Wahl, and Erik Shveima of Taylor & Francis, for their help in the finishing stages of what became an extended birthing process.

I am indebted to the two reviewers and to my colleague Ellie Irwin, whose comments were helpful in revising the text. I am especially grateful to my former student, Laurel Herman—an experienced editor and designer—who had just finished two years of graduate training in art therapy. Her detailed reading, questions, and ideas opened my eyes in many ways. She helped me to clarify what I was trying to say, and made useful suggestions for modifying both the format and content of the book. I also appreciate the help of the many art therapists and others in allied fields to whom I wrote or called with questions and requests, who are too numerous to name, but who were uniformly gracious and responsive.

Of course, I could never have written this book at all without my very best teachers—the patients, students, supervisees, consultees, and colleagues—from whom I have learned over the past 35 years. My gratitude for what they have taught me goes beyond words.

About Style and Saving Space

Before getting into the text, I should like to explain some stylistic decisions. Since the vast majority of art therapists are women, I have chosen to use the female pronoun when talking about the therapist. While patients are of both genders, I have arbitrarily chosen to use the masculine pronoun when referring to them in a general fashion. I hope this decision will not mislead or offend the reader, since it seems to make for a smoother flow in the text. While I have tried to be "politically correct" in terminology, I apologize in advance to anyone who feels offended by my preference for language that is familiar to me.

Because the book covers so much material, I have used two other stylistic modes to help the reader. One is the use of **boldface** type as a form of personal emphasis. Any boldface type in a quotation is *my emphasis*, and was not in the original. The second stylistic choice was putting all quotations in *italics*.

In addition, in order to reduce the amount of space needed to refer to journal articles, they have been abbreviated in the text as follows: AJAT = *The American Journal of Art Therapy*, AP = *The Arts in Psychotherapy*, AT = *Art Therapy*, *Bulletin* = *The Bulletin of Art Therapy*. Another mode of abbreviation has been to indicate only the year and first page of the article, rather than taking the space that would be required for a full reference.

The titles of some edited books which are frequently noted have also been abbreviated as follows: ATTP = *Art Therapy in Theory & Practice* (Ulman & Dachinger, eds., 1975); ATV = *Art Therapy Viewpoints* (Ulman & Levy, eds., 1981); *Advances* = *Advances in Art Therapy* (Wadeson et al., eds., 1989); *Approaches* = *Approaches to Art Therapy* (Rubin, ed., 1987); CATT = *California Art Therapy Trends* (Virshup, ed., 1993); WCAT = *Working with Children in Art Therapy* (Case & Dalley, eds., 1990). I have chosen brevity over proper academic style in order to allow more space to be used for words and pictures, as well as a list of References at the end.

For the same reason, the **publication date** of a book is not noted in the body of the manuscript, except as a means of distinguishing between one of several books by an author, and occasionally where the date of publication is germane to understanding the text. Similarly, books with more than one co-author are referred to with **et al.** Complete information about both the publication dates and collaborators can be found in the list of references.

I have occasionally referred to conference presentations, which can be found listed under the **Proceedings** in the reference section. If not otherwise indicated, the meeting referred to is the American Art Therapy Association (AATA) Conference. Other unpublished work has been cited occasionally, largely to present an accurate picture of the particular topic. My apologies to the reader for any undue frustration caused by these decisions.

Preface

Map of the Territory

ART AS A HELPER IN TIMES OF TROUBLE, *as a means of understanding the conditions of human existence and of facing the frightening aspects of those conditions, as the creation of a meaningful order offering a refuge from the unmanageable confusion of outer reality—these most welcome aids are grasped by people in distress and used by the healers who come to their assistance.*

RUDOLF ARNHEIM

Art therapy has grown so fast that, like a youngster who reaches puberty prematurely, it has sometimes seemed unable to keep up with itself. The literature, which was truly meager when I wrote my first book, has increased exponentially, and continues to grow at a rapid rate. Most books, however, like my own, have represented one individual's introduction to how he or she understands and practices art therapy.

What was needed, I felt, was an **overview of the field**, something broadly inclusive and reflective of the rich past and present of this new discipline. I had in mind an **introduction to art therapy** which could be a **guide**, a **resource**, a **sourcebook**. So when a publisher approached me with the invitation to write this text, I was delighted. My aim has been to review and to distill the story of this still-evolving profession. And I am pleased to be able to report that looking at the past as well as the present has been greatly encouraging. The field is growing, not only in size and scope, but in sophistication and sensitivity as well.

It is my wish that, despite its necessary brevity, this book will be sufficiently informative that the reader will want to explore the discipline in more detail. I shall attempt to offer a taste of some of the main ingredients of art therapy, hoping to stimulate an appetite for more substance than can be presented or digested here.

My plan is to broadly outline the history and current shape of the field, and to do so in a way that is fair and accurate. If I am successful, reading this overview will be like making an appealing new acquaintance, one the reader will want to get to know better in the future. This book is something like an aerial map of the territory, to be further explored at ground level by the interested traveller. As with a map, the reader may explore specific areas (chapters) in whatever order is most appealing.

Getting to know a person or a profession takes time. It is always risky to generalize from insufficient data. A little knowledge, in art therapy as elsewhere, can be a dangerous thing. And a little knowledge **about** art therapy is just that, only one aspect of a multifaceted discipline, with almost as many possible permutations as practitioners. No single instance represents the whole, yet each is part of a richly varied panorama. If I am successful, the overview provided in this book will give the reader an orientation with which to further explore this fascinating field.

PERSPECTIVES: PERSONAL & HISTORICAL

While I intend to present as many points of view and methodologies as possible, I realize that my psychoanalytic bias may inhibit the objectivity to which I aspire. Having been a therapist for over three decades, I have learned that it is impossible to consistently correct for the internal lenses through which you view reality. For in order to modify any distorted perception, you need to **know** it is there, and blind spots can obscure your vision. So I apologize in advance for any distorting effects of my personal theoretical lenses, and hope they will be received with tolerance.

I will try to give the reader a feeling for the drama of art therapy's development, as well as an introduction to some of the key players. Since I myself have participated over the past 35 years in a variety of ways, I shall include some personal experiences, to the extent that they seem to be illustrative of the story of art therapy.

I believe that the shape of the present can best be understood in the context of the past. Whatever kind of knowledge one wants to acquire, knowing what came before is extremely useful. In psychotherapy itself, clinicians differ greatly about the necessity of dealing with the past in the treatment. But all agree that some kind of **history** is vital for developing a sense of the problem and for deriving possible solutions. Even behavior therapists, whose focus is on the here-and-now, need to obtain what they call a **baseline** before initiating the process of psychotherapy. For this reason, each chapter includes foundations and early work in the area.

VISION: TRIPARTITE LEARNING PACKAGE

Classic Readings in Art Therapy

Because art therapy is a complex creative event, my vision of a full introduction to the field has evolved as I have worked on this book. This volume can offer the reader breadth, but it cannot provide depth. What is missing is the intimacy and immediacy of what actually goes on in art therapy, especially over time. The brief clinical vignettes and the single case study included here offer but a glimpse of the drama of the treatment situation. Writing this book has reminded me that some of the finest writing is out of print or hard to find, but might be made accessible in a book of readings. So I now plan a collection of annotated readings, entitled *Classic Readings in Art Therapy*, with an emphasis on detailed case studies, as part of a comprehensive learning package.

"Art Therapy: The Video"

When I told my husband I had signed the contract for this book, he asked if there would be a tape to accompany it, as is common in his field of speech therapy. I responded that although an audiotape would not have the same kind of value for such a visual discipline, a videotape would be extremely helpful. I had been involved in recording four art therapy pioneers on film (*Art Therapy: Beginnings*, 1974), and have also made three other films myself. This is because it seemed that only *in vivo* could the therapeutic power of art be effectively communicated. The very elements which make art therapy so powerful are difficult—if not impossible—to fully convey in words, even with pictures of the creative process and the art.

So my overall vision is to provide not only a verbal guide to the fascinating field of art therapy, but an audiovisual one as well. While the videotape will be free-standing like the book, it will further amplify what is possible in this exciting discipline. In an outreach born of unrealistic optimism about how quickly I could get started on that project, I placed a request for videos of art therapy sessions in a *Newsletter* of the American Art Therapy Association (AATA). Whether from beginning students or experienced clinicians, the videos I received were impressive. I now look forward to creating a far more energetic introduction to art therapy than words alone can accomplish, no matter how eloquent.

Words and Pictures

In a way, the complementarity of a videotape and a book parallels the nature of art therapy itself. The combination of genuine expressive art activity (Fig. 0–1) with some kind of thoughtful reflection on that process (Fig. 0–2) is really the essence of this field. In fact, it is what distinguishes it most clearly from related disciplines. In almost all approaches to art therapy, there is an image-making time and a reflection time. The proportions may vary, and the thoughtful component may be silent. Art therapy, however, is the **involved doing** (Fig. 0–3) plus the **relaxed reflection** (Fig. 0–4, p. xxv)—with or without words.

The combination, like psychotherapy plus medication for depression, is frequently more powerful than either one alone. Creating art can indeed be therapeutic, and verbal therapy can be very effective. But there is something about the two together that is really spectacular. Of course, there are times in art therapy when expressing or reflecting is the focus of a particular session or period of time, but the discipline, by definition, includes both elements. As with most alloys and hybrids, the synergistic mix is more sturdy than the individual elements alone.

Figure 0–1   A woman involved in creating.

Seeing and Doing

Although a videotape can offer useful illustration, there is nothing like observing an actual session for finding out what art therapy is all about. Even better than watching is **participating**. This kind of active and personal engagement in learning could occur in a workshop experience or in treatment—as an individual, as a member of a group, or as part of a family. Nothing conveys the power of art therapy as much as doing it, even if it is no more than a brief taste.

ART THERAPY: A RAPIDLY GROWING HYBRID

I am convinced that it is the synergistic potency of the combination of art with therapy which accounts for the extremely rapid growth of this still-young field.

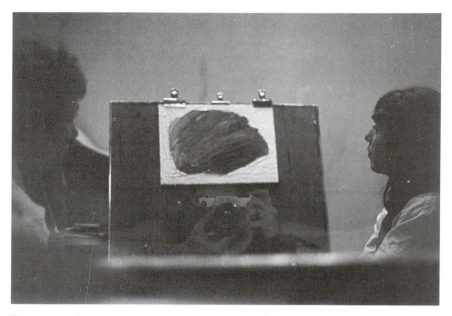

Figure 0–2 The same woman looking & reflecting.

This is especially remarkable, because the last decade has been a time of economic belt-tightening for all kinds of institutions that educate and employ art therapists in the U.S. Although the rate of growth has fluctuated, the field has been steadily expanding. New training programs and job opportunities have continued to develop, most often through the creative efforts of individual art therapists and others who believe in its potential. The American Art Therapy Association has grown in 28 years from a membership of 100 to almost 5,000. And there has been a worldwide expansion of the field of art therapy, with pioneers and new programs appearing around the globe.

While I imagine that the majority of readers of this book are likely to be students of art therapy, I hope that others will read it as well. For if more administrators, colleagues, and concerned citizens were aware of the power of art in therapy, I feel certain they would want to promote it. Perhaps even a brief introduction to this rich and wonderful discipline will stimulate the development of opportunities for more people in more places to have access to the healing power of art.

Judith Aron Rubin
October, 1998

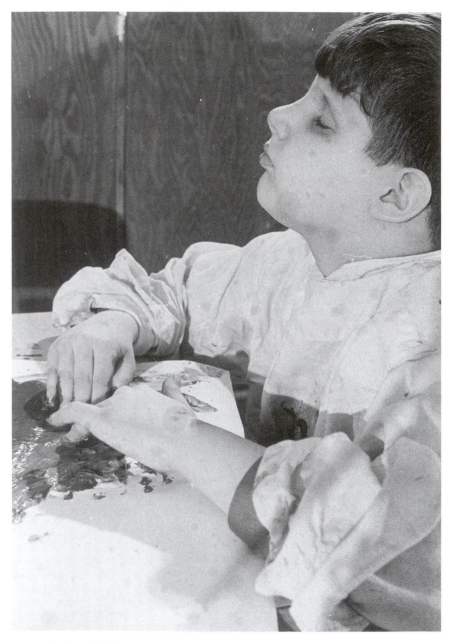

Figure 0–3   A blind boy deeply involved in fingerpainting.

Figure 0–4 The same boy talking about the experience.

Chapter 1

Previews . . .

The Many Faces of Art Therapy

What does art therapy look like? Art therapy is, always has been, and will continue to be a multifaceted field. There are a multitude of ways in which art can be used for either understanding (**assessment**) or for helping (**therapy**). But art therapy is a paradox . . . it is both extremely old and very young. Art for healing is as ancient as the drawings on the walls of caves, yet the profession itself is a child in the family of mental health disciplines. Art therapy is both primal and sophisticated, since making pictures appeals to a range of creatures, from apes to artists. Because art therapy is also extremely versatile, it has many different faces.

A Preview of Coming Attractions

Some years ago, I saw a little girl and her mother for individual art therapy, in tandem with a child psychiatrist who also met with each of them weekly. Lori would come into my art room, while Mrs. Lord saw Dr. Mann for 45 minutes. They would then switch places as well as therapists. Afterwards, Dr. Mann and I would meet and look at the pictures or sculptures done by Lori and her mom during their art sessions. Because ideas and feelings would appear in their art long before they were expressed in play or verbal therapy, Dr. Mann used to say that art therapy gave him a **"preview of coming attractions."**

Art therapy is vital for those who cannot or will not talk, like aphasic or electively mute individuals. At the same time, it is extremely helpful for people of all ages, even those who are verbally articulate. Art helps people like Lori and her mother to **see** what they are **feeling** or **thinking**. Art therapy can aid artists and nonartists alike, whether fluent or blocked.

This chapter is not a literal preview of what you will find in this book. Its images and short stories are close-up views of the art therapy terrain. That landscape will be surveyed from a more panoramic perspective in the chapters that follow, like a photograph taken with a wide angle lens. Yet, since art therapy happens between human beings—these glimpses are an attempt to capture some of the intimacy of the process.

We shall begin, therefore, with a quick tour of the territory, meeting some of the many individuals who developed the field of art therapy, citing just a few of their contributions. They represent a much larger number of people; some of whom will be introduced in later chapters, especially those dealing with history (Chapter 3) and approaches (Chapter 6).

PORTRAITS: Art Therapy Is . . .

ART THERAPY IS . . . a woman who founded a school where the arts were central (1914), and who developed *"Dynamically Oriented Art Therapy"* at a psychiatric hospital (1941), where she wrote her first book (1947). Her elegant charm and fierce conviction are both evident in this photograph, taken when she was in her prime. Her name was **MARGARET NAUMBURG**.

Figure 1–1   Margaret Naumburg, the primary "mother" of art therapy.

ART THERAPY IS . . . a gifted teacher who discovered that art had the power to liberate not only the creativity, but also the healthy psyches of *The Artist in Each of Us* (1951), and who began her work in New York City in 1920. Her name was **FLORENCE CANE**.

Figure 1–2 Florence Cane, with a young boy doing a Scribble Drawing.

ART THERAPY IS . . . a sensitive educator, who studied the nature of creative activity by teaching sculpture to blind children (1939), and who discovered that "handicapped" youngsters could be helped through what he called *"Art Education Therapy"* (1957). His name was **VICTOR LOWENFELD**.

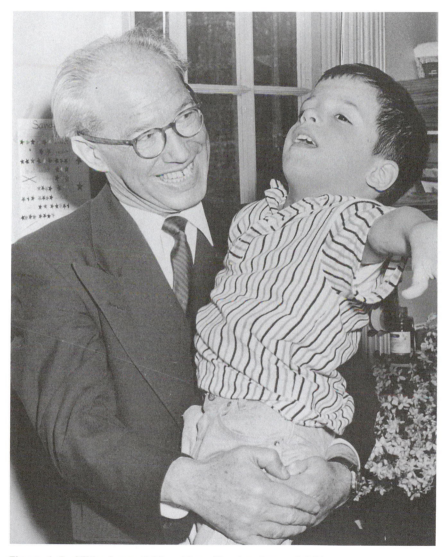

Figure 1–3 Viktor Lowenfeld working with a handicapped child.

ART THERAPY IS . . . an artist who taught painting to psychiatric patients in 1935 at the Menninger Clinic in Topeka, Kansas. In 1946, at a veterans' hospital, she created one of the first *art therapy studios* in the U.S. Her name was **MARY HUNTOON**.

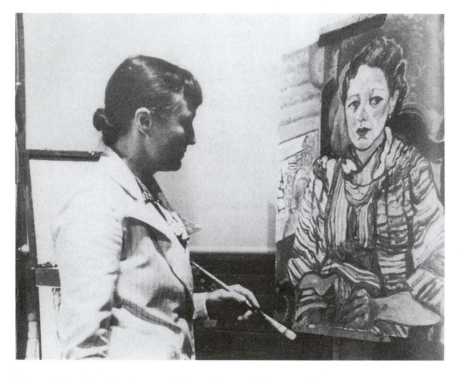

Figure 1–4   Mary Huntoon painting at the easel in her studio.

ART THERAPY IS . . . a man who found his own painting to be so therapeutic in his recovery from tuberculosis in 1938 that he promoted *"Art Therapy"* in hospitals, and wrote the first British book on the subject (1945). His name was **ADRIAN HILL**.

Figure 1–5 Adrian Hill conducting art therapy with an adult.

ART THERAPY IS . . . an artist and teacher who defined her theory of *Art as Therapy* in her first book (1958). The theory was developed at Wiltwyck, a residential school for emotionally disturbed children near New York City. Her name is **EDITH KRAMER**.

Figure 1–6 Edith Kramer working with two boys at Wiltwyck.

ART THERAPY IS . . . an artist and educator who did art therapy in the fifties at a general hospital in Washington, D.C.; and who later founded and edited the first journal devoted to the field, the *Bulletin of Art Therapy* (1961). **Her name was ELINOR ULMAN**.

Figure 1–7 Elinor Ulman in her garden.

Figure 1–8   Painting of a psychiatric patient by Don Jones.

ART THERAPY IS . . . an artist who worked in a mental hospital as a conscientious objector. His portraits of patients' anguish (Fig. 1–8) won him an invitation to develop art therapy at the Menninger Foundation in 1951. His name is **DON JONES**.

Figure 1–9   Don Jones looking at a drawing with a workshop participant.

ART THERAPY IS . . . a Polish sculptor who worked first at St. Elizabeth's (1955), then at the National Institutes of Mental Health (1958). At NIMH, she developed *Family Therapy & Evaluation Through Art* (1978). Her name was **HANNA YAXA KWAITKOWSKA**.

Figure 1–10 Hanna Kwiatkowska conducting a family art evaluation.

ART THERAPY IS . . . a California artist who wove the strands of many roles—teaching children, helping the homeless, and working in a growth center—into a fabric she called *The Gestalt Art Experience* (1973). Her name was **JANIE RHYNE**.

Figure 1–11   Janie Rhyne leading an art therapy workshop.

ART THERAPY IS . . . an artist who began his work at the Menninger Foundation in Topeka, Kansas, in 1960. Since 1985, he has also applied his clinical skills to helping ordinary people at *Ault's Academy of Art*. His name is **ROBERT AULT**.

Figure 1–12   Robert Ault working with a patient at a VA hospital.

ART THERAPY IS . . . an artist who worked at Hahnemann Hospital in Philadelphia, where her psychiatric colleagues helped her to initiate the first active
graduate-level *training program* in art therapy in 1967. Her name is **MYRA
LEVICK**.

Figure 1–13   Myra Levick teaching art therapy students.

ART THERAPY IS . . . a sculptor and psychoanalyst who blended his two loves into a way of working—in which he trained his students and about which he has written—which he called *Expressive Analysis* (1980). His name is **AR-THUR ROBBINS**.

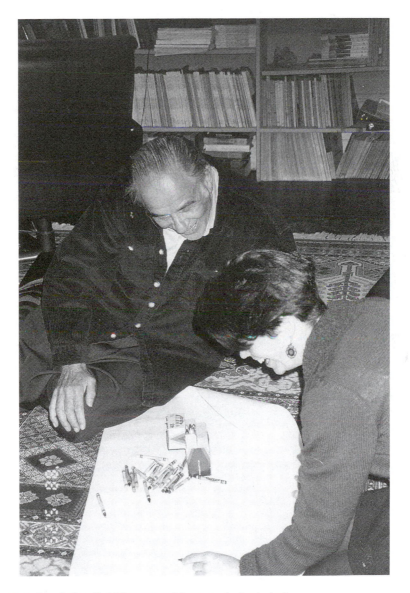

Figure 1–14 Arthur Robbins supervising a graduate student.

ART THERAPY IS . . . an artist who began her work with children and families at Cedars-Sinai Clinic in Los Angeles in 1967, and who devised many inventive techniques for what she called *Clinical Art Therapy* (1981). Her name is **HELEN LANDGARTEN**.

Figure 1–15   Helen Landgarten teaching art therapy to a workshop group.

ART THERAPY IS . . . a woman who was trained at NIMH in 1961, where she conducted some of the first *research studies* in art therapy. She later trained students and wrote and edited many books on art therapy. Her name is **HARRIET WADESON**.

Figure 1–16   Harriet Wadeson teaching a course on group art therapy.

Figure 1–17   Anthony's Portrait of a Group Member.

ART THERAPY IS . . . a young man working with patients who had been in a state hospital for many years, who discovered that some—like Anthony—were able to escape their isolation through art (Figure 1–17). He went on to define *Expressive Therapies* in training and in books. His name is **SHAUN McNIFF**.

Figure 1–18   Shaun McNiff with Anthony at Danvers State Hospital in 1975.

ART THERAPY IS . . . a young artist whose own battle with polio helped her to develop an *Art Studio* in a rehabilitation hospital (1967), where patients who had suffered trauma could create and heal. Her name is **MICKIE McGRAW**.

Figure 1–19 **Mickie McGraw** working with a patient in the Art Studio.

These "snapshots" of some of the pioneers and "early settlers" reflect art therapy's beginnings. Since then, the field has continued to develop in an increasing variety of places, with an ever-widening range of people being served. These images, then, foreshadow the even greater scope of art therapy as it is practiced today.

SHORT STORIES: VIGNETTES

The following are a few brief clinical vignettes from my own files which, like the "short cuts" from a film, offer a taste of what is to come. Some are adapted from *Child Art Therapy*; some are new. Although most of the names have been changed, the stories are true. I begin with some examples of my earliest learning experiences, in a hospital and at home. The first vignette is about Randy, one of the schizophrenic children I treated on a long-term inpatient unit at Western Psychiatric Institute & Clinic (WPIC) in 1963, under the auspices of the Child Development Department at the University of Pittsburgh. The second set of "clips" is about my own children, and what they taught me about the spontaneous use of art as therapy while they were growing up.

Art Helps a Psychotic Boy Return to Reality: **Randy** (12)

Randy suffered from an embarrassing symptom: soiling his pants. Although superficially in touch, he was inwardly unsure of the difference between reality and fantasy. Over a seven-month period, Randy had 23 individual art therapy sessions. He began by creating realistic images.

At his seventh session, Randy announced that he didn't want to paint that day, usually his first choice. Instead, he used markers to draw a picture of outer space, with a red planet—"Mars." He added some small yellow "pieces," explaining that they were bits of stars that had exploded. Some were "constellations," specifically "The King" and "The Queen." This drawing led to the creation of a book, *Our Trip Through Outer Space*, which Randy worked on steadily for the next five sessions, making a series of pictures about a Martian and myself in outer space.

He then shifted gears for the next four sessions and painted a variety of other topics. The following week, Randy told me about how people at his school teased him, and painted a picture of fantasied revenge (his "School on Fire"), then one of his "Enemies," and finally a "Volcano"—an apt metaphor for his messy, explosive symptom.

At his next session Randy returned to his space book. He made a cover, pointing out the "new earth," with a portrait of "you wearing one of the newest space hairdos," "your old pal, the Martian," and "me [Randy] wearing the newest style in space suits" (Fig. 1–20). The following week he painted the Sierra Nevadas with an "ice-capped mountain."

Randy's last five sessions were devoted to an *Earth Series*, similar to his *Space Series*, but more "down to earth." His oedipal wishes for some sort of romantic relationship with me became clearer in this less-disguised

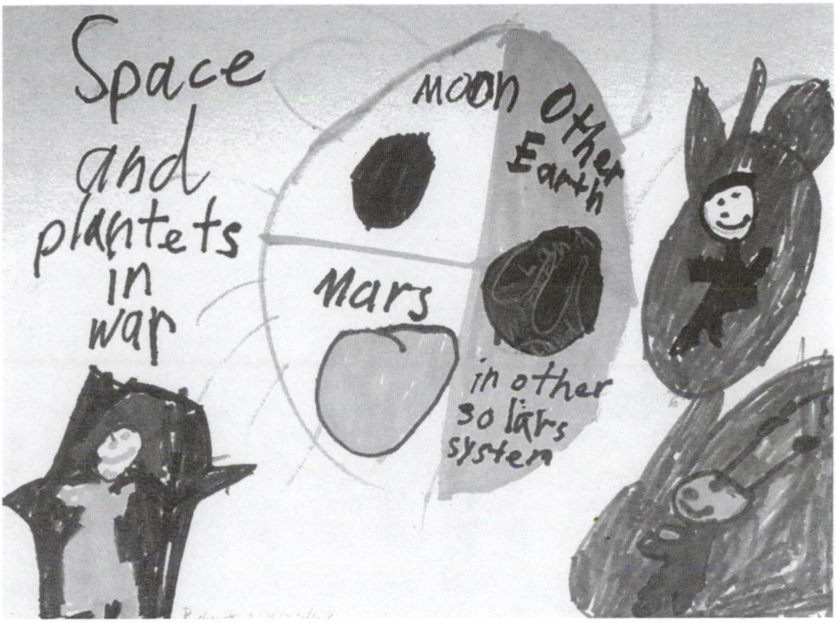

Figure 1–20 Randy's cover for his "Space Series."

sequence. The Martian dropped out of the story early, and the rest of the book was about our travels around the world. In "Our Visit to Egypt," Randy drew me in "fancy clothes, wearing a see-through dress . . . and a fancy hairdo." He drew himself giving me the jewels he found when he dug for buried treasure (Fig. 1–21). "Our Trip to Scotland" shows Randy as an adult holding on to my belt "so you won't trip" (Fig. 1–22).

Randy spent his last session reviewing his art in sequence, and was often surprised by pictures he'd forgotten. Best-recalled and most liked were the two series, which were also his most careful work. The last one of the earth series was a picture of me on the edge of a cliff in the Philippines, for which he made up the following story: *"A sailor from the Bounty was trying to kiss one of the island girls, and she backed off and fell down the mountainside, and then there was a war. The island girls fought the men and the men fought the sailors and the sailors fought the island girls. Everyone fought everyone!"* I wondered why the island girl had backed away from the sailor, and Randy replied, *"She backed off because **she already had a boyfriend**."* He then quickly drew "The Revolutionary War."

In Randy's two series he created his own symbolic framework, within which he could explore and gratify his curiosity and sexual fantasies regarding his female (mother) therapist. In the course of the story, he was working on resolving what is known as the "oedipal conflict," i.e., wanting to win mother, but acknowledging father's position ("she already had a boyfriend"). His impotent rage about losing this competition was at the

Figure 1–21 Randy giving Mrs. Rubin jewels: "For Me?"

Figure 1–22 Randy & Mrs. Rubin in Scotland.

root of his encopresis. In time, Randy accepted his "defeat," with the help of the therapeutic milieu, the art therapy, and the psychiatrist who saw him for individual and family therapy. As a young adult, he competed with an older candidate for political office, won the election, and was able to enjoy his victory and serve his constituency.

Art Contains Aggression at Home: **Jenny** (5), **Nona** (4), & **Jon** (4 & 14)

Jenny, our oldest child, was unable to express her jealousy at age five when her brother Jonathan was born. As when Nona had arrived three years earlier, Jenny was a model sister, offering help with household chores and baby care. While Jenny was acting equally angelic after Jon's birth, the drawing I found in her room told a more ambivalent story. She had drawn an "Ugly Mommy" and an "Ugly Daddy" who were missing eyes, hair, and limbs, along with a "Beautiful Jenny" (Fig. 1–23). The parents, she explained, had gotten ugly by making too many children. By the time she was six, Jenny was able to include both Jon and Nona in her drawing, although she still put herself on the periphery—and the dog in the attic (Fig. 1–24).

Nona, our middle child, was angry with me at age four because I had said she would have to get a haircut if she wouldn't allow anyone to brush

Figure 1–23 Ugly Mom & Dad & Beautiful Jenny.

Figure 1–24 Jenny's family drawing a year Later.

her hair. The day her hair was cut, she brought two paintings home from preschool. The first was entitled "A Girl who has Grown Long Hair and Locked her Mommy in the Garage" (Fig. 1–25). In the second painting, the girl is sitting triumphantly on top of the garage, the mommy (smaller) is still inside, and "The Girl Has the Key" (Fig. 1–26). Although Nona couldn't control me in reality, in art she could be more powerful than her mother.

Meanwhile, Jonathan, the youngest child and only boy in the family, also had some problems with aggression. When he was four, he dealt

Figure 1–25 "A Girl who has Grown Long Hair," by Nona.

with his scary monster dreams by painting pictures of his fears (Fig. 1–27). As he got older, he mastered his impulses through pictorial attacks on family members. Later, he drew armed ships and planes, as well as powerful soldiers and superheroes. By adolescence, he was reading science fiction, and creating humorous fantasy creatures (Fig. 1–28).

These early learning experiences convinced me that art could be therapeutic for all kinds of children, and that art therapy was the right choice for me too. Some of the following vignettes took place at the Pittsburgh Child Guidance Center, where I worked from 1969 to 1980; some happened on inpatient units served by the Creative & Expressive Arts Therapy Program at WPIC which I co-directed from 1981 to 1985; and some are from my private practice (1974–1998). All but the last two are presented in the order of the ages of the individuals involved, since art therapy can be a useful way to help people at all stages in the life cycle.

Art and Play Therapy for an Anxious Little Girl: **Amy** (3)

Amy was an adorable little girl who had been quite cheerful and well-adjusted until she started to wet her bed and to have scary dreams. Her mom had recently gone back to work, and worried that Amy was missing her. Amy's separation anxiety had indeed escalated, but behind it were

In the drawing:
A little girl

A garage with her Mommy in it

Figure 1–26   A girl has locked her mommy in the garage, and the girl has the key.

very mixed-up feelings. This was because, when mommy went on business trips, Amy got to be alone with daddy, which felt both good and bad. In fact, it felt great to pretend to be the mommy, but it frightened Amy that her scary-mad wish (to "get rid" of her mother) seemed to have come true.

She was very bossy and competitive with me, often reversing our roles in dramatic play. But the biggest breakthrough came after she drew what she called her "favorite picture." Her mom had just returned from a trip, and Amy was mighty relieved. The picture was of a King and a Queen, happily beaming at their little girl, the Princess (Fig. 1–29, p. 29). Amy announced that the Princess was going to a ball, where she would meet a man named Prince Charming, that they would soon be getting married, and that they would live in their own castle. Her symptoms gradually subsided, and she was soon able to finish her therapy.

Art Unblocks Grieving for a Little Boy: **Jeff** (6)

Six-year-old Jeff was referred for art therapy by his psychiatrist. Jeff's brother had died a year before this interview, and although Jeff had been in treatment for many months, he had not yet been able to deal with his feelings about the loss. In his first art interview, Jeff painted "A Monster

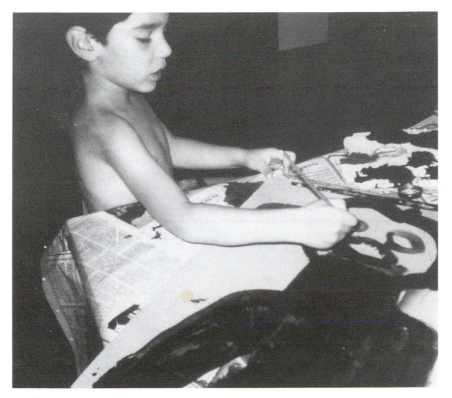

Figure 1–27 Jonathan painting a monster: Age 4.

Head" (Fig. 1–30, p. 30). Telling about the monster, Jeff expressed not only his awareness of his brother's death, but also his confusion about it.

"That's its hair. Know what happened to my brother? He died!" Then, about the monster: "He's gonna crush somebody up, maybe a snake. He'll go hiss . . . He'd blow poison dye right into the monster's face. Then they'll both die—Then they're gonna fight in heaven with spears." When I asked how old the monster was, Jeff said he was six, and that he was named "Purvungi, the Happy Monster. But he cried and he's sad." When asked why, he said " 'Cause his mother died. The people laid right on his mother. A big lightning bolt came down right into the cave and the mother monster got dead." Jeff's unresolved guilt, his identification with the dead brother who was one year older, and his fear of losing his mother, all came through eloquently in the story about his very first product.

After this initial diagnostic art interview, Jeff joined an art therapy group of children his age. One day, during snack time, the children were encouraged to make creatures out of marshmallows and toothpicks and to use them dramatically, like puppets. Jeff, whose brother's death had been caused by a cerebral hemorrhage, was able to express more openly some

Figure 1–28   Jonathan's "Funny Creature": Age 14.

of his mixed feelings about the event about which he had only giggled nervously in past group sessions. Stating that both of his marshmallow figures were boys, he put one down and said sadly, "His brother died . . . Then his father cried, and he felt sad, and he laughed." I wondered how it had happened, and Jeff said, "An accident . . . His mother was in the accident too, but she didn't die . . . His father said 'Don't die.'"

I asked if the brother died anyway. "Yeah, he died." Then I asked how the little boy felt, to which Jeff earnestly replied "Sad, sad, sad . . . Yeah! I was sad when my brother died!" "I bet you were," I commented, after which Jeff went on with images he had, until then, been unable to verbalize. "Yeah. My brother died, and the veins in his head broke, and all the blood came out from his veins. But my brother didn't have an accident when he died. His veins just broke."

Art Releases a Worried Boy's Energy: **Alan** (4 & 11)

Alan was a very tense little boy. Recently, he had begun to stutter and wet his bed. His parents, who had separated shortly before his symptoms appeared, were concerned about his increasing anxieties. During three years of weekly art therapy, Alan created dramatic disasters, like tornadoes and earthquakes, with blocks and clay figures, knocking everything and everybody down. He also painted many volcanoes (Fig. 1–31). Over

Figure 1–29 Amy & her drawing: King, Queen & Princess.

time, there were fewer and more manageable disruptions. By the time he decided to stop coming, he was a much more relaxed fellow.

Four years later, however, Alan began to have new versions of his old problems, something that often happens in the upheaval of puberty. While he no longer wet his bed, and his speech was fluent, Alan was inhibited in other ways. Though strong, he would allow bullies to taunt him without fighting back. He had also lost interest in playing with other kids.

His parents asked if Alan and I could try working together again, since it had helped when he was younger. At first he denied that he had any problems. But Alan also drew while he talked, mainly about how bored he was in school. The drawings offered clues to his inhibitions. After a few weeks of architectural designs, he began to describe and draw his plans for torture chambers, an interest he had when he was younger too (Fig. 1–32).

At this point, Alan was able to tell me about intrusive thoughts of awful things happening to his father, his mother, or both. My understanding was that he was once again having problems with his anger at his loving but busy parents. After several months of weekly sessions, Alan seemed more comfortable with his anger, but was still wanting a way to counter his "bad thoughts." So I told him about some cognitive-behavioral methods, using techniques like "thought stopping," and he figured out a few of his own.

Moreover, Alan's complaints about school were legitimate. A creative boy, he was stifled in his conservative school, so I suggested that he and

Figure 1–30   Jeff's painting of "A Monster Head."

Figure 1–31   Alan's painting of a volcano erupting.

Figure 1–32 Alan with a design for a torture chamber.

his parents explore other options. They finally settled on another place, where Alan's artistry was valued, and he began to enjoy school again. He even made so many friends that he asked to be allowed to stay for the after school program, and we were able to say goodbye again.

A Therapeutic Art Program Helps a Blind Girl: **Jane** (11)

Jane was legally blind, although she had more useful vision than most of her schoolmates. Still, like them, she was angry about being blind, and resentful and envious of the sighted adults on whom she was dependent. She didn't know about the intensity of her retaliatory rage, but was able to express it symbolically in a story about her painting (Fig. 1–33).

"This is a building which is a hospital, and in this hospital—there's just one patient in this hospital . . . The one patient is Mrs. Rubin . . . She had an accident. She bumped into another lady's car and . . . she punctured her eye." When asked what would happen, Jane said with a grin, "It's going to blind her!" She went on to explain how Mrs. Rubin would then be unable to work with children in art.

When I asked how she herself felt about it, she asserted with a sly smile, "I don't feel anything. My sight's coming back!" Having verbalized this wish, she went on to deny her disability completely—a fairly common phenomenon. "I can see just like a regular person!" In the course of group

Figure 1–33 Jane telling a story about her painting.

Figure 1–34 Some of Jack's cartoon characters.

art therapy, Jane was eventually able to accept her handicap—as well as her feelings about it—a necessary task for every blind individual.

Art Therapy Helps an Anxious Boy: **Jack** (12)

Jack had always been a difficult child, but his parents had resisted the suggestion that it might help him to see a therapist, thinking that he would outgrow it, and not wanting anything to be "wrong" with their beloved boy. Nevertheless, when he suffered a series of panic attacks, they became worried. They decided to consult a clinician, to see if therapy might help. Jack himself was extremely negative about seeing a "shrink," keeping his sessions a secret, even from his sister. Like many, he was afraid that he would discover that he really **was** defective, maybe even "crazy."

In his first session, he acknowledged that he had only come because his parents had insisted, and told me that he was to get a reward. At first, Jack demonstrated how well he could draw some of the cartoon characters he had invented (Fig. 1–34). He then began to work with clay, and created a series of increasingly massive and expressive heads. Initially the heads were fairly human, but soon began to look more like dinosaurs, with extensions of various sorts, including teeth, tongues, spikes, and horns (Fig. 1–35). Jack was proud of his sculptures, displaying them on a large table in my office, where everyone could "admire" them.

Jack talked constantly while he worked, about the "pressure" he felt to perform in sports and scholastics. Although he was competent in both, he vacillated between bragging and worrying. As he became more trusting, he began to disclose more about his feelings and anxieties, sometimes seriously, sometimes playfully. Over time, I grew to understand

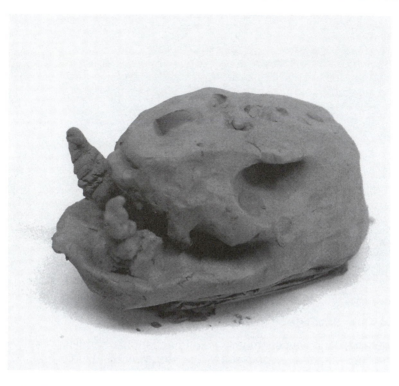

Figure 1–35   One of Jack's prehistoric creatures.

Jack's deep fears of inadequacy, of injury, and of his own aggression—which he usually masked with an air of bravado.

Occasionally his terror would break through at home, and he would
have another panic attack. Sometimes he would regress and have a tan-
trum, scaring himself and his family. Jack often manipulated his parents,
promising to do what they wanted if they would buy him one of the many
objects he desired.

Periodically, his parents would request a meeting to "touch base,"
sometimes because he was being oppositional in a passive-aggressive
fashion. His verbal attacks on family members increased for a time—a
common "side effect" when therapy uncovers repressed hostility. With
Jack's permission, I sometimes showed his folks his art work, which often
"explained" him better than my words. The meetings helped me to monitor
the effects of the therapy, since his parents could tell me more clearly
than Jack could about what was going on at home and in school. Our
sessions also helped them to understand Jack's puzzling behavior, so
that they could set limits as well as empathize with him.

As he began to get more comfortable with—and less frightened of—his
hostile and competitive impulses, Jack's performance anxiety lessened.
His art work changed too. He began a series of acrylic paintings, in which

he explored similar themes, but with more disguise. He received as much attention for these sublimated expressions of his concerns as he had for his sculptures. He was able to say goodbye after two years, as he entered adolescence. Without clay or a brush in his hands, I doubt that Jack would have been able to tolerate psychotherapy, despite his verbal fluency. With art, he was able to master his anxieties almost painlessly.

Art Therapy for a Painfully Shy Adolescent: **Lucy** (13)

From the time of her parents' divorce when she was three, Lucy had been a terribly timid child. Forced by a judge to move to her father's after a traumatic custody battle at age 12, she became increasingly withdrawn and depressed. By the time she was brought for the therapy that had also been ordered by the court, Lucy was justifiably suspicious, for the psychologist with whom she had met for the custody evaluation had not honored her stated wish to remain at home with her mother and brother.

Since she was so reluctant to speak, it was fortunate for both of us that Lucy liked using art materials. She began by carefully modelling tiny clay creatures, just a few inches high (Fig. 1–36). Though she worked in silence, Lucy was willing to talk for the figures in response to my questions, as if they were puppets. The little figures began to softly voice the angry feelings she had turned on herself, causing her depression.

After a few months, Lucy began to experiment with other media, like chalk, crayons, and all kinds of paints. She told me a great deal about her fantasy life in powerfully poignant paintings (Fig. 1–37) and poetry, long before she was able to speak freely and directly about her feelings.

She gradually adjusted to her new school, and became involved with a group of giggly girlfriends. After a year of weekly art therapy, Lucy was less depressed and more assertive—no longer terrified of her intense feelings—no longer frozen in silence. Although her father thought that she was so much better that therapy was no longer necessary, Lucy—who had been too afraid of her dad's temper to oppose him in the past—was able to speak up and to say that she wasn't ready to stop. She came for another year, and began to confront her more deeply buried fears and fantasies.

Art Therapy Helps a Talented Teenager: **Betty Jane** (14)

Betty Jane's parents had just announced that they were going to split up, her older sister had just left for college, and Betty Jane was becoming more and more depressed. She was also skeptical about therapy, since there was no way treatment could change the reality with which she had to cope. Her mother, however, asked her to come for one interview; and she agreed to my suggestion that she try a few sessions of art therapy.

A talented artist, Betty Jane enjoyed exploring different media. Although her art was more attractive than revealing, the pictures and her answers to my questions about them gave me clues to feelings of which she was not yet conscious (Fig. 1–38). Betty Jane continued to be ambivalent about our weekly meetings, especially disliking the ones where she

Figure 1–36 One of Lucy's tiny clay creatures.

would break down and cry or reveal something she later regretted. Nevertheless, she came reluctantly for several months, using her sessions mainly to express her distress about all the changes in her life.

Two years later, Betty Jane called, saying that, although she was "awfully busy" with plays and exams and activities, she'd like to come in again to work on some issues related to her final year of high school. Within a few sessions, drawing as she spoke (Fig. 1–39, p. 39), Betty Jane told me about some frightening dissociative episodes, when she had felt as if she were observing herself—like "out of body" experiences. While she hadn't said so, I wondered if she was worried that she had inherited the mental illness in her mother's family, so I suggested a diagnostic evaluation.

Happily, both psychological and neurological testing revealed that the cause of her spacy moments was anxiety and not biology. She was able

Figure 1–37 One of Lucy's Expressive Paintings.

once again to concentrate on her studies, and to win a scholarship to a prestigious art school. Betty Jane was also able to say goodbye to her parents, no longer worried about whether they could manage without her.

Then, this young woman—so skeptical about the value of therapy when we began, challenging me to show her how it could possibly help—asked if I knew a therapist in the city where she was going to college, "just in case." After her first semester, she reported with relief that, being among other artists, she discovered that everyone there was like her, and she no longer felt "weird"—like the Ugly Duckling when he found the swans.

Art Assessment with a Sullen Adolescent: **Melanie** (15)

Melanie, age fifteen, had been referred to the clinic because of her oppositional behavior. Her rebelliousness had already caused her aunt—who had cared for her since her mother's abandonment in early childhood—to kick her out of the house. She was living with her older brother, but did not feel happy or accepted in his home.

Like many adolescents, Melanie was reluctant to draw spontaneously, since she was "no good" at art. So I suggested that she make a "scribble" drawing, a technique used by art therapists to help people get started. She was able to "find" an image in her scribble, and to develop it (Fig. 1–40).

At first she said it was an "Eagle," then she changed her mind . . . "I think it's a 'Hawk' or something." Melanie went on to say that she would

Figure 1–38   An early drawing by Betty Jane.

like either to **be** the bird or to **take care** of it, eventually deciding that she
would rather be a caretaker. She went on to explain that eagles were in
danger of becoming extinct—through people's neglect—and that she
would like to work for the preservation of the species.

Figure 1-39 A later drawing by Betty Jane.

Figure 1–40   Melanie's endangered eagle/hawk.

Much to my surprise, Melanie was then able to connect these ideas about her drawing to her own strong and unmet dependency needs. The Eagle/Hawk expressed her loneliness, as well as her hunger for love, acceptance, and family. The sharp beak expressed her biting rage at those who had abandoned and rejected her, which was also reflected in the explosive, sullen, angry quality of her speech.

Art in Therapy with a Young Adult: **Sally** (22)

Sally was a graduate student who had always been an outstanding performer. But when she confessed to her advisor that she was having a hard time getting her work done, her teacher suggested that she see a therapist. Because Sally was very articulate, my first impression was that she was having an adjustment reaction to being so far away from home. After several months of therapy, however, she was still quite depressed.

Figure 1–41 One of Sally's expressive drawings.

One day I wondered if she had ever tried painting or drawing, and Sally said that she had loved art when she was little, but that she was sure she was "no good" now. Assured that the art was for therapy and not for show, she was able to start experimenting at home. When she brought in her first drawings and paintings, I was astonished (Fig. 1–41). They were not only beautiful; they also revealed the extent of her well-masked pathology, which included occasional paranoid delusions (Fig. 1–42).

Thanks to the clues in her art work, Sally was able to be placed on medication for her mood disorder before she had any psychotic episodes. Thanks to her hard work in therapy, accelerated by what she learned from her art work, she was able to finish her degree program. Sally's art became a welcome outlet at times of stress. When she left for a job in another city, her parting gifts were framed paintings and permission to use her story.

Art from Past Aids Therapy in Present: **James** (37)

When James was in his thirties, he sought therapy for his pervasive depression and persistent problems with women (Fig. 1–43). After several months, he shared with me his adolescent sketchbooks, in which he had continued to grapple with the mystery and mourning of the too-early loss of his mother at age six. His drawing of a lonely young man—feeling

Figure 1–42 One of Sally's poignant paintings.

alienated and alone and staring sadly out the window—represented his inner state of painful isolation (Fig. 1–44, p. 44).

His father, a distant man by temperament, was never emotionally available, even less so after his own loss. The one genuine human bond James had—with his mother—was repeatedly torn, first by the birth of his sister when he was four, then by his mother's illness, which led to too many separations, and finally her death from cancer. His last memories of her were of her face framed in a hospital window, echoing his self-portrait.

James was also an alcoholic, but had denied the extent of his addiction during his two years of therapy. Shortly after he terminated treatment, he met a woman whose concern helped him to finally go into rehabilitation. After completing the program, marrying the woman, and becoming a father, he returned for further therapy. This time he was able to express feelings he had hidden from me—especially, hurt and anger. His addiction had been a classic instance of the search for "mommy in a bottle."

Art Draws out Despair in Marital Therapy: **Mr. and Mrs. T**

I once worked with a couple for two years in weekly therapy, at first regarding their blind, multiply-handicapped daughter who was being seen by a child psychiatrist. We had used art during an initial family evaluation and in some of the diagnostic interviews. While not the main mode of communication for this concerned couple, it was especially useful in dealing with the most loaded and difficult areas of their relationship, which eventually emerged as significant factors in the girl's problems.

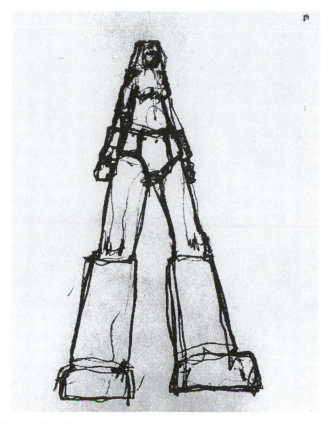

Figure 1–43 "An Aloof Woman," by James.

During one session, after much veiled expression of resentment from both about disappointment in their partner, I wondered if they could draw each other, working on opposite sides of an easel. These images actually became reference points for the remainder of the treatment. Mr. T. represented his wife as "The Rock of Gibraltar," a tower of strength and stability in the shifting currents of life (Fig. 1–45). At first he said that was how she **really** was. Then, responding to her hurt and anger at such unrealistic expectations, he acknowledged that he **wished** she would never show vulnerability or weakness, but that he had often been let down.

Meanwhile, Mrs. T. was in tears about how impossible it was to please her husband, how hard it was to get his sympathy and concern when she herself was needy, and how deprived and lonely she felt. She represented him as all wrapped up in his own activities, with no time left for his family—playing his guitar and daydreaming about his interests, none involving her or the children (Fig. 1–46). While at first defensive, Mr. T. finally agreed that his wife had a point, and remembered how he had placed himself far away from the others in his family drawing a year earlier.

Figure 1–44   "A Boy Looking Out a Window," by James.

Figure 1–45   "Mrs. T. as the Rock of Gibralter," by Mr. T.

Six months later, a good deal of work was accomplished by drawing together without talking during a number of sessions. In such a process, communication issues can be experienced and discussed in an affectively charged manner (Fig. 1–47). Since both Mr. and Mrs. T. tended to intellectualize often and well, art was extremely useful for helping them get in touch with their feelings.

Art Therapy for Abuse and Chronic Pain: **Elaine** (41)

Elaine was a middle-aged woman who had suffered from depression all of her life. She came for art therapy because fingerpainting had helped her to uncover and to express repressed memories of child abuse. She not only created art during her therapy sessions, but also at home—especially at times of deep distress. One of her paintings was a vivid statement of how imprisoned she felt by her psychic pain and depression. In it, a puffy, sad grey face looks out from behind black bars of raised paint (Fig. 1–48).

For Elaine, art therapy became a way of finding out what was inside, in a place that felt increasingly secure over time. She called it a "holding environment," and gave that title to one of her sculptures. In it, a person (Elaine) holding an infant (her small victimized self), leans against a well-rooted tree, her favorite symbol for support (Fig. 1–49, p. 49).

Figure 1–46   "Mr. T. and His Many Interests," by Mrs. T.

Figure 1–47 Two men drawing together without talking.

After many years of work, it was hard for Elaine to say goodbye to me and the safe space of the art therapy room, even though she had made a good attachment to another therapist during a long transition period. She took most of her art work home, but left a good deal with me too.

In her last art session, Elaine made a sculpture which reminded me of the one she had done four years earlier. The tree had not been in her work for a while, perhaps because she felt more grounded herself. In its place was a hand, cradling a person who is holding a baby (Fig. 1–50, p. 50). Although she traced the title—"Therapy"—into the wet clay, she called later asking me to smooth it out, feeling that the sculpture alone said it as well.

Art Gives Voice to Longing: **Hannah** (62)

For Hannah, a woman in her sixties who had been sexually abused by a family friend as a little girl, and who had been subtly rejected by her mother, her first foray into therapy was an anxiety-provoking event. She had come because one of her sons had gotten into drugs, and seemed to be on a self-destructive collision course. Like many mothers, she worried that she herself had been the cause.

Hannah was also restless, now that her children had left home and she was alone with her workaholic husband. She was unhappy with herself and with her own lack of direction, feeling that she had played roles defined by others all of her life. Although she couldn't say it, Hannah was really yearning for a sense of Self, wanting to find her inner voice.

Figure 1–48 "Woman Imprisoned by Depression," by Elaine.

Figure 1–49   "The Holding Environment," by Elaine.

Frustrated by the short time span of a regular session (45 minutes), since it took her the better part of it to "warm up," she had asked for a double session, which had worked out well. Invited to use art materials, she made a powerful clay head of a dog, and said it looked "very sad" to her (Fig. 1–51). We both saw it as a self-portrait, reflecting her discouraged state. Then, using a scribble as a "starter," she drew a pained head, mouth wide open. It conveyed how "hungry" she was, not so much for the extra time she had requested, but for what it symbolized—maternal love.

After a year of such weekly meetings, Hannah announced with pride that she thought she was ready to leave. She kept in touch for a time, with cards and the gift of a book about a talented child artist. In therapy,

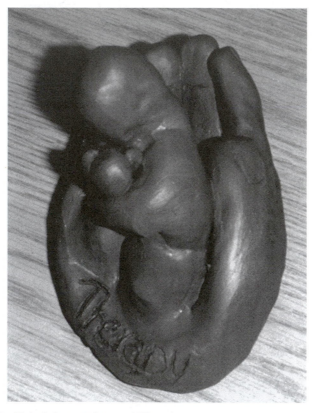

Figure 1–50 Elaine's later sculpture of "Therapy."

she had what she experienced as a new beginning, in which my nonjudg-
mental acceptance of her and pleasure in her timid steps toward self-
definition—which included trying art materials—enabled her to grow, at a
point in her life where she had almost lost hope.

The last two vignettes in this chapter concern Mrs. Lord and her daughter
Lori, each of whom saw Dr. Mann and myself every week, described earlier in
this chapter in "A Preview of Coming Attractions." Dr. Mann had requested
art therapy primarily for Mrs. Lord, who was so well defended that it was hard
to get past her glib rationalizations in verbal psychotherapy. In the session to
be described, Mrs. Lord used the routine she had developed in five months of
art therapy to cope with a situation that had rendered this chatty and articulate
woman temporarily speechless.

Art Therapy with a Depressed Woman: **Mrs. L.** (27)

Although she had come to the clinic because her formerly-cheerful
daughter, Lori, was sad, Mrs. Lord was also depressed. Both were reacting

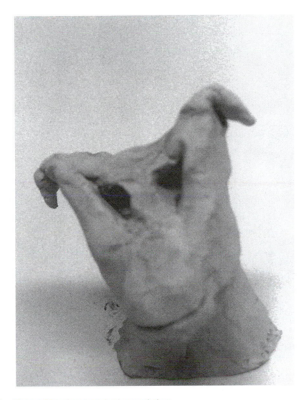

Figure 1-51 Hannah's clay head of a sad dog.

to Mr. Lord's recent announcement that he wanted a separation, and his subsequent move out of their home. Although Lori cried a lot, Mrs. Lord was generally able to hide her sadness behind a cheerful facade.

After five months of art therapy, she generally began a session by telling me what was going on in her life, while painting or drawing (Fig. 1-52). Then we would look at what she had made on the easel, which allowed her to feel less self-conscious than if she had to make eye contact with me—one of the reasons art therapy is effective (Fig. 1-53). Mrs. Lord had also learned by then to "associate" freely to her images, saying whatever came to mind as she looked at the pictures. After she had reflected on her verbal associations, we would attempt to figure out their relevance to her life.

One day Mrs. Lord arrived looking uncharacteristically somber. She said she had almost not come, and was so upset that she wondered if she would be able to talk about anything at all. I asked if she could **draw her feelings**, rather than trying to put them into words. She quickly selected a piece of black construction paper (12″ × 18″) and large poster

Figure 1–52   Mrs. Lord talking while drawing.

chalks, by then her favorite medium. She furiously scribbled a series of color masses whose brightness screamed out against the black—red, yellow, orange, magenta, and white (Fig. 1–54). Mrs. Lord then grabbed another piece of black paper, and quickly drew a series of multicolored lines which met, but did not intersect (Fig. 1–55, p. 55). Putting both on the easel, she looked at them.

She entitled the first drawing "Shock," and then, much to her surprise and embarrassment, this usually well-controlled woman began to sob. "All I have to do is break down and start crying," she said, "and **everyone will think I am crazy! . . . He's the one who should be here!**" She then said she had just discovered that her husband had a girlfriend, and that the affair had been going on for quite a while. Still agitated and tearful, Mrs. Lord went on to say how painful this **shock** had been.

The title for the second picture was less clear to her than the first. She groped for words, finally settling on: "Ambivalent, Dilemma, Uncertainty, and Confusion." She was unable to say much more, except that the image described as best she could her tangled emotions. By the end of the session, Mrs. Lord had regained her composure. While still visibly sad, she was no longer as tense as she had been when she arrived.

The art activity allowed Mrs. Lord to release some of the feelings which were flooding her. The drawings, which expressed her anguish and

Figure 1–53 Mrs. Lord associating to her drawing.

confusion better than any words, also helped her to sort out just what was happening, both internally and externally. She was then able to begin to consider how she might cope with the unwelcome news. In other words, articulating her inner world helped her to cope with the outer one.

Art & Drama Therapy Help a Child Say Goodbye: **Lori** (5)

The following vignette is from Lori's therapy, in which—like most young children—she spontaneously used both dramatic play and art materials (Fig. 1–56). She was four when her parents separated, and had seen very little of her dad since he had left the house. Although she first left him out of a family drawing, she later added him as the biggest figure in a wishful image of a family picnic. Sadly she said, "I love my daddy. He is beautiful. But he is not a live-at-home daddy."

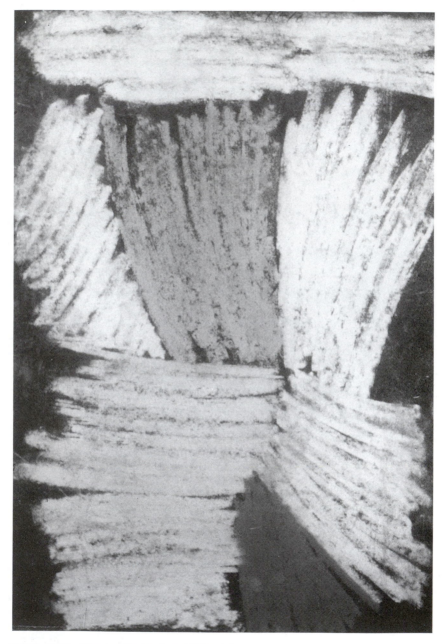

Figure 1–54 Mrs. Lord's drawing of "Shock."

Figure 1–55 Mrs. Lord's drawing of "Confusion."

Figure 1–56 Lori drawing a picture in the Art/Playroom.

Several months later, after the divorce, Lori drew a sad girl, saying, "That girl is crying" (Fig. 1–57). In response to my questions, she explained that the girl was crying "because her house falled apart . . . 'cause there was a big, big, storm, and lightning cut it in half." The picture-story was Lori's way of showing how violently her home had been split; how the divorce had been a bolt from the blue, shattering everything in its impact.

Later in that same session, Lori decided on a "new story" for her picture. Grinning impishly, she announced that the crying person was no longer a girl, but a lady . . . in fact, "You!" I wondered why I might be so sad, and she explained that I was crying "because I left you and I never would come back." Lori used a similar role reversal during her final art therapy session, which took place seven months later.

Lori began by reminding me that it was her last session, announcing that she intended to use **some of everything in the playroom**. After she

Figure 1–57 Lori's drawing of "A Sad Girl."

accidentally spilled some paint, she played at being a bossy mother while we both sponged it up, saying, "Do what I say! Don't step in this while it's wet!" Then Lori said that she didn't want to "make believe" that day.

She wondered if I had hidden the ice pick we had used to open clogged holes in paint shakers. When she found it in its usual place, Lori mimed stabbing me with it, saying that she wasn't **really** going to kill me, but was only making believe. Looking at her reflection in the mirror as she often did, Lori proceeded to put on soap crayon "makeup."

This time she commanded me not to watch, threatening abandonment if I disobeyed. "If you look, I'm goin' out the door!" When I wondered if she would rather go out the door herself on her last day than have me tell her it was time to leave, she nodded and said: "I **know** this is the last day, and I'll cry, and I said I'll miss you and Dr. Mann . . . I'm gonna leave here, and I'm gonna drive my own car, and leave my mommy. **But I might lost myself.** Then I might walk at your place cryin', 'I lost myself!'"

Lori then wondered if I might buy her play clothes for her birthday, and if we could exchange telephone numbers. She painted a huge, sloppy painting, and earnestly delivered her farewell address into the microphone of the small tape recorder we used for stories about her art. "Goodbye. I'm not gonna see you no more, but I'm gonna cry if I don't see you no more." I told Lori that I would miss seeing her too, and she went on: "Well, see, if I don't see you no more, I might cry. I wanna hear myself talk."

After listening to her speech on the tape recorder, a few faint smiles brightening her sad face, Lori said that we should kiss goodbye, and we did. She was thus able in her last session not only to express her anger, sadness, and sense of abandonment about the ending of her therapy; but also her affection and her growing autonomy.

PREVIEW OF COMING CHAPTERS

Now that you have gotten a peek at the process of art therapy, you will want to find out more about it. In Chapter 2, you will learn how art therapy is similar to and different from related fields. Chapter 3 tells the story of its development as a profession. Chapter 4 is about how the training of art therapists and the education of others have evolved over time. The ''basics'' of doing art therapy are outlined in Chapter 5, which also notes some of the basic reasons why art therapy works. Art therapy is conducted using many different theoretical approaches, noted in Chapter 6.

Art for assessment and diagnosis is described in Chapter 7, and some of the techniques used in treatment in Chapter 8. Since art therapy is used with a wide variety of people, some of the most common groups are identified in Chapter 9. Art therapy is also used in many different kinds of settings and for a broad range of purposes, some of which are noted in Chapter 10. Chapter 11 describes the evaluation of individuals, interventions, and programs (training and treatment), as well as research and ethical standards. Chapter 12 offers suggestions for further study, and some hypotheses about the future of the discipline. An Appendix follows, describing a single creative process and a case history, showing the process of art therapy over time. The book ends with a list of professional associations, journals, and books on art therapy and related areas.

Chapter 2

What Is Art Therapy?

Anything that is to be called art therapy
*Must genuinely partake of **both art and therapy.***

ELINOR ULMAN

ART + THERAPY = ?

In one of the first issues of the *Bulletin of Art Therapy*, when the field had only recently been born and named, editor Elinor Ulman wrote about how hard it was to classify this new discipline, with its roots and branches in many areas. Ulman concluded that art therapy needed to be true to both art **and** therapy. She defined **therapy** as *"procedures designed to assist favorable changes in personality or in living that will outlast the session itself"* (ATTP, p. 12). And she defined **art as** *"a means to discover both the self and the world, and to establish a relation between the two."* (ATTP, p. 13) She also called **art** *"the meeting ground of the inner and outer world"* (Ulman in Jakab, 1971, p. 93).

Despite Ulman's early and inclusive definition of the newborn profession, there was a series of what might be characterized as rather impassioned "custody battles." The biggest source of tension—still evident in varying forms—was whether **art** or **therapy** would be designated the dominant parent. Those who felt that art therapy's primary contribution was in the healing power of the creative process were drawn to what is often called "art **as** therapy." Those who felt that art therapy's primary value was as a means of symbolic communication sometimes called it "art **psychotherapy**." If you were to peruse the literature, you would notice that, while most refer to the field as "art therapy," some call their work by other names, such as "expressive analysis," "clinical therapy," "psychoaesthetics," or "expressive therapy."

ART THERAPY: WHAT IT IS AND WHAT IT IS NOT

Since art therapy overlaps many other areas, a useful way to define it is to compare and contrast it with closely related disciplines. Despite the fact that art therapy is much better known today than ever before, it remains a mystery to many. In places where little or no art therapy exists, it is still poorly defined and misunderstood (Fig. 2–1). Even when people have heard of art therapy, they

Figure 2–1   An amusing misunderstanding: Therapy for art!

are often unclear about just what it is. Art therapists contribute to this confusion, for they have different backgrounds and ways of describing what they do. So it is essential to know not only what art therapy **is**, but also what it is **not**.

Many people think, for example, that art therapy means working in art with those who are different from the norm. But the definition of art therapy does not depend on **who** is being seen, any more than it is a function of **where** the work occurs; but rather **why** it is being offered. When art materials are given to disabled or troubled individuals, the activities may well be educational or recreational. When providing art for the purpose of constructively filling leisure time, that is not art therapy. Even in a psychiatric setting, if the primary purpose of the activity is learning and/or fun, it is certainly **therapeutic**, but it is not art therapy.

The essence of art therapy is—as Ulman has said—that it must be true to both parts of its name—art and therapy. The primary **goal** of the art activity, therefore, must be **therapy**. This usually includes **assessment** as well as **treatment**; for any therapist needs to understand who and what they are treating. An art therapist also needs to know a great deal about the wide range of ways in which art can aid in understanding, as well as in helping people to grow and to change.

The field of psychotherapy is complex, encompassing many different ways of understanding human beings. It also includes many different ways of helping people to overcome difficulties in development or adjustment. In order to offer art as **therapy**, it is essential to be trained as a **clinician**. Even the most sensitive artist or art teacher is **not** a therapist, no matter who the student happens to be, or where the teaching takes place.

Just as it takes years of study and discipline to master the visual arts, so it takes time to master psychology and psychotherapy. As with all forms of therapy, understanding and synthesis in art therapy come only with experience. To integrate knowledge about art and therapy requires clinical training, involving thousands of hours of supervised work with patients. It is a lifelong task, one which cannot be mastered without ongoing guidance and continual self-inquiry.

ART THERAPY & ART EDUCATION

There is naturally an element of education involved in art therapy because the work includes helping others to create. But the teaching is secondary to the primary aim, which is therapy. In other words, if an art therapist teaches techniques, it is not for the sake of the skill itself, but rather in order to help the person to achieve—for example—a more articulate expression of a feeling, a higher level of sublimation, or an enhanced sense of self-esteem.

Similarly, there are therapeutic aspects of art education. The very best art teachers are growth-enhancing individuals who nurture a student's feeling of competence in a broadly beneficial fashion. And there is no question that art activities can be conducted so as to promote social and emotional growth. Art is intrinsically healing for many reasons, such as: discharging tension, experiencing freedom with discipline, representing forbidden thoughts and feelings, visualizing the invisible, and expressing ideas that are hard or impossible to put into words.

Invisible Differences

One reason why it is so important to distinguish between art for different goals is that the art activities themselves may not appear different to an untrained observer. An individual art therapy session can look like an art lesson, and an art therapy group may appear to be a class. The materials are the same, and approaches in both art therapy and art education range from open-ended to highly structured. Even the words of the therapist may be indistinguishable from those a friendly teacher might use. The primary distinctions are **invisible**—inside the mind of the art therapist and of the participant(s).

When an art therapist conducts an **art evaluation**, for example, she is looking with a clinically trained eye and listening with a psychologically attuned ear to what is happening. She is attentive to all aspects of behavior, hoping to understand as much as she can through the individual's interaction with her, with the art materials, and in response to whatever task(s) have been presented. From these clues, she does her best to assess where he is developmentally, what his primary conflicts are, and how he is coping with them.

Similarly, when an art therapist works with a family, she is interested in what their art and behavior can tell her about both individual and interpersonal dynamics. She looks at how they relate to one another, which helps her to understand the problems of the "identified patient" and of the "family system." Anyone watching a **family art evaluation** would see an exercise in which parents and children make things individually and jointly, and then talk about their art work (Fig. 2–2). If the family is relaxed, it might look like a pleasant recreational activity. The art therapist's interest, however, is in understanding family dynamics—through the symbolism of their art, in the context of their behavior. Similarly, **group art therapy** might look like an art class, but learning about art is secondary to learning about the self in relation to other people.

Participants "Know" the Difference

Eventually, the individuals involved in art therapy themselves become aware that this is a different kind of art experience, even when the goals have not been made explicit. While it is customary to explain to those who can comprehend the diagnostic or therapeutic purpose of the art activity, that is not always possible. But even the very young and those with language problems soon grasp the special nature of art in therapy.

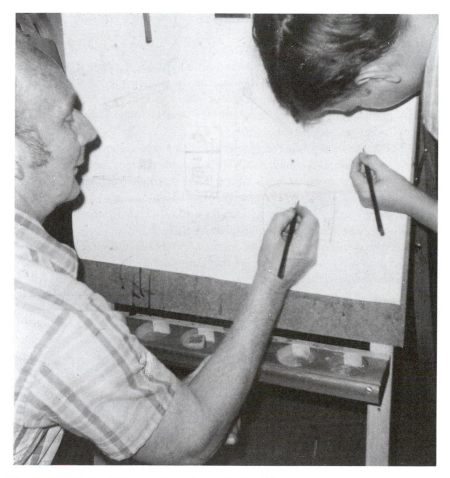

Figure 2–2 Father & Son work together in family art therapy.

I was reminded of this by the response of some children I saw in a pilot program at a school for the deaf. When some of the teachers asked to observe the art sessions, the children declined, perhaps needing to keep their often-angry imagery private. Similarly, a teenager signed out the window to his friend that he was with "an art lady who helped him with his problems," although we had never discussed the purpose of his visits.

So there **is** a difference, but it is not always visible or easy to explain. Of course, there are times in art classes when the activity is therapeutic, whether at the level of release or of reflection. Similarly, there are times when what goes on in art therapy is mainly educational or recreational, where learning or pleasure is focal for the moment. But the differences in the primary goals remain, for both teachers and therapists.

ART FOR PEOPLE WITH DISABILITIES

Educational Settings

The distinctions between art therapy and art education are especially likely to be blurred in the area of art with the disabled. In fact, two professionals with a foot in each field once diagnosed both disciplines as suffering from "**a shared identity crisis.**" The crisis was a territorial one, about who should be offering art activities to people with disabilities.

Although the kind of art therapy provided to disabled individuals often has a psycho-educational orientation, the two are overlapping but not identical. There is not only room; there is also a need for both teaching and therapy through art with this group. For example, in 1969 at the Jewish Guild for the Blind in New York, Yasha Lisenco taught art and Edith Kramer did art therapy—with similar sensitivity, but different goals.

While there will always be more teachers in schools and more therapists in clinics, it would be foolish to assume that the optimal division of labor would be in terms of **where** the work is done or **who** is being served. As noted earlier, **what** is done may look very similar, but **why** is the critical variable. When the need, for example, is for psychological evaluation, a therapist is the art-giver of choice. Only a trained clinician knows how to use art for assessment, or to identify the conflicts causing symptoms. When the goals of a given art intervention are social or emotional, a therapist—who understands interpersonal and intrapsychic dynamics—is more equipped for the job than a teacher.

Art therapists are trained to assess and to treat those problems that interfere with people being able to benefit from education—including learning art. Because of their clinical expertise, art therapists are often more comfortable than art teachers in working with the most severely and profoundly impaired students. As art has become more widely available to people with disabilities, art therapists often sensitize and train artists and art educators who offer creative experiences. Because they understand both the art process and the disability, art therapists are ideal consultants for other art professionals doing such work.

Medical Settings

There has been a similar kind of tension about roles and sharing the territory when artists have worked in hospitals or rehabilitation settings with the mentally or physically ill. In 1969 a New York group named Hospital Audiences, Inc. (HAI) started bringing musical performances to patients who could not get to concerts. Later, they offered activities in all art forms as well. Funded by the Rockefeller Foundation, HAI organized conferences on the healing role of the arts (1976 & 1977), inviting agencies, artists and arts therapists. An international meeting in 1982 resulted in a report: *The Healing Role of the Arts*, endorsing roles for **all** "who utilize the arts as a part of their rehabilitative efforts."

On the *Task Panel on the Role of the Arts in Therapy & Environment* of the *President's Commission on Mental Health* in 1978, there were deep philosophical differences about how best to help troubled individuals through art. Several panel members agreed with Joan Erikson (1976), developer of an activities program at Austen Riggs, a residential treatment center. Erikson felt that artists and craftsmen were the best people to bring creative activity to the mentally ill, arguing that using art as a form of therapy interfered with its intrinsically healing power.

The **art as therapy** approach is actually similar to Joan Erikson's position. It assumes, however, that deeper clinical understanding, rather than interfering, **facilitates** an artist's work with vulnerable patients. As its main spokesperson, Edith Kramer, had written:

> *"The artist who applies modern psychology in the field of art has to adapt his methods to the medium so that the therapeutic value of art is heightened and reinforced by the introduction of therapeutic thinking, not destroyed or weakened by the introduction of concepts and methods that might be incompatible with the inner laws of artistic creation" (1958, p. 6).*

Potter and poet M.C. Richards, while not an art therapist, was in favor of using art in therapy:

> *"Not everyone agrees that art should be used in a therapy situation. Some artists, some teachers, some doctors think it is demeaning to the seriousness of art to apply it as a kind of medicine or mending tape. I think they are wrong . . . Artistic experience is central to the human being and where it is sleeping, it should be awakened however modestly—for it is the person who will awake—and be strengthened—and aided in his growth and development" (1973, p. 32).*

In any case, after heated debate and covert anxiety about sharing what seemed like a rather small pie, a broad set of recommendations was articulated by the Task Panel. The healing potential of a wide range of possible art interventions was made explicit in the report. Twenty years later, an even greater openness to avenues of healing through the arts is evident in a growing movement in both the U.S. (Palmer & Nash, 1991) and Great Britain (Kaye & Blee, 1996; Senior & Croall, 1993), sometimes referred to as "**Arts Medicine.**" Within the last decade, there is a new **Society for the Arts in Health Care**, an **International Arts Medicine Association**, a journal, and many creative programs, such as "Art for Recovery" at San Francisco's Mt. Zion Hospital, led by an artist and a physician since 1988.

A person helping hospitalized patients to paint might be a nurse, a volunteer, an artist, a teacher, or an art therapist. The difference is found primarily in the **goals** of the activity. An art therapist makes use of art and therapy to assess, to treat, and to remediate those psychological problems that interfere with adaptive

Figure 2–3 Phototherapy at the Pgh. Center for the Arts (PCA).

functioning—which might include being able to use art media or to attend a painting class.

Room for All: Teamwork

Just as there is room for more than one approach in providing art to the disabled or the mentally ill, so it is in work with hard-to-reach individuals that a team of arts professionals is often ideal. In 1973, I coordinated a creative arts program for poor children, who are at increased risk for social and emotional maladjustment. The program was funded by Pittsburgh Model Cities (part of a national "War on Poverty"), and was administered through my employer, the Pittsburgh Child Guidance Center.

Since I was not restricted to hiring people from any specific discipline, I chose individuals with the personal and professional qualities that seemed most critical. The result was a team of twenty staff members—artists, art educators, and art therapists. All of them shared a sensitivity to the cultures of the children and families who lived in the neighborhoods being served. Equally important, all had experience and skill in helping others to create in their particular art form.

Since 1993, I have worked with an established organization, the Pittsburgh Center for the Arts, to develop a **Community Arts Education Network**. Like other art therapists, I have functioned in a variety of roles, depending on the need. I have been a consultant to a weaving program for people with chronic mental illness, a photography program for delinquent teenagers (Fig. 2–3), a workshop on healing art for cancer patients, and an arts enrichment program for alienated adolescents. I have also co-led group therapy with a drama therapist for women in an addiction rehabilitation program (Fig. 2–4).

As noted earlier, there can and should be room for artists, art teachers, and art therapists, for each has special skills to offer. And people with problems—mental, physical, socioeconomic—deserve all the help they can get, whether their difficulties are temporary or chronic. Happily, multidisciplinary efforts are becoming increasingly available.

ART THERAPY AND CHILD THERAPY

Play Therapy & Child Art Therapy

There is understandable confusion about the distinctions between play therapy and art therapy with children. Here, too, the differences are not always visible on the surface. A session of art therapy with a child or a group might look very much like play therapy, especially if there is any media exploration or dramatization. This is true in several vignettes in Chapter 1, like those about Amy, Alan, Jeff, and Lori. Art and play are closely related, since playfulness is part of any creative process, and there is considerable artistry in good play therapy.

These overlappings are, however, analogous to the educational aspects of art therapy and the therapeutic aspects of art education. In art therapy and art

Figure 2–4 Art therapy group, Sojourner House Women (PCA).

education, the **modality** (art) is the same, but the **goal** (therapy vs. education) is different. In the two types of child therapy, the **goal** (therapy) is the same, but the **modalities** (art vs. play) are different.

Even when dramatic play occurs in art therapy with children, there are still distinctions between art and play therapy. Although most play therapists provide some art materials, they are usually offered along with a range of other play equipment. A recent collection of "favorite play therapy techniques" included many which used art media, but usually in structured activities designed for specific purposes. Art therapists are more likely to foster free self-expression, even when specific tasks are utilized. Art therapists also generally provide a greater variety of art materials, and are able to teach children how to use them effectively.

In the 1994 book *Family Play Therapy* (Schaefer & Carey, eds.), several chapters mentioned using art materials. One, for example, described the "**Collaborative Drawing Technique**," a highly structured 15–minute exercise designed by a clinical psychologist. Each family member uses one color of crayon, and takes turns drawing on a 12″ × 18″ piece of paper. The turns are timed by the therapist to get progressively shorter until the task is done. In contrast, art therapist Helen Landgarten's chapter on "**Family Art Psychotherapy**" described many creative diagnostic and therapeutic art activities using varied materials; which promote free and individual expression, at the same time that they clarify interaction patterns.

Pediatric Art Therapy & Child Life Programs

There is also some overlap and interaction between art therapy with young people and pediatric art therapy, as well as a field which is as young as art therapy—"Child Life." The **Association for the Care of Children's Health** (**ACCH**), founded in 1965, is a multidisciplinary organization which promotes the psychosocial well-being of children and families in health care settings. Child Life Specialists work to reduce the psychological trauma for hospitalized children and their families.

In the past, most play programs in hospitals for children were staffed by volunteers. In 1964, a Child Development student running a play program at the Children's Hospital in Pittsburgh asked if I would teach the volunteers how to use art in their evening activities. In 1971, an art therapy intern travelled through the wards, offering art materials and support to children before and after surgery, as well as during long hospitalizations (Fig. 2–5). And a "Hospital Drawing Book" was such a success that we were able to retrieve only one finished copy. Perhaps because of these earlier efforts, the Director of the first Child Life program at that hospital requested inservice training in art therapy for her staff.

Art therapists in other parts of the country are even more directly involved in this area of work. One, for example, was Director of the "**Art & Play**

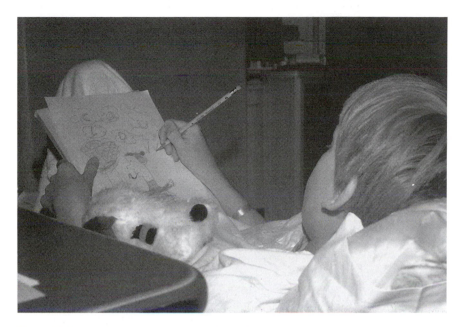

Figure 2–5 Child drawing after surgery in the hospital.

Therapy Program'' in the Pediatric Department of San Francisco General Hospital (CATT, p. 219). Another, trained as both an art therapist and a Child Life Specialist, directed the **"Creative Arts Child Life Program''** in a New York hospital where 80% of her staff were registered art therapists (AT, 1995, p. 104). In an equally humane **"Arts Medicine''** program, doctors, nurses, and artists-in-residence provided services on a pediatric oncology unit in Gainesville, Florida—led by a physician.

Art Therapy & Art Counseling

Another overlapping area of work with young people is occasionally referred to as "art counseling." "Counseling" is sometimes a synonym for "advice" and at other times for "psychotherapy." Counselors tend to be employed in education or rehabilitation settings, and specialize in many different areas. Those with an affinity for visual expression have integrated art into their work. One was James Denny, author of "Art Counseling in Educational Settings," who published several other articles in the *Bulletin* (1969, p. 25; 1972, p. 117) about his work with college students.

John Allan, who worked with school children in Vancouver, authored two books which describe ways of using art and writing to counsel children in schools (1988, 1992). Many art therapists act as consultants to art and classroom teachers, as well as to guidance personnel, in schools for both normal and disabled youngsters. The American Counseling Association has published a book on the use of the *Creative Arts in Counseling* (Gladding, 1992), and the George Washington University Counseling Center, for example, has offered art therapy since 1978 (AJAT, 1981, p. 101).

OTHER CLINICIANS WHO USE ART

Occupational, Recreation, & Activity Therapy

There are many superficial similarities between art therapy and other ancillary treatments that use art activities. In the sixties, Occupational Therapy departments were usually psychodynamic. Since such approaches stressed the dangers of repression and the values of expression, it was natural that art and craft activities were central in O.T.

When I was asked to consult to the large and well-equipped O.T. program at Western Psychiatric Hospital and Clinic in 1969, art therapy pioneer Margaret Naumburg advised me not to do so. She was in favor of my consulting to the new Day Hospital (like today's "Partial Hospitalization" programs), because what they were doing was "real therapy" (group psychotherapy).

There was much overlap at that time between art and occupational therapy in materials and approaches, and pioneers like Naumburg feared that the young field might be engulfed by its more powerful older sibling. Occupational therapy has since become less psychodynamic, and has moved away from its earlier emphasis on arts and crafts activities. Nevertheless, many art therapists began their careers under the job title and/or the supervision of an **occupational, activity** or **recreation therapist**.

All of these fields use art as one of many possible activities, forms of recreation, or ways of being constructively occupied. All of them also tend to provide art as an activity for some **prescribed purpose**, usually specified by the referring physician. Although the social and emotional well-being of the patient is of interest to other activity-based therapies, art therapists focus on the psychological aspect of the work. In addition, these other therapies are always **adjunctive**, while art therapy often is not.

Art therapists—because of their greater familiarity with media and processes—can serve as resources for these other professions, and can learn from them as well. The woman who taught crafts to the same hospitalized children I saw for art therapy in 1963 had been trained in occupational therapy. She taught me "**task analysis**," a method of breaking a task into its smallest components. This kind of thinking is especially valuable in selecting, offering, and evaluating art activities for those who are neurologically impaired and/or developmentally disabled.

Art Therapy & Other Uses of Art in Psychotherapy

Art therapy is actually more similar to other psychotherapeutic approaches which use art materials than to its activity therapy relatives. For example, projective drawing tasks were originally the province of clinical psychologists, and social workers used art materials in activity group therapy. Psychodynamic therapists have been especially attracted to the use of art in their work because of the ability of imagery to bypass defenses. And since art materials can be used by a wide range of people without specific training, it is no wonder that many clinicians have offered art media to those they are interviewing (e.g., Coles, 1992), and especially to their clients in individual, family, and group psychotherapy.

Despite the fact that many in the field seem to feel remarkably proprietary, art therapists do not **own** art, any more than they own therapy. What they do have to offer, that is unique, is a highly developed expertise in the use of art as a central modality in therapy. This is true whether the art therapy is adjunctive to verbal psychotherapy, or is the primary treatment itself. At first, art therapy was usually adjunctive, though it was sometimes used by psychoanalytic clinicians as a major form of expression in treatment. Lately, more art therapists are functioning as primary therapists, probably because of the growing sophistication of trained art therapists, as well as changes in human service delivery.

As for the many others who also use art in healing, Elinor Ulman pointed out long ago (1977) that *"Painting and sculpture are subject to such a broad range of therapeutic and educational applications, that the boundaries between art therapy and other disciplines are inevitably blurred"* (p. 7). She also observed that *"patients are not ordinarily concerned with professional distinctions, so they will occasionally turn out sculptures in occupational therapy sessions and make ashtrays in the art room"* (p. 37). Ulman's parting words were that all those *". . . who use art in their practice must live with the task of sharing their common ground as peacefully as possible and must learn to respect each other for the special knowledge and skills that are unique to each professional group"* (p. 39).

ART THERAPY & EXPRESSIVE THERAPIES

It is easy to tell the difference between art therapy and close relatives like music, movement, dance, drama, or poetry therapy—at least when each is offered separately. But there is considerable confusion about approaches which use multiple modalities. Multimodal approaches are usually called by names like **"expressive [arts] therapy"** or **"creative [arts] therapy."** Although there are a few individuals with the ability to evoke and to facilitate expression in more than one art form, such people are rare. More often, a therapist has training in one creative art modality, along with an openness to and comfort with others.

The following vignette is about the close relationship between all expressive modalities, which come naturally to young children. This close relationship between different modes is also present in adolescents and young adults, who simply need more help to access their creativity. Although Carla's treatment was primarily through art, she also used drama and film-making in her therapy.

Expressive Therapy Ends Nightmares: **Carla** (8)

The oldest of four little girls, eight-year-old Carla had been a pretty happy child. But shortly after the birth of the latest baby, she began to have nightmares almost every night, often wetting the bed as well. Her tired mother brought her to a clinic, and she was referred to me for weekly individual art therapy. For many months she refused to talk about or to draw her scary dreams, but instead painted beautifully colored "bars" behind which the monsters were hidden.

One day when she couldn't decide what to make, I suggested a "scribble drawing." Carla must have been ready to find and to represent her "Nightmare Monster," for that is what she made, telling the story as she drew (Fig. 2–6). The monster caught first one little girl, then another, then Carla too. After showing all three girls in the monster's clutches, she drew one yelling "Help!" Picking up a red tempera marker, she pounded vigorously on the paper, calling the blotches "soldiers," who she hoped would be able to rescue the children. Throughout most of the drama, Carla was uncertain about the outcome. At the very end, however, she declared with relief that the soldiers would win and the monster would be killed.

For months Carla drew monsters of all shapes and sizes, using a variety of media. For a while, she cut out the monster drawings and placed them inside cut-paper cages she had carefully constructed. And for two weeks, she insisted that the caged monsters be locked in my desk drawers. As Carla became more familiar and comfortable with these images, it was possible for her to extend the fantasy in dramatic play.

One week, she spontaneously used soap crayons and painted my face as the nightmare monster, asking me to pretend to attack her. The following week, she reversed roles and became the monster, attacking me as the fearful child (Fig. 2–7). It was during this period that the nightmares stopped. Art allowed Carla to **see** the scary-mad monster, while drama allowed her to safely **feel** her anger. Over the course of another year, she was able to become comfortable with her jealous and hostile feelings—to integrate them. When the time came for her therapy to end, Carla was sad.

For her last project, she decided that she would make an 8 mm. film about monsters, suggesting that I show it to other children with fears like hers. She cut out monster heads which moved (magically, through simple animation) around the walls, finally scaring a little girl (Carla) at the sink. The girl then came to see me, we returned to look at the heads together, and presto! They had disappeared! The film was a creative way for Carla to review the main problem for which she had been in therapy, reminding herself of what she had learned. It was also a way to deal with her envy of future patients (siblings), by transforming her jealousy into generosity through the defense of reaction-formation.

Mixing Modalities In Treatment

My own experience with other expressive arts therapists began in a **study group**. The group, which had been organized by a child psychiatrist, also included a

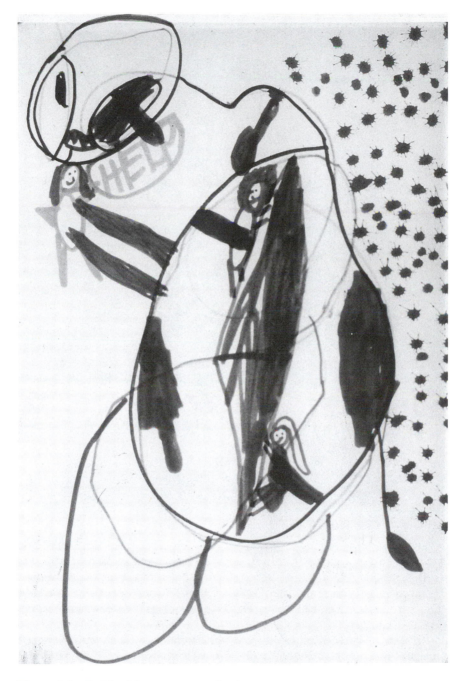

Figure 2–6   Carla's nightmare monster drawing.

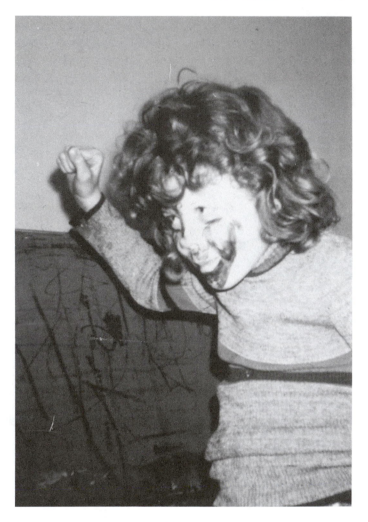

Figure 2–7 Carla attacking me as the nightmare monster.

drama and a dance therapist, as well as psychologists and social workers inter-
ested in the arts. We initially worked **side-by-side** with the same children in a
Therapeutic Day Camp, and later **jointly** in ''**Art-Drama**'' groups with children
(Fig. 2–8), adolescents, and adults (Fig. 2–9), as well as ''**Parent Play**'' groups
(Fig. 2–10, p. 79).

In such an interdisciplinary mix, it was natural to want to learn from one
another. As a result, I added simple musical instruments and dramatic play
equipment like puppets, dolls, and props to the art materials in my playroom.
Nevertheless, while the children were able to use the others spontaneously, I
was still best at facilitating expression with art materials. My colleague, Ellie

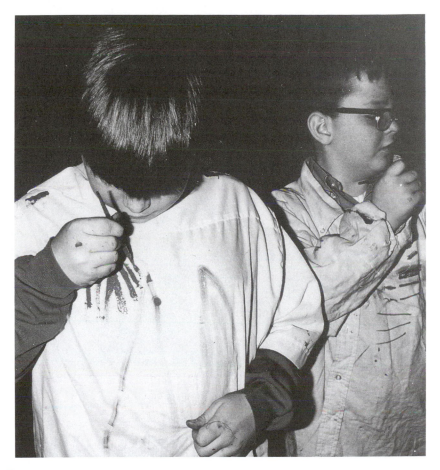

Figure 2–8 Two boys create soldier "uniforms" for a drama.

Irwin, similarly added art materials to her playroom, but she was more skilled at helping children in drama.

There have been a few individual art therapists who have been able to facilitate expression in more than one modality. At the 1973 AATA conference, for example, art therapist Mildred Lachman (Chapin) who was also a trained dancer, offered a workshop on ''**The Use of Movement in Art Therapy.**'' At the 1976 conference, Harriet Wadeson described ''**Combining Expressive Therapies in an Experience Group**'' for adults in long-term psychiatric hospitalization, something which was common in the era before effective anti-psychotic medications. Her **multimodal group**—using relaxation exercises, movement, music, drama, fantasy, and art—seemed to be the only way to reach these severely withdrawn patients.

Figure 2–9 A woman & her mask: Art-drama therapy group.

Sharing & Collaborating

The trend in art therapy **training** programs has been to focus on expertise in the visual arts, though some have fostered exposure to other expressive modalities as well. Many **service** programs have also expanded to include more than one creative arts therapy. A similar process is reflected in the story of one **journal**, which began in 1973 as *Art Psychotherapy*. First, articles in other creative arts therapies were accepted, then there were separate editorial boards, and in 1980 the name was changed to *The Arts in Psychotherapy*. The stimulation of cross-fertilization is a major fringe benefit of communication. This is evident in recent books from Great Britain, which include chapters by art, music, dance, and drama therapists on practice, training, and research.

Despite the fears of some individuals that involvement with other groups would dilute or contaminate art therapy, the advantages of working with music, drama, and dance therapists are great. In addition to the expansion of service and training programs, political coalitions have been formed and have been quite effective. Although some worried that the natural rivalry of creative arts siblings

Figure 2–10   A woman blows bubbles: Parent play group.

for jobs and recognition would be destructive, that has not generally been the case.

The **National Coalition of Arts Therapy Associations** was formed in 1979. The member groups of NCATA have worked together, holding Joint Conferences (1985 and 1990), as well as regular meetings to address common political concerns. While a closer administrative relationship among the member organizations has been proposed, it has yet to occur. Cooperation for political and economic purposes has been acceptable to all members of the coalition; but an underlying tension between autonomy and collaboration remains. In European coalitions, relationships among the different creative arts therapies seem to be similarly ambivalent. The ongoing debates concern both practical and philosophical issues.

Training Issues

Many art therapy educators question the feasibility or desirability of training students in more than one creative modality. Most express anxiety about producing shallow dilettantes, though some have become more comfortable with multidisciplinary approaches. Two training programs in the U.S. were in ''**expressive**

therapies'' from the start. Several others have added some kind of **exposure**—if not training—in other art forms. However, even those with multimodality orientations require students to **specialize** in one of them.

Connie Naitove, who formed the National Educational Council of Creative Therapies in the seventies, called what she did **''multi-arts therapy.''** Connie preferred to be a **generalist**, seeing the arts as historically interwoven; but she also respected those who wanted to be specialists. Her position statement and Myra Levick's response were published in 1980 (AP, p. 253). Levick described how programs training music and dance therapists were added alongside the already-existing art therapy training program at Hahnemann Medical College. Like Gladys Agell, who debated Shaun McNiff on the same topic at the 1982 AATA conference (AJAT, 1982, p. 121), Levick saw training competent generalists as impossible.

One of the first art therapists to advocate a multimodal approach was Shaun McNiff, whose training program at the Institute for the Arts & Human Development of Lesley College was in the ''Expressive Therapies'' from its inception in 1974. In several of his books, McNiff has described his rationale for a multimodal approach to expression and training, noting its roots in **shamanism** and ancient healing rituals.

His colleague, Paolo Knill, has also argued for an interdisciplinary approach. In one article, he explored the connection between expressive therapies and related phenomena in both the arts and psychotherapy (AP, 1994, p. 319). His theories were further articulated in a book subtitled *Intermodal Expressive Therapy* (1995). Knill agrees with the critics that a superficial acquaintance with different techniques is meaningless, stressing instead what he calls **intermodal** understanding, comparing it to art forms like opera, film, or performance art.

Stephen Levine, who co-directs a training program in expressive arts therapy in Toronto (ISIS-Canada) has a similar philosophy and approach, which he articulated in *Poesis* (1992). Ellen Levine, co-director of ISIS, has also contributed her ideas about such work in *Tending the Fire* (1995). Along with others, the couple is involved in a Canadian multimodality organization called **C.R.E.-A.T.E. (Creative & Expressive Arts Therapies Exchange)**. The area of multimodal ''expressive therapy,'' is growing, as is evident in the recently organized (1995) **International Expressive Arts Therapy Association**. Although most art therapists are still trained and skilled primarily in the visual arts, there seems to be a greater openness to the use of other art forms than in the past (Cf. Levine & Levine).

Choosing a Multimodal Approach

Certain groups naturally evoke multimodal expression. In my work with young children, related modalities often emerged spontaneously, as with Carla. A child might use fingerpaint as make-up, and create a role (Fig. 2–11). He might create a prop, like a sword, and then use it to attack in a drama (Fig. 2–12). Or he

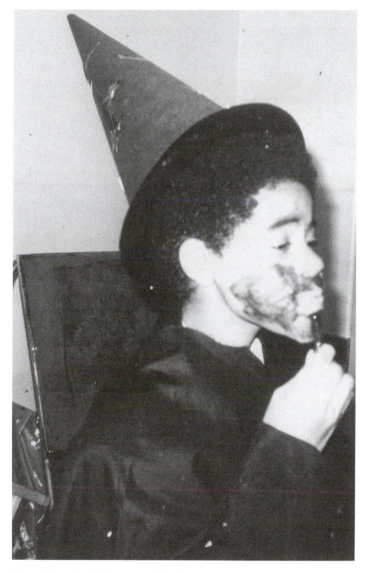

Figure 2–11   A boy in art therapy decides to be a wizard.

might pick up a clay sculpture and start to speak for it as if it were a puppet. Violet Oaklander, a Gestalt therapist, has used art and other creative modalities in her work with children and adolescents. And Natalie Rogers, who first worked as a play therapist, has advocated the use of all of the arts with people of all ages.

In addition to population as well as personal and philosophical predilections, geographic isolation and the search for kindred spirits is probably a factor in the adoption of a multimodal orientation, as with C.R.E.A.T.E. in Toronto. In

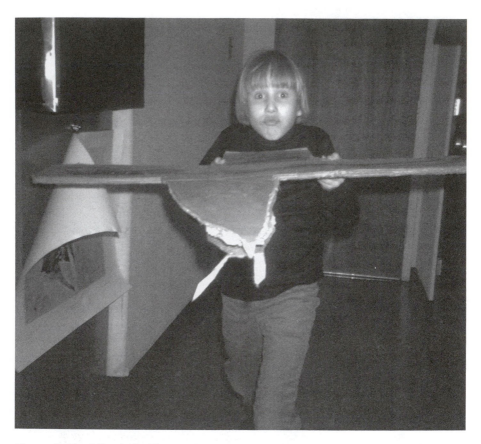

Figure 2–12 A Boy in Art Therapy Attacks with his Sword.

Pittsburgh, for example, there were so few creative arts therapists that in 1973 we founded a multi-arts organization, The Pittsburgh Association for the Arts in Education & Therapy (PAAET).

One of our colleagues at the Pittsburgh Child Guidance Center was Penny Bernstein Lewis, author of several books on dance therapy. She later published another in which she used art, drama, and music as well as movement. Penny's embrace of multiple creative modalities may have been enhanced by the many groups she and I co-led with Ellie Irwin, our drama therapist colleague.

A multimodal expressive therapies approach seems to many to be as natural as children's play or religious ritual. But it is not for every client or for every practitioner. It has always been popular in the "human potential" movement, from its early beginnings in the sixties to its revival in the nineties. This is evident in the numerous multimodality arts workshops offered at growth centers like Esalen or Omega, and described in periodicals like *Common Boundary*.

In 1981, Ellie Irwin and I were asked to develop a department at the **Western Psychiatric Institute & Clinic (WPIC)**. We chose to have a multi-arts therapy team, and hired music, dance, drama, and art therapists. We called it **CEAT (Creative & Expressive Arts Therapies)** because we couldn't choose between the richness associated with both **expression** and **creation**. An article written about our program was entitled *"Words Can't Say it All"*—like a recent book on expressive art therapies, subtitled *"When Words are Not Enough"* (Levy et al., 1995). As we had by then discovered in our clinical work many times over, no single art form says it all, or is right for every person or for every purpose.

There is as yet no consensus about the meaning of terms like "expressive" or "creative" therapies. As they are currently used, they deal with two different phenomena. One involves arts therapists from distinct disciplines working together collaboratively. The other is a genuinely integrated expressive arts approach by an individual therapist, who has primary expertise in one art form but who offers others as well. And, since the word "**art**" can refer to all creative modalities, there are even times when "art therapy" means "**arts** therapies." Similarly, there are times when "**creative therapy**" refers not to many art forms, but to one alone. To Dr. Margarethe Hauschka in Germany, for example, "**artistic therapy**" means "**painting therapy**."

ART + THERAPY = ART THERAPY

The definitions of art therapy currently offered by both the **American Art Therapy Association*** and the **British Association of Art Therapists**** allow for a wide range of activities, with varying degrees of emphasis on either component of the mix. There is clearly a **continuum** in the use of art for therapeutic purposes, from the intrinsically healing experience of the creative process to the diagnosis and treatment of specific conditions. Although the debate about the definition of art therapy continues, most practitioners would agree with Elinor

---

*Art therapy is a human service profession that utilizes art media, images, the creative art process and patient/client responses to the created productions as reflections of an individual's development, abilities, personality, interests, concerns, and conflicts. Art therapy practice is based on knowledge of human developmental and psychological theories which are implemented in the full spectrum of models of assessment and treatment including educational, psychodynamic, cognitive, transpersonal, and other therapeutic means of reconciling emotional conflicts, fostering self-awareness, developing social skills, managing behavior, solving problems, reducing anxiety, aiding reality orientation, and increasing self-esteem" (AMERICAN ART THERAPY ASSOCIATION, 1997).

**Art Therapy is a process involving a transaction between the creator (the patient), the artefact and the therapist . . . Art therapists provide for their patients an environment, art media, and very importantly, themselves—in terms of time, attention and a clearly defined relationship. The aim of the session(s) . . . is to develop a symbolic language which can provide access to unacknowledged feelings and a means of integrating them creatively into the personality, enabling therapeutic change to take place. The therapist's focus is not particularly on the aesthetic merits of the art work . . . but on the therapeutic process—that is, the patients' involvement in the work, their perception of it, and on the possibility of sharing this experience with the art therapist" (STANDING COMMITTEE FOR ARTS THERAPIES PROFESSIONS, 1989).

Ulman, that whatever is called ''art therapy'' needs to partake in an authentic way of both art and therapy.

Learning the history of the discipline, like the history of an individual or a family, is an excellent way to understand how art therapy came to be what it is today. In 1980 psychologist Rudolf Arnheim gave the keynote address at an AATA conference. His understanding of our genetics was simple: ***Psychology and art may be called the father and the mother of art therapy.*** The next chapter will look more closely at the broader question of our complicated heritage, asking ''Where Did Art Therapy Come From?'' exploring the origins of Art Therapy and the history of the profession.

Chapter 3

History

ART THERAPY IS NOT A MODERN INVENTION. *"If men of worth did know what delight [art] breedeth,"* wrote Nicholas Hilliard, Court painter to Queen Elizabeth I, *"how it removeth melancholy, avoideth evil occasions, putteth passions of grief or sorrow away, cureth rage and shorteneth the times, they would never leave until they had attained in some good measure or more their comfort."*

Writing more than 300 years later, Jung made much the same observation:
"A patient needs only to have seen once or twice how much he is freed from a wretched state of mind by working at a symbolical picture, and he will always turn to this means of release whenever things go badly with him."

ANTHONY STEVENS

IN THE BEGINNING: ORIGINS OF ART THERAPY

Multifaceted Metaphors

I have been trying to figure out just how to introduce the reader to the multifaceted origins of the field of art therapy. Like most artists, I favor visualization, so I found myself thinking of images. First I thought of a **Tree**, its roots extending in many directions underground, drawing upon nutrients in the soil, while its leaves and limbs absorb nourishment from the atmosphere. As an image of art therapy, it combines the deep and ancient roots of the field with its constantly developing, newly budding branches. These have taken in much from the surround, and already bear a remarkable array of blossoms, in their short but fruitful history.

Another way to picture art therapy's history would be as **Streams**, flowing from different sources into a larger body of water. Many streams of varied origin have fed the pool of knowledge that is art therapy. The larger body of water could be a lake or a pond, within which all kinds of life can germinate, continually expanding and enriching the mix. The history of the field is in many ways like that of **still water**, much developing unseen until it emerged. As with a natural pool, the presence of art therapy in many places has facilitated the growth of other kinds of life around it.

On the other hand, the destination of the many streams could be a **flowing river**, which picks up and deposits all kinds of substances as it wends its way.

The history of art therapy has in many ways been like that of a river, fed by formerly-icy and later rapidly-melting creeks. In fact, there has been a gradually onrushing quality to the development of art therapy in America over the course of the past fifty years. Although it has never reached dangerous flooding proportions, it has at times threatened to overrun its own banks, and has had to work rapidly to shore them up by strengthening its standards of training and of practice.

Like any body of water, whether still or in motion, the fortunes of the field of art therapy have been affected by all kinds of environmental factors. Skeptical attitudes have thawed and climates have warmed, allowing the flowering of many developments in the profession. The pressures of societal tides and currents have also shaped the course and tempo of art therapy's development. Both trees and water are organic images, part of the natural world—also the foundation of art therapy.

Natural Beauty is Soothing

In fact, the bedrock, the underground source of healing through beauty—whether taking it in or creating it—is not only art, but the natural world from which it springs. Many have found in nature's eternal wonder an echo of something deep in the human soul; whether it be in the rhythm of the waves, the rustling of the leaves, or the howl of the storm. I have often soothed myself, when too troubled to create, by searching for a peaceful spot. Then I can drink in the delicate shape and shifting tones of a wildflower, the linear tracery patterns of trees silhouetted against the sky, or the majesty of a brilliantly-hued sunset.

The power of the aesthetic, the beautiful, to quiet and to calm, to contain even ugly passions, is so profound as to be incalculable. Why else would we derive such joy from natural beauty or such pleasure from the arts? It seems that the nonverbal forms we treasure are so very valuable because they mirror, echo, and express the ineffable, unspeakable feelings we all carry within, from birth until death. And when we touch and shape materials in making art, we experience our impact on the world; indeed, we feel our very existence.

Creating Comes Naturally

Creating seems to be natural to our species, involving a spontaneous impulse, if not an actual need. Making marks comes so easily in fact to infants and toddlers, that we were not terribly surprised to learn from anthropologists like Desmond Morris that our closest animal relatives—apes and chimpanzees—also love to draw and paint, sometimes enough to postpone food or sex while engaged in creating (Fig. 3–1). Those that have learned sign language even name their scribbles, just like toddlers.

I once had the good fortune to accompany art therapist David Henley on a visit to the Lincoln Park Zoo in Chicago, where he had been going for weekly art sessions with the animals (Fig. 3–2). Though his chimp friend made it clear

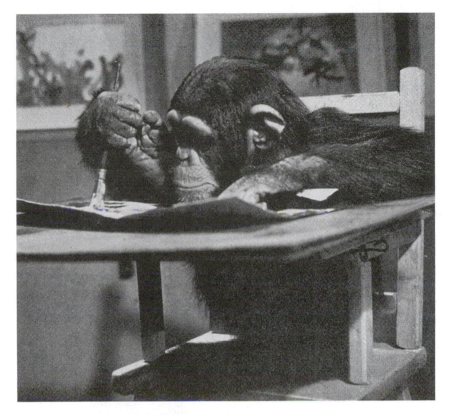

Figure 3–1 Congo the chimpanzee painting a picture.

that she didn't feel like painting that day, I did get to watch a mother elephant and child painting side by side, brushes held in trunks, both rhythmically swishing colors back and forth on the paper.

I had the further pleasure of observing a gorilla named June create a crayon drawing, which I treasure as a memento of the visit. June's drawing itself was unremarkable, like a child's scribble. But watching her concentrate on the activity for a full five minutes in a large cage full of noisily playing apes was astonishing. Although I have often seen people similarly absorbed in drawing (Fig. 3–3), I felt like I was witnessing first-hand the primal pleasure of a deep engagement in the creative process.

Art for Healing is Ancient & Universal

So the origins of art therapy lie in many different natural realms. Although its emergence as a newly-defined profession is relatively recent, its roots are ancient and universal. Prehistoric artists who drew animals on the walls of caves (Fig. 3–4), or who carved fertility figures, Egyptian painters of protective symbols on

Figure 3–2 David Henley painting with a chimpanzee.

Figure 3–3 A young boy deeply absorbed in drawing.

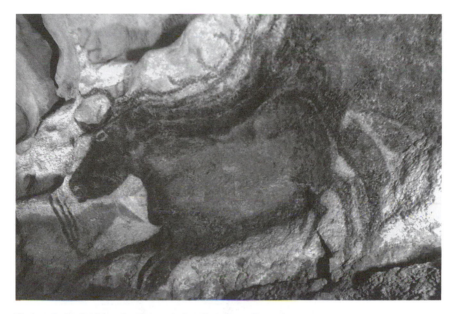

Figure 3–4 Prehistoric cave painting (Lascaux, France).

mummy cases, Tibetan Buddhist creators of sand mandalas, African carvers of ritual masks, Byzantine painters of sacred icons, Ethiopian artists who drew on parchment healing scrolls, Zuni carvers of magic fetishes—all represent one powerful stream flowing into the basin of modern art therapy.

Like the unconscious mind itself, this source is ever-present as a part of the human condition. The "magical thinking" behind such things as faith healing and voodoo effigies is not simply an ancient relic or exclusive to primitive cultures. It is, in fact, present in us all, not only when we are children but eternally, in that part of the mind not accessible to rational thought. It may well be the source of the "placebo effect" and the success of mind-body approaches to healing. What art historian/psychoanalyst Ernst Kris called the "**magic power of the image**" is very real for human beings, and we who work with art in therapy know and respect it. Man's profound belief in this phenomenon may even be the primary reason that art has always been so therapeutic.

Equally ancient is the use of symbolic expression in order to heal. In most "primitive" societies, the visual arts are evident in the ritual decoration of body, costumes, masks and other props, the beautification of the sanctuary, and the creation of a setting for the ceremony. More dramatic still is the use of magical visual symbols, such as fetishes, talismans, or sand paintings. Medicine men and shamans have been thought of as the forerunners of modern psychiatrists. They are even more clearly the ancestors of creative art therapists.

Because of the universality of art-making and image-magic, and because of the related power of the symbolic mode, healers past and present have utilized many different art forms in their work. Most healing rituals incorporate the rhythm of the chant, the beat of the drum, the movement of the dance, and the drama of the story, along with the power of many visual elements. One summer in New Mexico I accidentally came upon a Hopi Rain Dance, an event not normally open to the public. One need only witness such a ritual, with its total and passionate community involvement, to sense the awesome power of the arts in a culture where they are still central and very much alive.

The Climate Was Ripe for Art Therapy

In spite of these deeply entrenched roots, the climate had to be ripe for growth. We would probably not have discovered so many ways of using art in, for, and as therapy, had not the late 19th and early 20th century been so fascinated by the concept of the **unconscious**. This idea was made popular not only in the depth psychologies of **Freud** and **Jung**, but also in the novels of James Joyce and the poetry of the French Symbolists. Artists have always delved within for the source of their imagery as well as their creative power. It was not until quite recently, however, that exploring, knowing, and representing the inner world was articulated as a respectable aesthetic goal.

Around the time that **psychoanalysts** were beginning to plumb the mystery of dreams, Western **artists** were in the process of giving up the representation of the outside world for the mysterious goal of expressing the inner one. They were attracted to what seemed more pure, less fettered expressions of man's spirit, such as the masks of Africa or the prints of Japan. And they set out—not to reproduce external reality as before—but to reflect the reality of the soul. This was the goal of such artistic techniques as Automatic Drawing. And it was the essence of movements like Expressionism and Surrealism—to depict emotion through color and line—as in Edvard Munch's "The Scream" (Fig. 3–5), or to show the irrational landscape of the dream, as in the paintings of Salvador Dali.

Meanwhile, the artist himself was becoming more and more of a social outcast. No longer automatically supported by social structures like the church or royal patrons, he became more starkly than ever the lone seer—a prophet who saw and told of things we didn't always want to know. And perhaps even more than in earlier eras, the artist became a creature of glamour, as did the creative process itself.

Psychiatric Interest in Patient Art

Also during the late 19th and early 20th centuries, some psychiatrists, stimulated by the possibility that what had been thought to be irrational might make sense after all, became fascinated by the **spontaneous art of the mentally ill**. People caught up in the turmoil of a psychotic break, threatened by loss of contact with reality, frequently felt compelled to create something as a way of coping with their confusion (Fig. 3–6). Sculptures of bread dough, and drawings on scraps of toilet paper or walls, had long been noted in institutions housing the insane.

Figure 3–5 "The Scream" by Edvard Munch.

Around the turn of the century, a few psychiatrists began to collect the spontaneous art work of their patients. Although most "regarded them only as curiosities" (Plokker, 1965, p. 83), there were some notable exceptions. Paul-Max Simon, a French psychiatrist, published the first serious studies of the drawings of the mentally ill (1876, 1888). He was joined by Cesare Lombroso (1887), whose linking of genius with insanity is still being debated today. In 1901, a French psychiatrist named Reja wrote about the art of the mentally ill, noting three types. These early workers appreciated, even before the advent of depth psychology, that patients' products were related to their conflicts—that, as confusing as they often were, they made a kind of **psycho-logical** sense.

Figure 3–6   A patient & his sculptural creation at an asylum.

With the arrival of psychoanalysis, those studying the mind began to find ways to unlock the puzzle of **"primary process"** (unconscious, illogical) thought. They were thrilled to be able to decode the meanings of images, whether in dreams, reverie, or the art of the insane. In 1918 Paul Schilder, the psychiatrist who originated the concept of the **"body image,"** published a monograph in which he compared art by one of his patients to the avant-garde work of the time, suggesting what while both seemed "mad" to the layman, they also made psychodynamic sense.

In 1921, a Swiss psychiatrist named Morgenthaler published a case study of Adolf Wolffli, a gifted paranoid schizophrenic artist (recently translated by an art-loving analyst). The soil that nurtured expressionism and psychoanalysis was rich with the excitement of discovering buried treasure. In 1922 a Viennese art historian and psychiatrist named Hans Prinzhorn published the most extensive study ever of the art of the mentally ill (trans. 1972), and part of the collection toured the U.S. in 1985. The most recent survey of the topic is by art historian James MacGregor (1989) (Cf. also Jakab, 1998).

Interdisciplinary Exchange

Interest in the **"Psychopathology of Expression"** has continued. For many years, psychiatrists, art historians, and art therapists from around the world have met regularly in an interdisciplinary organization. The **International Society for Psychopathology of Expression (I.S.P.E.)** was founded in Europe in 1959; the **American Society for Psychopathology of Expression (A.S.P.E.)** in 1966. In addition to representing one of the interest areas leading to the emergence of art therapy, the meetings of the A.S.P.E. facilitated communication among art therapists in the U.S., especially before there was a national association. In addition, the published *Proceedings* (Jakab, ed.) provided invaluable written resources for art therapists, when literature in the field was still extremely scarce.

Another forum for interdisciplinary exchange was provided by Mary Perkins, an art teacher at the Dr. Franklin Perkins School (for retarded children) in Massachusetts. Mary organized a series of meetings in the seventies entitled **"The Arts in Education International Seminar Series."** In 1972, the topic was "Order and Discipline in Art as Models for Effective Human Behavior." As a participant, I had the pleasure of meeting many interesting people, including my roommate, pioneer British art therapist, Diana Halliday. In her paper, Diana quoted Professor Carstairs:

> *"Art expression is as old as Paleolithic man, and as young as psychedelics. It has been the medium for profound explicit commentaries on the state of the world, on the nature of man, and also for the relatively formless emotional outpourings of lyricism—or of torment."*

A similarly fruitful interdisciplinary dialogue was facilitated through a series of symposia and publications in the eighties, about *Psychoanalytic Perspectives on Art* (Mary Gedo, Ed.), which were organized by a team of an analyst (John Gedo), an art historian (Mary Gedo), and an art therapist (Laurie Wilson).

Creativity & Madness

Another interdisciplinary series of conferences, held in artistically-rich settings, have been sponsored since 1983 by the American Institute of Medical Education. The meetings, occurring several times a year, and a book, *Creativity and Madness: Psychological Studies of Art & Artists* (Panter et al., Eds.) are organized by a multidisciplinary group (psychiatrist, internist, artist, art therapist).

Studies of the psychopathology of expression are related to the ongoing debate about the relationship between creativity and madness. The nature of the connection is, of course, relevant for art therapy. It is now known statistically, as well as anecdotally, that the incidence of bipolar (manic-depressive) disorder is significantly greater among creative artists than in the population at large (Jamison, 1993). It is also known that some individuals are more productive during episodes of illness, while the creative output of others suffers in both quantity and quality. Did Van Gogh and Munch paint **because of** or **in spite of** their ailments? The question is a complex one at best, and there is as yet no clear consensus.

What is less debatable and more relevant is that people suffering from acute mental distress are often better able to express themselves through the more direct language of paint, clay, or pastels. When the verbal mode is absent (as in catatonia or mutism), or so confused as to be largely indecipherable (as in the "word salad" and neologisms of some psychotic states), "image-talk" can be a vital form of communication, and a welcome release of tension. Psychotic imagery is sometimes childish, primitive, and confused; but it can also be very beautiful. Its aesthetic appeal is probably more significant than its symbolic meaning in terms of its persistent popularity.

Art Brut & Outsider Art

Since the turn of the century, artists and art critics have been intrigued with the art of untutored individuals, including the spontaneous and lively work of young children. As noted earlier, the Impressionists were fascinated by the art of primitive tribes and exotic cultures. Many artists and critics have valued work by those with no formal training—called "naive" or "primitive"—from the Frenchman Henri Rousseau to the American Grandma Moses.

Since the late forties, painter Jean Dubuffet and others have been drawn to what is known as "**Art Brut**" (Thevoz). This is a broad characterization covering all kinds of "raw" creations, including artwork by those with mental illness. Also called "**Outsider Art**" (Cardinal, 1972; Hall & Metcalf, 1994; Trechsel, 1995), both names capture the sense of alienation associated with untamed expressions of the human spirit—whether by indigenous peoples, children, naive adults, or those with mental disorders.

Art in Diagnosis & Therapy

A similar vein fertilizing the soil for the eventual emergence of the field of art therapy was the growth of "**projective testing**" in the field of clinical psychology. Fingerpaint, from the time of its invention by teacher Ruth Shaw in 1931, was thought to be potentially diagnostic as well as therapeutic. My own first exposure to the idea that art could show something significant about people was in a 1954 child psychology class, where my teacher, Mrs. Alper, shared her discovery that children from different socioeconomic milieus did very different kinds of finger paintings. When she held up the pictures, her excitement was contagious.

In addition to being attracted to the use of art for the purpose of **assessment**, it was natural that analytically-trained clinicians of all sorts would be drawn to employ it as a means of **psychotherapy**. In fact, almost all of the references I found on the "psychology of children's art" for a 1957 seminar (with the exception of those by art therapy pioneer Margaret Naumburg) had been written by psychologists or psychiatrists. One was Ernest Harms, who first published in English in 1939, later founding *Art Psychotherapy* (1973). There were also

Figure 3–7 Psychiatrist Joseph Berke with Artist Mary Barnes

papers by the team of psychologist Ernest Zierer and his artist wife Edith, who began using "creative analysis" at Hillside Hospital in 1943.

Some responsive therapists whose psychotic patients began to spontaneously communicate through art encouraged them to do so and utilized it as part of the treatment. There were many such clinicians, including Marguerite Sechehaye in France, Ralph W. Pickford in Scotland, Marion Milner and Joseph Berke (Mary Barnes) in England (Fig. 3–7), Ainslie Meares in Australia, Ingrid Naevestad in Norway, and Sigrid Ude-Pestel in Germany. Their case studies demonstrate how their capacity to "hear" their patients' "symbolic speech" was crucial to their success.

Therapeutic Art Education

While these developments were occurring in mental health, educators were discovering the value of a freer approach to art in schools. Inspired by Froebel's "kindergarten" in Germany and Montessori's "infant schools" in Italy, many were persuaded that children needed to learn in more direct, personally involving ways. Those in "**progressive education**" were especially convinced that creative experiences in art were vital to healthy emotional development.

Early art education had been rigidly didactic, involving the copying of "good" art and the learning of basic principles of color and design. With the growth of the **child study movement**, along with the value placed by psychoanalysis on the dangers of repression and the virtues of expression, things began to change. In Vienna an art teacher named Franz Cizek, who coined the term "*Child Art*," encouraged children to paint and draw in a natural fashion—then a radical idea (Viola).

There was another Viennese who observed Cizek's methods, and who was especially sensitive to the value of personal expression in helping children to achieve what he called "**self identification**." He was also exposed to psychoanalytic ideas during the formative years of his career, and was taught by Oskar Kokoschka, an Expressionist painter. Because he wrote a textbook in 1947 which has been used to train art teachers for over 50 years, **Viktor Lowenfeld** has had a profound influence on art education.

Since his early work had been with blind and partially-sighted children (1939), Lowenfeld was attuned to the perceptual and emotional impact of a handicap on a child's self-concept (Fig. 3–8). In a 1957 chapter omitted from later editions of *Creative & Mental Growth*, he described what he called an "**art education therapy**" for children with various disabilities. Although he made it clear that he was not advocating that teachers do counseling, Lowenfeld

Figure 3–8 Viktor Lowenfeld with a handicapped child.

himself was briefly employed as an "art therapist" at institutions for the blind and the retarded in 1938 and 1939.

Lowenfeld was not alone in championing the psychological value of spontaneous expressive art for children. In England, freer art teaching was being advocated by Herbert Read and others. One was Maria Petrie, an art teacher who had fled Nazi Europe. In Part III of *Art & Regeneration* (1946)—entitled "**Art & Therapy**"—she described how art could help those suffering from physical, sensory, mental, medical, and societal ills.

In the U.S., another refugee, Henry Schaeffer-Simmern, described his "experiments" in teaching art to several atypical groups (1948), including delinquent and retarded individuals (Cf. Sarason). In New York City, Florence Cane, an art teacher to whom psychiatrists referred patients, wrote a book about her methods for evoking creativity and promoting healing (Fig. 3–9), which she called *The Artist in Each of Us* (1951).

Artists in Hospitals

The history of art in psychiatric settings is almost as old as the units themselves. As early as 1907, a teacher of clay modeling was working at Massachusetts General Hospital; and in 1929, William Alan White, superintendent of St. Elizabeth's Hospital in Washington, presented a paper on "The Language of the Psychoses," with many references to patient art. During the Depression, one of President Roosevelt's "New Deal" agencies, the Works Progress Administration (WPA), employed artists in the **Federal Art Project**. Through this avenue, art teachers were enabled to offer classes during the thirties to psychiatric patients in various settings, such as Bellevue Hospital in New York City (Cf. Bender).

By the forties the ground had been prepared, as it were, for the planting and budding of this new discipline. Most of the early work on the psychopathology of expression had been done by European psychiatrists. However, the same political situation that drove Petrie to England and Lowenfeld to America richly fertilized the soil in the United States, largely due to the influx of analysts and of psychodynamic thinking.

ART THERAPY IS BORN

Naumburg & Kramer

Two remarkable women were primarily responsible for the planting, tending, budding and blossoming of the American art therapy garden. Their contributions were distinguished not only by their pioneering work, but also by their articulate prose, which defined the new field. Both **Margaret Naumburg** and **Edith Kramer** were sophisticated in their reading and understanding of analytic theory, child development, art, and education. They were unusually well-qualified to

Figure 3–9   Florence Cane with a group of students.

synthesize these understandings into a theoretical basis for the newly-emerging discipline of art therapy. And both were scholars, exploring other domains, like archeology or ethology, to deepen their grasp of art therapy. Each of them was also extremely independent—as a person and as a thinker.

Although both relied on psychoanalytic theory, their definitions of art therapy were quite different—one stressing the **therapy** and the other the **art**. Margaret Naumburg saw art as a form of **"symbolic speech,"** coming from the unconscious like dreams, to be evoked in a spontaneous way and to be understood through free association, always respecting the artist's own interpretations. Art was thus conceived as a "royal road" to **unconscious symbolic contents**, a means of both diagnosis and therapy, requiring verbalization and insight as well as art expression. Edith Kramer, on the other hand, saw art as a "royal road" to **sublimation**, a way of integrating conflicting feelings and impulses in an aesthetically satisfying form, helping the ego to synthesize via the creative process itself.

Margaret Naumburg was also influenced by her sister, Florence Cane, the analytically-oriented art teacher mentioned earlier. Naumburg herself was a pioneer in education as well as in art therapy. She founded a school named Walden in 1914, explicitly rooted in psychoanalytic principles, which (like the discipline she mothered) is still alive and well (Naumburg, 1928). A remarkable woman, she had studied with the pioneer educators John Dewey and Maria Montessori. Naumburg had been so impressed by the infant field of psychoanalysis that she had urged all of the teachers at Walden to be psychoanalyzed. For several years, beginning in 1920, the art teacher at Walden was Florence (Naumburg) Cane.

Margaret Naumburg had the good fortune, as did other pioneering art therapists, to meet a psychiatrist who already felt that art could be a useful tool in both assessment and therapy. Dr. Nolan D. C. Lewis had in fact published two papers himself in the twenties on the use of art in psychoanalytic treatment. He was the "fairy godfather" who opened the doors of the New York State Psychiatric Institute to Naumburg from 1941 to 1947, during which time she worked with individuals using art, and published a series of case studies in psychological journals.

Naumburg collected her child case studies in a 1947 monograph. She was intent on presenting her research as scholarly, since she wanted art therapy to be taken seriously. Margaret Naumburg remained a tireless ambassador for art therapy throughout her life, lecturing far and wide in order to acquaint other professionals with this new field. She published three more books (1950, 1953, and 1966), as well as many book chapters and catalogs for exhibitions of patient art (Fig. 3–10).

Naumburg was something of a rebel, no doubt an essential quality for anyone choosing to challenge the establishment. In her theory too, she was unusually eclectic for the period. Having experienced both a Jungian and a Freudian analysis, she saw values in each which were relevant for the use of art in therapy. She was also open-minded about the meaning of visual symbols, choosing to rely on the artist's own associations.

The other most influential writer and theorist was Edith Kramer. An artist who fled Prague just before the second world war, Kramer had been exposed to a rich diet of psychoanalytic thinking, as well as to Lowenfeld's ideas about art education. Having already seen the value of art for the refugee children she taught before leaving Europe, Kramer was ripe for a job in 1951 as an art therapist at Wiltwyck, a residential school for disturbed children in New York, obtained with the help of her "fairy godmother," child psychiatrist Viola Bernard. Her first book, *Art Therapy in a Children's Community* (1958), was inspired by this work (Fig. 3–11).

Figure 3–10 Later portrait of Margaret Naumburg.

Figure 3–11   Edith Kramer doing an art evaluation.

Kramer's thinking was different from that of Naumburg, whose theory of art therapy reflected the emphasis in early psychoanalysis on **making the unconscious conscious**. Kramer learned analytic theory in a milieu which stressed **ego psychology**. It is also relevant that Kramer's work was always as an **adjunctive therapist**, allowing her to freely concentrate on the inherent healing properties of the creative process; whereas Naumburg's role increasingly became that of **primary clinician**. Kramer also contributed greatly to the literature, publishing two more books (1971, 1979), and many important articles (ATTP, ATV).

Other Art Therapy Pioneers in the United States

Actually, one of the odd things about art therapy is that, since it was indeed **an idea whose time had come**, even its acknowledged "mothers" did not give birth entirely on their own. Not only are there many genetic roots; art therapy is a child with multiple parents, all with "legitimate" claims. In fact, as art therapy came to be better known, many individuals in different places appear to have given birth to remarkably similar ideas around the same time, often unknown to one another. In other words, it seemed—after there was better communication—that there were many people doing "art therapy," sometimes even calling it by the same name.

Figure 3–12   Bernard Levy Teaching an Art Therapy Class.

Often there was another individual, one who already had credentials for being there, who opened or widened the door for the neophyte art therapist. **Elinor Ulman**, for example, had a friend in artist/ psychologist **Bernard Levy**, with whom she worked at D. C. General Hospital during the fifties. He helped her start the first journal in the field, as well as an early training program—at George Washington University, where he was Chairman of the Psychology Department (Fig. 3–12). The three East Coast pioneers were well known, primarily because Naumburg and Kramer wrote the first books, and Ulman published seminal articles in the **Bulletin of Art Therapy**, some of which she later collected in two edited books (ATTP, ATV).

There were also other art therapy trailblazers who had toiled in the hinterlands for many years. With the soil so fertile in the predominantly psychoanalytic world of mental health, and in the ''progressive'' domain of education, artists and teachers doing something ''therapeutic'' were springing up all over, like wildflowers after a Spring shower.

Although the Menninger Clinic is in the wide open prairie of the Midwest, it is also one of the most sophisticated psychiatric treatment centers in the world. Because of the vision of the founding family, it has pioneered in all of the activity therapies. From 1935 to 1937, an artist named **Mary Huntoon** was invited by Dr. Karl Menninger to offer classes in painting and drawing to psychiatric patients. In 1946 Dr. Menninger asked Huntoon to organize one of the **first art therapy studios** in the U.S., at the new Winter Veterans Administration Hospital, also in Topeka, Kansas.

In l951, art therapy at the Menninger Foundation began another phase with the arrival of **Don Jones**, an artist who, as a conscientious objector, had worked in a psychiatric hospital during WWII. Jones, who stayed at Menninger's for 15 years, later trained an artist named **Robert Ault**, who was hired in 1960, and who subsequently trained **Charles Anderson**, hired in 1968.

Both Ault and Jones were on the Steering Committee that formed the **American Art Therapy Association** after Jones had moved to Harding Hospital in Columbus, Ohio. Both also pioneered in developing some of the first **clinical internship training programs**. There were many others in different places in this country who were usually invited into a psychiatric setting by a psychiatrist or a psychologist, and whose primary identity was as an artist or educator. Many of these individuals, like **Marge Howard** in Oklahoma or **Elsie Muller** in Kansas, gathered with the East Coast pioneers and their students at meetings of the A.S.P.E., led by another psychiatric "fairy godmother" of art therapy—**Dr. Irene Jakab**. As one of the founders of I.S.P.E. in Italy in 1959, she was quick to found and to lead the American society in 1966.

In the nation's capital, yet another pioneer art therapist was learning her trade in prestigious institutions. She was a sculptor from Poland named **Hanna Yaxa Kwiatkowska**, and she had the good fortune to work first (1955) at St. Elizabeth's Hospital—which actually had had an "art therapist" since 1943 (**Prentiss Taylor**)—and then at the National Institutes of Mental Health (1958). At NIMH she gave birth—with the support of her psychiatric colleagues doing seminal work in the new field of family therapy—to **family art therapy** and **family art evaluation**.

Myra Levick, who started the **first graduate training program** in art therapy at Hahnemann Medical College in 1967, was an artist who had been invited to work with psychiatric patients at Hahnemann Hospital in Philadelphia by Dr. Paul Fink, a psychiatrist and psychoanalyst who became her ally and guide. Together, they started a service program and graduate-level training. They also got the national organization of art therapists under way by hosting a critical meeting in Philadelphia in 1968.

Levick (along with Ault, Jones, Ulman, and Felice Cohen from Texas) was on the Steering Committee that incorporated the **American Art Therapy Association**, which was actually "born" at a second meeting at the **University of Louisville** in 1969. As the first President of AATA, Levick presided in 1970 at its inaugural meeting, with 100 people (including myself) in attendance. The first **"Honorary Life Membership"** award (HLM) was presented to Margaret Naumburg, widely acknowledged as the primary parent of the field of art therapy. Additional information about the beginnings of art therapy in America may be

Figure 3–13 Edward Adamson with patients in his studio.

found in *A History of Art Therapy in the United States* by Maxine Junge and Paige Asawa.

Art Therapy in Other Countries

If Naumburg is the "**grandmother**" of art therapy, the most likely candidate for "**grandfather**" would be her British counterpart, an artist named **Adrian Hill** who published two books, in 1945 and 1951. Hill wrote that he had coined the term "art therapy" in 1942, to describe the value of doing his own painting while he was recovering from tuberculosis in a sanatorium. Invited to offer art to other convalescents, Hill was as enthusiastic and energetic a campaigner for art therapy in Great Britain as Naumburg was in the United States.

Although the story of art therapy in England is as long and varied as in America, the growth of the discipline has not been as rapid. Even though the **British Association of Art Therapists** was formed earlier (1964), Diane Waller's history suggests that political and economic pressures complicated the development of both jobs and training programs. But there were "fairy godfathers," like psychiatrist E. Cunningham Dax, who in 1946 hired artist **Edward Adamson** to set up a studio at Netherne Hospital (Fig. 3–13).

The primary "fairy godmother" in Great Britain was **H. Irene Champernowne**, a Jungian analyst who, with her potter husband, Gilbert, founded a residential treatment facility in which the arts were central. **Withymead**, a creative therapeutic community, was operated from 1942 to 1967 (Cf. Stevens). Adlerian "social clubs" were run by Dr. Joshua Bierer in London, where pioneer British art therapist **Rita Simon** began her work in 1941. And Jungian art therapist **E. M. Lyddiatt** developed studios in many mental hospitals beginning in 1950, which she described in her 1971 book (Cf. Thomson).

Canadian art therapy also had its indigenous pioneers—like **Marie Revai**, who was art therapist at the Allan Memorial Institute in Montreal, **Louise Annett** who ran a sheltered workshop for retarded "craftsmen," and psychiatrist **Martin Fischer** who started the Toronto Art Therapy Institute. Because of Canada's vast size, many worked for long periods in isolation, like **Selwyn Dewdney**, who was the art therapist at a psychiatric hospital in London, Ontario, from 1947 to 1972. He and his wife **Irene**, who joined him in 1956, published several papers during the sixties in the *Bulletin* (ATTP, ATV). Art therapy is currently alive and well in all regions of Canada, with associations and training programs in each.

While the growth of art therapy in other countries has been slower, recent decades have seen the development of budding programs around the globe. In the **Netherlands**, "**creative therapy**" has been practiced since the fifties, with formal training since 1980. It seems to be largely an "**art as therapy**" approach; in contrast to **Finland**, where psychoanalysts have supported its development as an "**art psychotherapy**" approach.

In **Japan** the founding fathers were psychiatrists, like Dr. Tokuda, who themselves had been using art in therapy since the fifties. Even in this culture, so radically different from our own, art therapy has been incorporated into treatment settings like Ureshino Hospital, operated according to traditional Japanese principles of healing (as described by Michael Campanelli at the 1990 ASPE Conference).

It seems that, even if the seeds were planted early in other countries, they have usually taken longer to germinate than in the U.S. For example, in **France** the **Association Francaise de Recherches et Applications des Techniques Artistiques en Pedagogie et Medicine** was formed in 1974, yet it was not until 1988 that the **Federation Francaise des Arts-Therapeutes** was born. In England the **BAAT** was founded in 1964; yet only recently have British art therapists begun to publish extensively.

In 1989, California art therapist **Bobbi Stoll** created a much-needed structure by founding the **International Networking Group of Art Therapists (ING/AT)**, which sponsors a biannual *Newsletter*. The **European Consortium for Arts Therapies Education** was formed in 1991, and has since held several international meetings. The **European Advisory Board of National Art Therapist Associations** met for the first time in 1993 in **Germany**, with the goal of working "on the recognition of the different arts therapies professions." The British agreed to develop "a questionnaire to determine the current situation of art therapy in a given participating country." These developments are reminiscent of the early stages of information-gathering and organizing among art therapists in the U.S.

Currently, communication is becoming possible with some societies formerly closed to the West. In **Russia**, a meeting of expressive therapists from the U.S.

and Europe was held in 1993, and a Conference on the arts in psychotherapy and other fields in 1995. That year, a delegation of art therapists consulted with mental health colleagues in **China**, and in 1996, a similar group visited **Indonesia**. What is impressive about all of this international networking is that in 1998, the *Newsletter* of the ING/AT listed 64 countries, covering every continent on the globe. Even more noteworthy is the existence of 38 national art therapy associations and 22 journals of art therapy; and it should be noted that these numbers represent only those **known** to the ING/AT.

In addition to training initiated by indigenous groups, many Americans have taught courses abroad, and a number of educational institutions in the U.S. and Canada have established satellite programs in Europe and Israel. The journal, *The Arts in Psychotherapy* has always had an international Advisory Board, frequent contributions from abroad, and two issues devoted to "**European Perspectives on the ... Arts Therapies**."

Although the soil and atmosphere in different parts of the world might germinate a variety of art therapy plants, some sturdier than others, it seems clear that the discipline, at least for now, is here to stay. It is still growing in the United States, despite massive budget cutbacks and radical changes in human services. Since the places where art therapists work and the work they do have continued to proliferate, it would appear that continued growth is inevitable, at least in the foreseeable future (Cf. Waller, 1998).

Given the blossoming of art therapy all over the world, it seems fitting to close this chapter with a statement written two centuries ago by a German poet, novelist, and scientist, whose studies included an elaborate theory of color and the emotions. Johann Wolfgang von Goethe (1749–1832) has been admired by people as diverse as Rudolf Steiner, father of the rather spiritual philosophy of Anthroposophy, and Sigmund Freud, rationalist father of the highly verbal theory of Psychoanalysis. In *My Italian Journey*, published in 1787, Goethe wrote:

*"We ought to **talk less and draw more**. I, personally, should like to renounce speech altogether and, like organic nature, communicate everything I have to say in sketches."*

I have no doubt that Goethe would have welcomed the development of art therapy.

Chapter 4

Education

Training Ourselves
Informing Others

THUS, THE ART THERAPIST COMBINES SEVERAL DISCIPLINES.
He is at once artist, therapist, and teacher.
To maintain a sound balance between his several functions is his greatest skill.
EDITH KRAMER

EVOLUTION OF ART THERAPY EDUCATION

This chapter is primarily about the development of educational programs in art therapy, the training required to be a competent art therapist, and some of the unique aspects of learning in this field. The chapter is also about the education of other professionals and of the public. Although the discipline is still quite young, it can fairly be said to have "come of age" in many of those areas distinguishing the professions.

In order to promote art therapy education, the **American Art Therapy Association**, founded in 1969, first needed to define **a competent practitioner**, and then to articulate **guidelines for training**. The development of **standards** for both individuals and training programs is described in detail in Chapter 11. To understand how art therapy education has evolved, we will first review some of the many paths people have taken to become art therapists. In describing how today's learning routes have developed, I shall use my own experiences when they seem relevant to the issues at hand.

BECOMING AN ART THERAPIST

First Generation Pioneers: Individual Paths

As might be imagined from the story of how art therapy grew, each of the pioneers took a slightly different route, learning their skills along the way. As is true in most disciplines before any kind of formal training is available, education was largely informal and idiosyncratic. In countries where there are as yet no organized programs, training is still self-designed, as it was for those who parented the discipline in the U.S.

Most first generation pioneers were truly self-taught, like theorists Edith Kramer and Margaret Naumburg—each inventing her ideas about art therapy from her own experience. Also self-educated were artists like Edward Adamson in England and Mary Huntoon in America, who worked with hospitalized mental patients in a largely intuitive fashion. The guidance they received—from the psychiatrists who initiated and supported their presence—was usually to do what came naturally.

The idea in most settings where art was offered to mental patients was to make available the healing properties of the creative process itself. From the outset, there was a fear of compromising the therapeutic potential of art by "psychologizing" it. Clinical training, therefore, was not always seen as desirable for art therapists—something I was surprised to learn at the beginning of my career, as you will see in the following story.

Intuition: The Initial Instructor

In my first use of art in a psychiatric setting, I encountered this attitude from Professor Erik Erikson of Harvard. My contact with him, while brief, had an impact which lasted for years, delaying my search for training for almost a decade. Although my experience was hardly typical, it may be helpful to review, since it contains within it many questions about the best kind of training for art therapists confronting the new field.

Beginning in the fall of 1963, I had been meeting for weekly individual art sessions with hospitalized schizophrenic children. Probably because the setting was psychiatric, these meetings were referred to by others as **"art therapy."** Although my bachelors degree had been in Art, my masters was in Education, and I did not in any way feel like a "therapist." My activities were funded by a research grant to the Child Development Department, which was housed in Child Psychiatry. Professor Erikson, who had taught in that program, visited annually, and would always comment on a child case at a Grand Rounds to which the community was invited.

I was asked to participate because of the art work of Dorothy, whose story is told below. Her drawings and paintings were unusually eloquent, and had attracted the interest of all who had seen them. Dorothy's art was especially striking because it stood in sharp contrast to her speech and demeanor, which were bizarre and virtually unintelligible. In the case presentation, attended by many professionals, the director of the unit and Dorothy's psychiatrist discussed her history, diagnosis, and treatment. I showed slides of her art work and described her behavior during our sessions. Professor Erikson critiqued the material, and suggested ideas for further treatment.

When I met afterwards with my Chairman and our distinguished visitor, Erikson complimented me warmly on my work. I told him that I felt I could help even more if I understood better what was going on, and that I was longing for further training. For months I had been concerned that I didn't comprehend enough about what was happening with these children, that I was "flying by the seat of my pants" while conducting the art sessions. I felt uncertain about what I was doing, despite the fact that I attended staff meetings, collaborated with the psychiatrists, and met weekly with Dr. Margaret McFarland, the clinical psychologist who had first suggested the "art therapy" program.

Much to my surprise, Professor Erikson was adamantly opposed to further training of any sort. He suggested that it might well ruin—or at least interfere with—something of value in the spontaneous/intuitive approach I was, by default, forced to follow. Years later, after learning more about him, I had some hypotheses about why he had cautioned me with such conviction. Erikson himself had first been an artist and then a teacher, prior to becoming a psychoanalyst. In addition, he was analyzed by another self-educated innovator—Freud's daughter Anna—one of the architects of both ego psychology and child analysis.

It is also relevant that his dancer wife, Joan, had started an activity program at Austen Riggs, where craftsmen and artists worked with the patients (1976). By the time he was advising me, she was the artist in the family and he was the therapist. Fifteen years later, when Joan Erikson and I served together on an advisory panel, I learned the depth of her conviction about the hazards of "therapizing" art (AJAT, 1979, p. 75). She also told me that she had observed poorly-done "art therapy"—a common problem before adequate training programs and standards of practice were in place. As Marge Howard said in 1962, at that time "anyone with a paintbrush and a patient" could claim to be an art therapist (!) (ATV, p. 102).

Art Clarifies a Child's Fantasies: **Dorothy** (10)

Dorothy was the girl with "childhood schizophrenia" whose art Erik Erikson saw at Grand Rounds. Her story, described in more detail in *Child Art Therapy* (Rubin), is briefly told here. Dorothy was a strange looking and odd acting little girl, who sometimes flapped her arms and chirped like a bird or meowed like a cat. Her speech was unintelligible, except for her perseverative plea to "Go Home!"

But Dorothy loved her weekly individual art sessions, taking to them immediately. First, she did a series of beautiful, brightly-colored birds, always outlining them in pencil before filling in the colors with crayons or paint. One day I wondered if she'd like to try painting freely at the easel without drawing first. She was elated, creating then and in subsequent sessions a series of monsters (Fig. 4–1), sometimes attacking humans.

These pictures allowed fearful Dorothy to safely discharge her pent-up aggression. Her articulate images also helped the professionals to understand the multiple meanings of the bird for her. It symbolized not only her wish for freedom, but also her violent wishes and fears (Fig. 4–2).

Because of the relief she felt after this explosive artistic expression of unconscious fantasies, Dorothy was able to turn her attention from her

Figure 4–1 Dorothy's first Painting of the Bird Monster.

inner world to the outer one. She proceeded to draw highly perceptive portraits of the other youngsters on the ward. These drawings were so accurate that they delighted the other children, and Dorothy became less isolated.

She also drew a series of pictures about cats and cat families, which poignantly expressed her longings. Though Dorothy had been unable to form attachments to many people, she had felt close to her art provider. The ending of her therapy was caused by my pregnancy, not her readiness, but she was able to express her anger after I had left, in a picture of "Mrs. Rubin being Attacked by Soldiers for Being Bad" (Fig. 4–3).

Learning by Doing

After Professor Erikson's visit, I tabled my explorations and plans for further study, at least for a time. My curiosity about art therapy was channeled primarily into reading, especially the eagerly-awaited issues of the *Bulletin of Art Therapy*,

Figure 4–2 Dorothy's bird attacking a human being.

to which Margaret Naumburg had suggested I subscribe in 1963. In 1966, Fred Rogers, whom I had met through Dr. McFarland, invited me to be on his new public television program. As "the art lady" on "**Mister Rogers' Neighborhood**", I used my ad-libbed segment to communicate the therapeutic values of art (Fig. 4–4).

During that same year, I also began teaching courses in Art Education at a local college. Since the school was receptive to a course in the "**Therapeutic Aspects of Art Education**," I had the pleasure of designing and teaching those classes. They were similar to the many individual **courses in Art Therapy** which had begun appearing in the fifties in educational institutions around the country. Like the other instructors, I was teaching a class about a subject I had never formally studied myself (!).

Like many of my colleagues, I also learned a great deal by developing programs in a variety of treatment settings. In 1967, I was invited to start an Art Department at an institution for orthopedically-handicapped youngsters—the Home for Crippled Children. I was aghast at how few children were seen by the professionals as being able to participate.

Figure 4–3 "Mrs. Rubin Attacked by Soldiers for Being Bad."

Thanks to my experience with the hospitalized children, I was able to design a rudimentary "**Art Assessment**," to determine who might benefit from art. The following vignette about Claire, while fairly dramatic, was not so unusual. Happily, everyone in the institution was capable of doing something, though many required creative adaptations to do so (Fig. 4–5). The program itself was modelled on my partly-digested understanding of the ideas of art educators like Lowenfeld, Cane, and Robertson; as well as the theories of art therapists like Kramer, Ulman, and Naumburg.

Figure 4–4 A "Mister Rogers' Neighborhood" segment.

Figure 4–5 Children with spina bifida working on trays.

Art Reveals Capacities   : **Claire** (10)

Claire had just come back from the dentist. Inside, she was screaming with the agony of the encounter, but she had no words, not even gestures, with which to express the impact of this traumatic experience. For Claire was a deaf-mute, crippled and in a wheelchair. Before she drew her first picture, she had been withdrawn from school and speech therapy, since the staff felt from her behavior that she was profoundly retarded.

As it happened, Claire's art evaluation was scheduled right after a visit to the dentist. She wheeled herself up to the table, grabbed a marker and paper, and drew a picture which—more eloquently than any words—told what it feels like to be invaded by the dentist's tools, to be open and vulnerable and terrified (Fig. 4–6). Though helpless, like any patient in a

Figure 4–6   Claire's picture of "A Girl at the Dentist's."

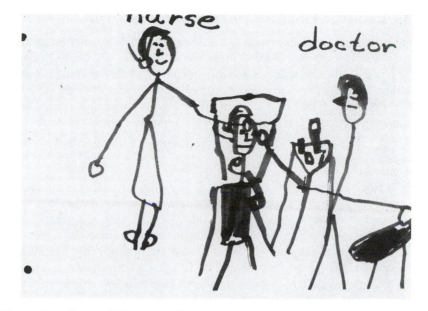

Figure 4–7 Nurse, girl & doctor in Claire's talking book.

dentist's chair, Claire could master the traumatic event by expressing her feelings in art, effectively turning passive into active.

More important for her future, the age-appropriate drawing revealed that Claire's intelligence was much higher than anyone had imagined. She was again placed in a classroom and resumed language therapy. In both settings, she used a "Talking Book" to communicate with others. The pictures were drawn by Claire and then labelled by the teacher or speech therapist, as in this picture of the doctor and the nurse (Fig. 4–7).

Learning by Sharing With Others

By that time, I had heard of a child psychiatrist named Marvin Shapiro who was interested in the arts therapies, and went to see him in 1968. He invited me to join a weekly **Expressive Arts Study Group** he had recently started at the Pittsburgh Child Guidance Center. Due in part to those discussions—and in part to my case presentation on Dorothy five years earlier—I was offered the opportunity to start a **Pilot Program** at PCGC.

The memory of Dorothy's art must have been vivid, because the Chairman of Child Psychiatry referred to it several times when we met. He agreed to support a one-day-a-week trial of art therapy at the department's outpatient clinic. This incident illustrates a major factor in the growth of art therapy: the impact of **pictures** that are indeed "**worth a thousand words**" on decision-makers.

Learning Through Psychotherapy & Supervision

Having consulted with both Margaret Naumburg and Edith Kramer in the early sixties, I again sought the advice of these pioneers. They were most generous with their time—meeting with me, allowing me to attend classes, and to observe art therapy sessions. Their ideas about art therapy were quite different from one another, but their advice about learning to be a good clinician was not. Each, independently, had said that there were two key things I needed to do if I was going to become an art therapist. One was to **engage in my own psychotherapy**, which I had already initiated in 1967. The other was to **be supervised by an experienced clinician**.

Both pioneers said that a supervisor's professional discipline mattered less than his or her respectful support of art therapy. I was very fortunate to have an enthusiastic mentor in Marvin Shapiro. Most of the "fairy godparents" who facilitated the hiring of art therapists trained them too, as in my case. The supervision was frequent and intensive. Dr. Shapiro, who was also a child analyst, observed numerous art therapy sessions (diagnostic, therapeutic, individual, family, and group) through a one-way observation window. We met for two hours every week.

Both of us knew that art therapy was "**on trial**" at PCGC. We needed to prove—to those in the established disciplines of psychiatry, psychology and social work—that art therapy could offer something unique. Most early art therapists were required to demonstrate the value of this unfamiliar discipline to those in charge. This is still true whenever art therapy is new to any setting. Although such pressure is stressful, it is also a powerful stimulus for creative problem-solving.

Apprenticeships, Early Courses, & Training Programs

Like artists through the ages, some who were in a setting that already had an art therapist obtained an **apprenticeship**. At first, these were individualized situations, like Don Jones training Bob Ault at Menninger's, or Hanna Kwiatkowska training Harriet Wadeson at NIMH. In most institutions, art therapists also learned other specializations by working with colleagues. Depending on the setting, an art therapist might learn about psychoanalytic theory, family or group therapy, or how to conduct experimental research. Just as the early courses were precursors of organized training programs, so these apprenticeships foreshadowed the development of formal clinical internships in art therapy.

Like the profession itself, art therapy education had a long incubation period prior to one of rapid growth. Although isolated courses and some certificate training programs had started earlier, the formation of the American Art Therapy Association in 1969 was a tremendous impetus to the development of formal training. When the *Bulletin* was first published in **1961**, there were five institutions offering seven courses, taught by four art therapists. Both Kramer and

Figure 4–8 Margaret Naumburg teaching a seminar.

Naumburg taught introductory courses in New York throughout the sixties (Fig. 4–8). Both taught at the New School for Social Research, Naumburg at NYU, and Kramer at the Turtle Bay Music School. In Washington, courses were taught by Elinor Ulman and Hanna Kwiatkowska at the Washington School of Psychiatry. And **Janie Rhyne** offered workshops through the San Francisco Gestalt Institute.

By 1971, the demand for training opportunities was much greater than the available supply. Three institutions were awarding masters degrees; and several clinical internships were also available. Although the graduate schools had initially offered one-year programs, within a short time they all added a second year of full-time training—a step taken in the nineties in England. In less than a decade (1979) there were 22 graduate programs with a concentration or degree in art therapy, 41 undergraduate programs, ten clinical programs, four certificate programs (for post-graduate training), and eight special programs. Moreover, 28 colleges were identified on the **AATA Education List** as offering one or more courses in art therapy.

Over time, the period of rapid proliferation has yielded to one of consolidation, although the number of graduate programs has continued to climb. By **1997**, there were **55 graduate programs** (36 degree programs, four institute and 15 certificate/diploma programs). In contrast to 1979, by 1997 there were only 25 undergraduate degree programs. Although many of the early academic programs had been undergraduate, there was intense debate within AATA about the adequacy of such preparation. A masters degree was ultimately recognized as the entry level, primarily because of the maturity required to do art therapy.

Graduates of baccalaureate programs in art therapy no longer receive credit toward registration. Instead, bachelors degree programs are viewed as preparation for graduate work, not for training clinicians. Nevertheless, during the three years in which this book was being drafted, the number of undergraduate programs with majors in art therapy began to grow once again. This trend may be related to the fierce competition for the limited number of spaces in graduate degree programs. It may also reflect the current attempts to cut costs in all areas of service delivery by "downsizing." In psychiatric hospitals, for example, senior clinicians are being laid off, and those with bachelors degrees are being hired as "milieu therapists." Individual courses in art therapy are now so widespread that the listing formerly provided by AATA is no longer necessary.

EVOLUTION OF CONTINUING EDUCATION

Even before Continuing Education credits were required to maintain Board Certification (instituted in 1994), there had been a growing interest among art therapy practitioners in expanding their skills and knowledge. Since **1982, Pre-** and **Post-Conference Mini-Courses** have been offered by AATA, usually with university and C.E. credits available. In addition, since **1988, Regional Symposia** have been organized by AATA, and are available at no charge to the sponsoring local chapter. Each symposium is led by presenters who are invited because of their expertise on the topic.

As the field has expanded and grown, so have the interests of its practitioners. Just as many entered art therapy from other fields, many have studied other areas. The goal was not to change their professional identity, but rather to deepen understanding of their work as art therapists. Over time, individuals have studied various specialties, such as marital, family, or group therapy, as well as psychoanalysis. Some have earned degrees in counseling, social work, or clinical psychology. A few have learned specific skills, like sign language or hypnosis. Others have obtained doctorates in a variety of fields, including interdisciplinary ones in art therapy itself.

Learning Through Further Education

My own story, the beginnings of which were described earlier, is also relevant here. Professor Erikson had indeed succeeded in discouraging me from seeking further training in 1964. Working at PCGC in January of 1969, I was soon supervised on a regular basis not only by Dr. Shapiro, but by two other experienced child psychiatrists. I was also collaborating with experts in research, family therapy, projective drawing assessment, and group dynamics on different projects, learning from each joint venture.

Since PCGC was an academic center for many disciplines as well as an outpatient clinic, there was a great deal of inservice training available, which I took advantage of whenever possible. I have gone into detail, because even these rich and varied resources were not sufficient to compensate for my areas of deficit. In fact, I had not been there very long, before I began to wish again that I understood more about what was happening with the patients I was seeing in art therapy.

Fortunately, my primary supervisor (Shapiro) was as **encouraging** as Erikson had been **discouraging**. By then I had spent several years in the individual psychotherapy recommended by both Naumburg and Kramer, and I was being supervised by experienced clinicans, as they had also suggested. Unlike my earlier adjunctive work in the hospital, this therapy was outpatient, and I often became the **primary therapist** for nonverbal youngsters. I therefore felt an even greater responsibility to deepen my rudimentary clinical skills and understandings.

Since my undergraduate major was Art and my master's degree was in Education, I first investigated doctoral studies in Psychology, the area in which I felt weakest. By the seventies, however, psychology departments were less interested in training clinicians than researchers. They had also become less psychodynamic and more behavioral in orientation. I chose instead to study **psychoanalysis** at the local Institute, primarily because my best supervisors and teachers had been analysts.

Halfway through my training analysis, I discovered that my feeling that I didn't "need" a Ph.D. had neurotic roots. In fact, it became clear that, for me, the degree represented a penis, which I felt I didn't "need" in order to be recognized. While it is true that I didn't require a phallus to be a therapist, I was denying the realistic benefits of having a Ph.D.

I was fortunate to find a **doctoral program** in the School of Education in **Counseling**, where I could obtain credit for my master's degree and for courses at the Pittsburgh Psychoanalytic Institute. I was also able to meet the dissertation requirement by writing a book about art therapy with children. One of the reasons the proposal was approved was that in 1975 it was easy to demonstrate the need for more art therapy literature, since there were very few books by art therapists.

The doctorate required that I become competent in six areas: research, consultation, supervision, systems theory, group dynamics, and theories of psychotherapy other than Freud. The psychoanalytic training required that I conduct six supervised analyses (three adults and three children), attend courses, and complete the required personal analysis. That training lasted from 1973 through 1983, while the Ph.D. was completed in 1976. Weekly microscopic supervision using detailed process notes was one of the most helpful aspects of analytic training. The tripartite integration of theory and practice with my analysis was a wonderful way to learn. It also validated the requirements which were being developed for art therapy training: a combination of didactic instruction and supervised clinical work (see Chapter 11).

RECOGNITION OF ART THERAPY

Obtaining Relevant Credentials

The most useful fringe benefit, for me, of obtaining the doctorate had not even been a goal of mine when I went back to school, because at that time art therapists in agencies did not need credentials. But what turned out to be most practical was being able to qualify after two more years of practice to sit for the *Psychology Licensing Exam.* When I left the university in 1985 for private practice, it was extremely helpful to have the license—a credential respected by most insurance companies—which would reimburse the patient for all or part of the cost of therapy. Although a license no longer automatically guarantees coverage, it is still useful and often vital.

Having a credential that is recognized by others eventually became a need for many practicing art therapists. For those teaching in an academic setting, a doctorate was desirable, if not essential. In a university, a Ph.D. is not only a way of obtaining respect among colleagues; it is also a means of achieving advancement and security. If the individual's need was primarily for clinical credentials that would make her eligible for licensure, she might pursue a master's degree in a more established field for which there is licensure in some states, such as Social Work or Marriage & Family Counseling. Since Psychology is licensed in all states, many art therapists have gotten a Ph.D. in Clinical Psychology or a Psy.D., a degree focussed specifically on clinical training.

Political Action & Networks

The need for licensure in art therapy itself has become increasingly evident. It is even more pressing now, due to massive changes in health care delivery during recent years, especially the development of "managed care." Like a growing child, the field in its youth was much more concerned with internal familial issues than with the outside world; so it took some time before art therapists started to pay attention to political realities. This ostrich-like posture was rarely challenged because, during the years of art therapy's most rapid growth in the U.S., ample funding was available for many kinds of human service activities.

Although art therapy was sometimes recognized by public figures—like **Eleanor Roosevelt**, pictured at an exhibit of art from Wiltwyck School with art therapist **Edith Kramer** (Fig. 4–9)—there was no organized effort at gaining recognition. Thanks to a gradual dawning of awareness, however, AATA slowly developed mechanisms for identifying and influencing relevant political activity.

Just as it might be hard for newcomers to believe that there was ever any question about the wisdom of forming a national association (Chapter 11), it might be equally surprising to learn that just 20 years ago there was a similar ambivalence about being politically active. Thanks to the foresight of a few individuals, an early ad hoc group with a tiny budget grew into a **Governmental Affairs Committee**, and AATA distributes a *Legislative Handbook*. No one would now question the importance of being alert, nor of supporting lobbying activity at both state and federal levels.

Much has been accomplished for art therapy by working with other creative arts therapy groups, both in legislative coalitions and through **The National Coalition of Arts Therapy Associations** (**NCATA**), formed in 1979. At the

Figure 4–9   Edith Kramer with Eleanor Roosevelt in 1958.

national level, there have been significant achievements. In 1975, art and dance therapists lobbying together enabled both modalities to be included in legislation regarding those with disabilities (PL 94–142, the **Education of all Handicapped Children Act**, updated in 1990 as PL 101–476, the **Individuals with Disabilities Education Act (IDEA)**.

In 1979, the creative arts therapies obtained **Federal Civil Service job classifications**. In 1980, they were noted in the Senate and House Report (96–712) on the **Mental Health Systems Act**. In 1992, art therapy was included in the **Older Americans Act**. In 1993, art therapy was described in some detail in the Report of the Panel on Mind/Body Interventions (National Institutes of Health, **Office of Alternative Medicine**). And in 1996, art therapy was included in the standards for **Day Treatment Programs**.

Creative arts therapists in many states have worked in alliance with other unlicensed master's level clinicians to become recognized as legitimate service providers. The networking between music, dance, drama, poetry, and art therapists at the local and regional levels has been at least as important as at the national level, and is becoming even more vital as the health care system reorganizes.

Communication with other art therapists in all geographic areas was greatly facilitated by the establishment within **AATA** of local **Affiliate Chapters** in **1982**. Some state art therapy groups actually predated the national one, like the Wisconsin and Buckeye Art Therapy Associations. The need for communication and representation finally overcame the complications of modifying local by-laws. These groups can now become Chapters of AATA by meeting relevant criteria. Each chapter sends delegates to an annual **Assembly of Affiliate Societies**, which then elects a Speaker, who sits on the AATA Board of Directors. To further grass roots access to the decision-making process, each Board member acts as liaison to a group of Chapters, of which there were 41 in 1997.

These regional organizations throughout the country provide a network for sharing political information, as well as the ability to respond rapidly when necessary. This is especially helpful whenever pending legislation requires quick action, as with a licensing bill in Pennsylvania which included art therapists along with other masters' level clinicians. After receiving requests to contact my representatives, I called the State Senator for my district, whose legislative assistant agreed to encourage him to co-sponsor the bill. She was favorably inclined because she had taken a course in art therapy, and was therefore eager to help in the effort to gain recognition. Art therapy in the U.S. has often been in the fortunate position of having friends in the right place at the right time. These allies in key positions have made possible a number of significant events, which have been critical in the rapid growth of the profession in this country.

Public and Professional Awareness

As already noted in Chapter 3, many promoters of art therapy facilitated the development of both treatment and training programs. In addition, several critical steps toward gaining recognition were made possible by art therapy's **"friends in high places."** When psychiatrist **Bertram Brown** was Director of the National Institutes of Mental Health, his support facilitated many things, including the publication of two bibliographies of art therapy literature (see Chapter 12).

Starting in the sixties, the **Maurice Falk Medical Fund** supported studies and films on dance, drama, and art therapy in Pittsburgh. In June of 1979, **Philip Hallen**, President of the Fund, suggested and funded a two-day **Conference on the Creative Arts Therapies**. This Washington meeting, sponsored and hosted by the **American Psychiatric Association**, was a marvelous opportunity to inform the invited decision-makers.

The next issue of *Hospital & Community Psychiatry* included a report on the conference, and an article by Dr. Israel Zwerling on "The Creative Arts Therapies as Real Therapies." In a related effort at educating those who at that time hired the majority of art therapists, an entire issue of the *Journal of the National Association of Private Psychiatric Hospitals* was devoted to the creative arts therapies.

Another outcome of the APA conference was a pamphlet, *The Use of the Creative Arts in Therapy*, summarizing the presentations. Perhaps the most important outcome was to follow the advice of the decision-makers who attended: to stop competing and to combine forces, in what soon became the National Coalition of Arts Therapy Associations (NCATA).

Meanwhile, AATA had been invited to attend meetings in 1976 and 1977 on **"The Healing Role of the Arts,"** organized by Hospital Audiences, Inc.

(HAI) with the support of the Rockefeller Foundation. And, thanks again to Philip Hallen of the Falk Fund, I was able to serve as a consultant in 1978 to the **Task Panel on the Arts in Therapy & Environment** of the President's Commission on Mental Health, where I (as President of AATA) could speak in support of the lone, beleaguered creative arts therapist in the group. Together, we were eventually able to persuade the other members to include the arts therapies in their recommendations.

From 1976 to 1982, I served on the Board of the **National Committee * Arts for the Handicapped** (**NCAH**), which is now **Very Special Arts**. At this critical period for public awareness of art therapy, it was very helpful to have a voice for the creative arts therapies in that group. NCAH also funded a meeting co-sponsored by the **American Art Therapy Association** (**AATA**) and the **National Art Education Association** (**NAEA**). This two-day working conference took place in August of 1980, and resulted in the publication of the condensed deliberations of the group, *Art in the Lives of Persons with Special Needs*. In addition, a special issue of the NAEA journal was devoted to ''Art Therapy & Art Education,'' with articles by those experienced in both fields.

As with the APA Conference and the Task Panel, these are examples of the kinds of public information activities which were essential to the growth and development of the new discipline of art therapy. Recognition by those doing the hiring, credentialling, or seeking of art therapists was the major objective. These activities were also aimed at reassuring those whose boundaries overlapped ours, such as other creative arts therapists, artists working with the mentally ill, or art educators specializing in work with the disabled. The goal was to be able to pool our resources in collaboration, rather than wasting them in competition. Happily, such cooperative efforts are going on all over the country today with those in other allied health professions.

BECOMING AN ART THERAPIST TODAY

Requirements

The standards for all kinds of educational programs recognized by AATA are combined in one document, *Education Standards*. There is now a general consensus on both the prerequisites for, and the basics of, an art therapy education. In order to be eligible for graduate study, a student needs to have a bachelor's degree or its equivalent, a portfolio of original art showing competence with materials, 15 credits in Studio Art and 12 in Psychology (including Developmental and Abnormal).

AATA's requirements for graduate training programs are clearly stated in *Education Standards*. It specifies in detail the minimum standards for qualified faculty, for required courses in Art Therapy (21 credits), and for closely supervised practice (600 hours). There are also standards for facilities (space, library) and for student and program evaluation. In addition, the program must take no less than two years or its equivalent for the student to complete its requirements.

Settings

Art therapy is a **hybrid**, reflected in its name, its origins, and its history. So it is natural that training programs have evolved in a wide variety of settings. Those in **colleges and universities** may be found in schools of Medicine, Education, Allied Health, or Arts & Sciences. The program itself may be a separate department. It may be housed administratively within another department, like Art Education or Counseling. Or it may be interdepartmental—run collaboratively by two separate departments. Sometimes art therapy programs are in an Art Department or a School of Art. Full academic programs all result in the granting of a master's degree, but because of their varied auspices, the degree can be M.A., M.S., or M.Ed. Some are unusual, like Hahnemann's M.C.A.T. (Master of Creative Arts Therapy) or Pratt's M.P.S. (Master of Professional Studies).

Internship programs are housed in treatment settings, usually those which offer multiple levels of care (inpatient, partial, and outpatient). **Institute** programs are the most autonomous, in that they are free of the institutional constraints of academic and treatment settings. They are therefore likely to have a clear art therapy identity, but there are variations here, too. AATA publishes an annual list of all graduate-level programs, indicating which ones have been ''Approved'' by the Educational Program Approval Board, which is described in Chapter 11. Suggestions for students interested in graduate programs are found in Chapter 12.

Publications

Art therapy educators have met annually since 1978, a tradition initiated by Sandra Kagin Graves and still ongoing as a regular pre-conference event. There are, however, few articles and even fewer books on the topic of training. The first book, by Shaun McNiff (1986), described the history of training in all of the creative arts therapies. McNiff cited the development of itemized ''**Competency Evaluations**'' for becoming registered as a critical event. Those competencies, which art therapists agreed were essential, were the basis for a survey conducted in the course of preparing the **Certification Examination**, first given in 1994.

The second book (1992) was a description of Bruce Moon's approach to the training of art therapists in the context of a clinical internship program (Fig. 4–10). Two other art therapy educators who discussed training in their books were Arthur Robbins (1980, 1995) and Harriet Wadeson (1987, 1989). Both stressed the importance of self-awareness; and each described creative ways for the art therapist to explore her responses to staff, supervisors, patients, and their families.

Teaching Methods

Training in art therapy involves a combination of didactic classes and supervised practicum experience, which is common in all clinical disciplines. What is different is that, in addition to lecture and discussion, slides and works of art are also

Figure 4–10 Bruce Moon working with a graduate student.

central to the learning process. Many programs require or recommend personal psychotherapy, as well as some kind of active involvement in artistic expression—ranging from open studios for interns to more structured classes. Required art therapy groups in which students learn about group dynamics also facilitate self-awareness.

Figure 4–11   Gladys Agell teaching graduate students.

It is also not surprising that art therapists often use **art activities** as a way of conveying information, from understanding theories by representing them graphically to feeling what it's like to be a patient. For example, creating art using blindfolds or the non-dominant hand seems to enhance empathy for disabled clients. Similarly, role-playing family members doing art exercises is also a powerful way to understand how it feels to be in family art therapy. Hanna Kwiatkowska, Mildred Lachman, and their students described their reactions during a group art therapy learning experience (ATV, p. 121).

Just as art students sometimes **copy** artwork of the old masters, some art therapy instructors have required students to copy psychotic art. The reason for this exercise, like working with blindfolds, is to help foster empathy. A similar task is to **mirror** another person's process of using artistic media, by imitating it as closely as possible while watching. These are just a few examples of the many ways in which art therapy students learn about all sorts of things—even theory—using materials (Fig. 4–11).

Supervision

Supervision is the most vital and delicate aspect of clinical training in any therapy, and is the one most often discussed in art therapy literature (Fig. 4–12). There have been useful papers by educators from many countries on art therapy

Figure 4–12 Charles Anderson supervising an intern.

supervision—its stages, different models, and flexibility in meeting student needs. *Supervision & Related Issues* by Cathy Malchiodi and Shirley Riley (1996) is the first and, to date, only book on the topic of supervision in art therapy. In addition to the usual verbal and audiovisual modes of reviewing clinical practice, art therapy supervisors—like art therapy teachers—also use art.

Educators have described many inventive ways of using art materials to help students to more deeply know themselves and their work. The most common themes dealt with are transference and countertransference, and the artistic task might be to **draw a patient**, to **draw your reaction to him**, or to *draw with a patient or supervisor*, etc. The many creative possibilities for the use of art activities in relation to clinical work are limited only by the imagination of the supervisor.

Self-Awareness

The need for students to grow in **self-awareness** seems to be one on which all art therapy educators agree. Some insist that only therapy will do it; others feel that self-inquiry need not take that form. For myself, I think Naumburg and Kramer were right to recommend that I become a patient in psychotherapy. I have often wondered if being an **art therapy** patient would have been an even more useful learning experience. It is my belief that **personal psychotherapy** is an essential part of a full educational experience for all therapists, including art therapists. The work is so intense, and in some ways so intimate, that blindness about unresolved personal issues is a real danger. It is easy to rationalize one's responses, and the only antidote to acting out on the part of the therapist is self-knowledge. Even after years of therapy, experienced clinicians often seek consultation or even treatment in regard to difficult cases.

Being an art therapist is not easy, and wishful fantasies of rescue and repair are soon replaced by a need to accept the inevitable frustrations and failures of the work. Like all clinicians, art therapists need to face their "**dark side**"—the rejected parts of themselves. Therapists cannot help patients to deal with their "shadows" if they have not made peace with their own. Experienced workers have written about the powerful effect on the art therapist of confronting her own "underside" as well as the patient's (AP, 1989, p. 133; AT, 1990, p. 107). Art therapists also need to deal with their grandiosity and narcissistic reactions to idealization as well as to devaluation. Art therapy, like any other kind of psychotherapy, can be stressful. As noted earlier, making art is a fine way to reflect on a difficult session, patient, or colleague, and has been recommended by many.

Images of Supervision

As a supervisor, when frustrated by my inability to communicate with a blocked supervisee, I would sometimes imagine a sow's ear actually turning into a silk purse. Happily, helping most neophytes to become good therapists does not require such an impossible transformation. My own favorite metaphor for the hazardous shoals of supervision is a book from my childhood, *Epaminondas and His Auntie*. It is a wonderful teaching tale about how foolish it is to apply suggestions which are appropriate for one situation to another one where they simply don't fit.

The story is that Epaminondas went to see his aunt every day, and she always gave him something to take home to his mother. The first item was a big piece of cake, which the boy put in his fist "all scrunched up tight," and "by the time he got home there wasn't anything left but a fistful of crumbs." After his mother yelled at him for being so foolish, she told him that "the way to carry cake is to wrap it all up nice in some leaves and put it in your hat." So when his aunt gave him a pound of butter, Epaminondas wrapped it in leaves, put it in his hat, put his hat on his head, and came home. Since it was a very hot day, the butter melted. Again, his mother gave Epaminondas some very good advice about how he should have wrapped and carried the butter. As you might imagine, that is how he handled the puppy dog he got the following day, with equally sad results.

The message of the book is relevant for any supervision which suggests what **could** or **should** have been done at any particular clinical moment. Most supervisors do not give direct advice, preferring to explore the situation in question with the trainee. It is clear that learning how to **figure out** good answers is much more useful than **knowing** any number of them. The wish to have a "recipe book" or a "script" is understandable, and is even common among the creative people who become art therapists.

Promoting Creativity in the Art Therapist

The **creativity** of the therapist is, however, critical to any effective therapy, including art. Many have been concerned about "the search for the formula" among art therapists, and have suggested that a clinician needs to be able to use her artist self in a flexible, yet disciplined way. But promoting inventiveness in the context of self-discipline is far from simple.

In fact, the notion of **creativity** is almost as slippery as catching fish with your bare hands. Harold Benjamin, the Dean of Columbia University's Teachers College once wrote a satire on education called *The Saber-Tooth Curriculum* (1939). It's about a stone-age "experimental institution" called "the School of Creative Fish Grabbing." To quote: *"The creative part is the heart of the whole movement—just to catch fish—That's nothing—but to grab fish creatively—Ah! That is something!"* Happily, despite the complexities and challenges of the work, doing art therapy is much more creative and infinitely more satisfying than grabbing fish.

Becoming an Art Therapist: Professional Identity Formation

Making the transition from training to practice can be hard. Susan Makin, a recent graduate, dealt with her frustrations by writing a book. In today's economic crunch, young professionals rarely get the kind of close and detailed supervision that used to be provided in the workplace. Obtaining some kind of post-graduate supervision, whether individual or group, however, is essential to growing as a clinician, not to mention qualifying for Registration. The support and feedback of a study or "peer supervision" group with other (art) therapists can also be immensely helpful. For example, when dealing with severely abused clients, all therapists are at risk for "vicarious traumatization"—addressed in an art psychotherapy stress reduction group run by Shirley Riley (AP, 1996, p. 407).

Establishing and consolidating a professional identity takes time in any profession. It may be especially difficult in art therapy, because of the inevitable tug of war between the clinician's artist-self and therapist-self. Even if the issue of their relative importance has been settled, there is still the pragmatic problem of finding the time and energy to make art. This has been a source of discontent, personally as well as philosophically, from the inception of the field.

It was, in fact, the theme of the 1976 AATA conference: "**Creativity and the Art Therapist's Identity**." Robert Ault, art therapist at the Menninger Foundation who had continued to do his own painting, put it quite simply in a talk at that meeting (p. 53). He had been asked: "If someone shook you awake at 3:00 in the morning and asked 'Are you an artist or a therapist?' how would you answer?" Bob then said that he had found himself deciding in favor of "artist," but that he also resented having to make a choice.

Mildred Chapin and Mari Fleming addressed the same issue from a slightly different angle in "From Clinician to Artist; From Artist to Clinician" (AJAT, 1993, p. 70). Art therapy students whose training programs are in art schools are sometimes seen as "**second-class artists**." And in treatment settings, because of their low position in the hierarchy, art therapists often feel like "**second-class therapists**." No wonder a drama therapist noticed a "**shame dynamic**" in the expressive arts therapies.

CONCLUDING THOUGHTS

Nevertheless, despite the difficulties of learning to be an art therapist and of honing one's skills—not to mention the obstacles to recognition by others—the discipline continues to grow. It is impressive that a large percentage of students in art therapy training programs are pursuing a second career. They are often artists, teachers, or other health care professionals, who want to use their ability to help others to create in a more deeply satisfying fashion.

Because of the complexity of doing responsible art therapy, the required two years of full-time training—in theory, practice, and self-knowledge—are an essential first step. In order to become **Registered**, the neophyte art therapist must accumulate at least 1,000 hours of supervised work beyond the master's degree. To be **Board Certified**, the Registered art therapist must pass a written examination, and must accumulate 100 **Continuing Education Credits** every five years to maintain it.

Serious art therapists have always continued to learn, even before continuing education was mandated. And the motivation to do so is great, because being an art therapist is both terrifically challenging and intrinsically rewarding. I believe that art therapy is such immensely satisfying work because it calls on so many human resources—feeling and intellect, heart and mind. Despite the complexities of doing a good job, unlocking someone's creativity is a profoundly gratifying experience. This is especially true if you love to watch people—as well as the unique images they create—being, in a very real sense, (re)born.

Chapter 5

The Basics

THE ART THERAPIST IS A SPECIALIST
who combines the qualification of being a competent artist
with specialized skills in the field of psychotherapy and education.

EDITH KRAMER

Art therapists know about art, about therapy, and about the interface between the two—doing art therapy. In contrast to the broad range of theoretical perspectives on art therapy and the wide variety in ways of working; most art therapists agree on the basic skills and understandings necessary for effective work. In *The Art of Art Therapy* (1984), I described in detail what I think art therapists need to know about each of these areas. This chapter will first outline the **basic elements** of art therapy, and will then note some of the **basic reasons** why it is effective.

Although knowledge about art and therapy are essential, no amount of knowing leads to effective art therapy without two **basic beliefs** shared by all art therapists . . . first, in the healing power of art, and second, in the capacity of all human beings to be creative with art media. Necessary personal qualifications (AATA, 1997) include: sensitivity to human needs and expressions, emotional stability, patience, flexibility, a sense of humor, a capacity for insight into psychological processes, the ability to listen attentively, to observe keenly, and to develop a rapport with others.

THE ART PART

Materials

Whether entering the field via art or some other avenue, art therapists are familiar with a wide variety of materials, tools, and processes. These include the surfaces on which people work, like different types and weights of paper; as well as the tools used with different materials, like various kinds of brushes or clay modeling implements. They also include the basic media for drawing, painting, modelling and constructing. Art therapists are familiar with the specific qualities and particular capacities of each type: pencils, chalks, crayons, markers, fingerpaints, water colors, tempera, acrylic, oil, clay, plasticine, wood, wire, and less common materials. Since art therapists are also artists, they have had **personal experience** with most media and processes; such experience is the best way to get to know them, and to help others learn to use them in a comfortable way.

For practical as well as psychological reasons, the materials used in art therapy tend to be **simple** and **unstructured**. Since art therapists value the importance of each individual's creativity, whatever is offered needs to allow for personal expression and definition. Even if limited in quantity, the materials in art therapy are generally of good enough quality to be utilized energetically. Supplies and tools used in art therapy are also sturdy, and are stored and cared for with respect.

Individual Differences

Many considerations affect decisions about which materials are offered and how. Some are **pragmatic,** like budget and population; others are more **personal.** There are in fact differences of opinion within the field about how many different materials should be made available, seemingly unrelated to theoretical preference. At one end of the continuum are those who are convinced that a few expressive materials are sufficient for most circumstances. At the other end are those who believe in offering as many choices as possible. Most art therapists fall somewhere in between.

Anyone who reads widely in art therapy will note a great variety of opinions about the most desirable materials and processes. Sometimes preferences are explained as reasonable for a particular population, setting, or purpose. Although such variables are indeed relevant, there are also more subtle influences on an art therapist's choice of materials. One of my mentors, a psychologist named Margaret McFarland, taught that a child will develop positive feelings about any materials or activities that are especially valued by his mother (or surrogate). Thus, a preschool teacher noticed that her pupils must have known how much she liked easel painting, because there was so much activity in that corner when she led the group. Yet when the same children were taught by a woman whose interest was in modelling, there was a preponderance of clay work.

In a similar fashion, an individual art therapist's enthusiasm for a particular medium or process is likely to stimulate interest in it for those with whom she works. In after-school workshop groups at a Child Study Center, I used to call this the **"Pied Piper Effect."** If I wanted to get the youngsters to try any art activity, all I needed to do was to start doing it myself. They would usually come, look, and eventually become engaged.

As for media offerings, my own preference has been for a broad selection under most circumstances. This approach seems sensible to me, because I sincerely believe that any individual does best with materials that allow him to feel as comfortable as possible. I also trust, because of my experience with many different populations, that even those with poor ego boundaries tend to choose materials they can control. However, I know myself well enough to be aware that my need for people to have choices is not limited to my work in art therapy, but extends throughout my life, from menus to maps. So, like most, I have managed to justify making materials available to people in a way that is syntonic with my personality.

The processes of working with art materials are as varied as the media themselves. Art therapists, regardless of individual predilections, are familiar with a wide range of materials, tools, and ways of working. Most practitioners draw upon an extensive awareness of many different possibilities for creative work. The range of what can be used and how is limited only by the knowledge and creativity of the individual clinician.

Keeping Up with New Media

Since the definition of art is continually expanding, offerings in art therapy do too. For example, recent technological developments have tremendous potential for all kinds of creative work. Since I cannot sit comfortably in a desk chair since having had back surgery, the laptop computer on which I wrote this book allowed me to type while sitting in a recliner. For me, a notebook computer is a welcome convenience. For those who are severely disabled, it might be a critical prosthesis; which can be used to create pictorial images as well as words. For anyone wanting to animate artwork, the computer offers an exciting and efficient avenue.

New art materials and tools are continually being developed. These can be especially useful for particular expressive needs. Tempera markers, for example, are perfect when a person wants to pound aggressively with paint, or to use paint in settings where there is a need to minimize the mess. Specific materials can make possible the successful expression of visual ideas. Staying informed about these is as important as keeping up with professional literature; since knowing media is as critical to art therapy as knowing pharmacological drugs is to medicine.

Understanding/Analyzing Materials

In 1978 two art therapists proposed a way of understanding and of classifying both materials and processes. It was called the "**Expressive Therapies Continuum,**" and was the product of a collaboration between Vija Lusebrink and Sandra Kagin (Graves) (AP, 1978, p. 171). It was based on Kagin's earlier work, in which she had defined "media dimensions variables." The system itself is not used by all art therapists. But the kind of thinking it embodies—about the nature and properties of work with materials—is part of any competent art therapist's decision-making process (Lusebrink, 1990).

Although materials are an essential component of our work, they have not been written about by many art therapists, perhaps because we take them for granted. Edith Kramer discussed the properties of different media in her 1979

Figure 5–1 An art therapist observes a child working.

book, to which Laurie Wilson also contributed a section on "Pre-Art Materials." There was a brief chapter on "Art Materials" in Arthur Robbins' first book (reprinted 1994), and Helen Landgarten described work with a resistant adult, focussing on her rationale for choosing both the media and the tasks (1981). The **"task analysis"** approach can also be helpful in media selection (Wilkinson & Heater, 1979).

The Creative Process

Understanding and being able to **facilitate** a genuinely creative process is also part of every art therapist's armamentarium. While there are many individual differences in how each worker goes about accomplishing this, all agree on its importance. Like being familiar with media and tools, this is one of the ways in which art therapists differ significantly from other clinicians who use art materials in their work. Facilitation sometimes involves teaching—often of techniques, always of ways to express the self authentically. As with knowing media, personal experience of the artistic process (see Appendix) is critical in helping others to achieve the altered state of consciousness required for creating.

Equally central in effective art therapy is knowing how to **observe** another's creative process acutely, sensitively and unintrusively. Becoming aware of all of the temporal, spatial, and other nonverbal aspects of people's behavior with materials takes time and practice (Fig. 5–1). It is a major component of training, because the more an art therapist can see, the more she can figure out, and the more effectively she can intervene to help. As Robert Ault once said, a picture may be "worth a thousand words," but "to **observe** the making of a picture is worth **ten** thousand words" (Unpub. 1983 manuscript).

Artistic Products

As with the other elements of "the art part," there is essential agreement about the centrality of the product, along with a variety of opinions about its place in art therapy. Although the person being served is always more important than either product or process in art therapy, the very existence of a **concrete product** makes art therapy unique among clinical disciplines.

In addition to helping the artist to see himself in a new way (Fig. 5–2), creative products often enable others on the treatment team to understand a patient better. They can also be useful with family members and other clients (Fig. 5–3). They are a silent but eloquent form of education, whether displayed in the treatment setting or at a gallery. And at the end of the therapy, art products offer a vivid way for participants to **review**—to re-live and to assess what happened during the therapeutic journey.

Those who emphasize the **art** in art therapy are more likely to view the **quality** of the product as related to the success of the therapy. This group includes those who espouse an **"art as therapy"** approach; as well as those who find special value in the **image,** and who come from a wide variety of theoretical orientations.

Those who emphasize the **therapy** in art therapy are less likely to be concerned with quality, and more likely to focus on the **communicative value** of the artistic product. They too are interested in the image, but primarily for **what** it says, rather than **how well** it speaks. Janie Rhyne, who studied line drawings of feeling-states based on George Kelly's "personal construct" theory, described such creations as **"visual languaging."**

All art therapists value authentically expressive work, whether crude and primitive or sophisticated and refined. This is true regardless of whether they stress art or therapy in how they define their work. Margaret Naumburg, for example, though she wrote primarily about the value of art as **"symbolic speech"** emanating from the unconscious, encouraged and valued powerful visual products. This is apparent in the vivid images she selected to illustrate the case studies in each of her four books.

In all art products, there are two elements that can be identified and understood—**form** and **content.** Some art therapists focus more on one or the other; most value the importance of both. Edith Zierer sometimes had students view patient artwork upside down, so that they could focus on the formal element of "color integration" undistracted by either content or competence (Fig. 5–4). Rita Simon's approach to art therapy emphasized **style.** And in Janie Rhyne's

Figure 5–2 Sandra Kagin (Graves) helps someone view art.

Figure 5–3 Christine Wang discusses some art products.

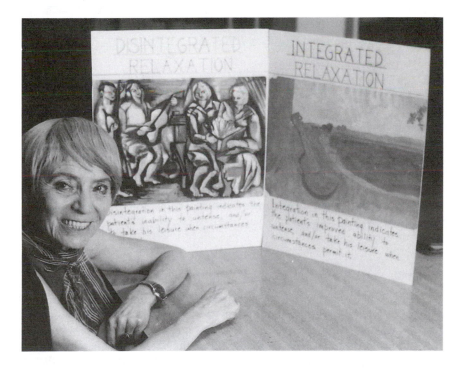

Figure 5–4 Edith Zierer with two contrasting paintings.

use of "personal construct drawings," the **form** itself became the **content** of the communication.

The **subject matter** is significant too, and—like the manifest content of a dream—may be disguised. Understanding the nature of metaphor and symbolic expression is, therefore, critical to any translation or artistic meaning. A literate understanding of the *language* of both form and content is vital to an art therapist's functioning. The complex intertwining of these two variables constitutes the **grammar** of art, which is mastered by art therapists in order to develop **visual literacy** in their work.

Clinically sophisticated vision can decipher artistic information about development, about psychodynamics, and about psychopathology. Art therapists learn to "listen" to what art products have to "say." While there are many different ways to look at or to think about art, doing so sensitively and coherently is central to doing effective art therapy.

Understanding the **art part** of art therapy, then, involves knowing a great deal about **materials, the creative process,** and **artistic products.** As with art media and the creative process, most art therapists are highly respectful of the products created therein. Whether and where they are displayed or stored depends on a large number of variables, some of which are discussed in Chapter 11. But they are always handled by art therapists with the utmost care. Since artistic products are also statements by the individual—whether garbled or articulate—they are treated with the same confidentiality accorded verbal communication.

THE THERAPY PART

Development

The second major component of art therapy is the **therapy part.** Whatever preferred theoretical orientation they eventually adopt, all art therapists have some basic frame of reference about human psychology. They have a picture of **normal development,** in order to identify **deviations** therefrom. In addition to knowing something about both cognitive and emotional growth, art therapists are familiar with **normal development in art.** Art therapists are also informed about a variety of developmental perspectives, so they can selectively choose and/or synthesize their own.

Dynamics

In a similar fashion, art therapists understand **psychodynamics,** both **within** and **between** individuals. Whether they end up being partial to a **conflict** or a **deficit** theory of **psychopathology,** art therapists are familiar with both ways of thinking. Art therapists are also knowledgeable about different understandings of both **intrapsychic** and **interpersonal** dynamics. The latter includes **dyadic** (2-person), **triadic** (3-person), and **group** dynamics.

Pathology

Like other clinicians, art therapists are familiar with the major theories of personality and psychological functioning. All therapists need to have some coherent way of thinking about what is wrong (pathology), so they can figure out how best to help (therapy). Eventually, most practicing clinicians choose to deepen their understanding of one preferred frame of reference, so that theory becomes integrated with technique.

Because psychopathology has been defined **descriptively** as well as **etiologically,** art therapists are trained to understand the meaning of the current **diagnostic classifications.** The specific **languages** individual art therapists utilize depend mainly on where they work. For example, those who are in **psychiatric** settings understand the thinking behind systems like **ICD-9** and **DSM-IV,** the most widely-used forms of classification. Similarly, those in **special education and rehabilitation** are familiar with relevant categories of **exceptionality** and **disability.**

Planning

In addition to knowing the terms used to define different diagnostic groups in human service settings, art therapists are also familiar with the various languages used to describe the **process of helping.** Whether writing a **Treatment Plan** in a hospital or an **I.E.P.** (individualized educational plan) in a school; art therapists are multilingual, though fluency in any one language develops through usage. Regardless of the setting, competent art therapists understand ways of describing what is wrong, planning to help, and evaluating the effectiveness of their intervention.

The Therapeutic Dyad

Another core area of understanding about therapy has to do with the importance and meaning of the *relationship* with those who are served. Whether or not an art therapist fosters or utilizes the symbolic aspects known as **"transference,"** all schools of thought about helping people to change recognize the significance of the climate between clinician and client. As noted in Chapter 4, art therapists are usually encouraged—and sometimes required—to get to know themselves better through their own psychotherapy. This is essential, so that their own issues do not interfere with their ability to use themselves in their work with other people.

Many outcome studies, involving a wide range of theories and techniques, have found the most critical variable in the therapeutic equation to be the **"fit"** between patient and clinician. Art therapist Aina Nucho found that therapist-patient pairs who were matched according to their artistic preferences had more successful treatment outcomes than those who were assigned at random (in Jakab, 1981).

Art therapists of all theoretical stripes agree on the importance of the **"thera-peutic alliance."** Freud once suggested that this critical relationship provides the "anesthetic" which makes possible the sometimes-painful "surgery" of an interpretation. "Alliance" in psychotherapy means trust and commitment, not social or physical intimacy. Ethics committees in service disciplines report that most patient complaints involve "boundary violations," the dark side of the immense power in the relationship itself.

Although some argue that art therapy dilutes the intensity of the transfer-ence—because of the more active teaching component in the therapist's role and the existence of the art object as an intermediary—I do not agree. In fact, it appears to me that art therapists, because we draw on and expose the innermost private parts of the human soul, often have an even more "intimate" relationship with our clients than talk therapists. And, since a great deal of physical activity (with materials, tools, products) is a necessary component of the work, we may have increased potential to do harm as well as to heal. In any case, knowing the importance, meaning, and power of the relationship—both real and symbolic—is basic to being a responsible art therapist.

The Process of Change in Therapy

Equally basic to comprehending the therapy part of the work is having some understanding of the process of change. Although there is such a thing as "one-trial learning," most psychological therapies take time and go through **stages.** This is true whether the treatment is short-term or long-term, and whether it is open-ended or time-limited. There are many variations, depending on multiple factors, but art therapists have a sense of the shape of the therapeutic process over time.

As with theories and techniques, clinicians often disagree about the names or the nature of the sequential stages or phases in treatment; but most agree that they occur and that they are, in a general way, predictable. There is always a beginning, a middle, and an end; and the worker needs to understand the goals and interventions appropriate to each period. Otherwise, doing art therapy would be like flying blind, a situation unlikely to induce security in either the pilot or the passenger(s).

NECESSARY CONDITIONS: THE FRAMEWORK

Understanding therapy is as central for an art therapist as knowing art. In order to facilitate authentic expression, the clinician needs to create what I have called a **"framework for freedom"** (1978). The **conditions** which are necessary for effective art therapy tend to cut across theoretical and stylistic preferences. Because of the concrete nature of the modality, they are **physical** as well as **psychological.** Although it is rare that an art therapist finds or creates a perfect set of conditions for her work, some are fundamental. Political as well as psycho-logical, they are intertwined.

A Supportive Setting

For example, before an art therapy program can take place in any kind of setting, somebody needs to be convinced of its desirability. Depending on the chain of command between the person(s) with the power to decide and those who implement, the support can vary. If those choosing art therapy are able to facilitate positive attitudes in other staff members, achieving good conditions becomes a feasible goal. However, it is not uncommon for a busy administrator to hire an art therapist, who arrives only to discover that she is viewed suspiciously by her co-workers, sometimes even by her immediate supervisor.

In order to establish the basic conditions necessary for good art therapy, it is necessary to have a **supportive administrative matrix.** This requires preparatory and ongoing education of the person responsible for overseeing the art therapy program, who needs to understand just what its value can be in that particular setting. If he or she is well-informed and can educate others, the potential for effective work is greatly enhanced. It is not sufficient to simply create an art therapy position or program in any setting. Whether brand-new or established, solid support for the physical and psychological conditions needed for good art therapy must also be present. As with any partnership, maintaining the alliance is essential.

Assuming that such support is available, then it is possible to create conditions which are as good as possible under the circumstances. Art therapists learn to be flexible about the fact that optimal conditions are rare. Knowing what would be ideal, however, helps an art therapist to maximize the potential of any particular situation, and to work towards improving it. It is similar to having a model of a mentally healthy person in mind, while helping each patient to come as close as he or she can to that goal.

Physical Conditions

An ideal physical setting for art therapy is private and protected from intrusion, has adequate light and working surfaces, contains within it an easily accessible water source, and has sufficient space for storage and display of art supplies and products. In the best of all possible worlds, it does not need to be shared or used by anyone else. While it would be lovely if all could operate under such conditions, that is rarely the case. More often, the art therapist must access her own considerable creativity in order to make the best of a less-than-ideal situation. Although art therapists are usually required to accommodate to the setting and its deficits, a clear understanding of the importance of a safe and secure physical framework helps in obtaining administrative support.

Psychological Conditions

It could be argued that a safe and secure psychological framework for all therapy, including art therapy, is even more critical. It is probably that which accounts for the remarkable fact that powerful art therapy can take place in suboptimal situations; like a child's bedside on a crowded hospital ward, or the corner of a hectic shelter for battered women. "Art is a quiet place," even in a noisy room or in June's cage at the zoo (Chapter 3).

Despite the possibility of conducting art therapy under difficult circumstances, a stable set of physical and psychological conditions is still best. This requires the same kind of **steadiness and predictability** from an art therapist as from a talk therapist. What is added is a need for clarity and consistency in offering materials, evoking their use, facilitating expression, and dealing with artistic products. Creating an environment in which people can feel metaphorically **"held"** and secure is as much an art as a science, regardless of the actual setting.

This is something with which art therapists are especially concerned, because of the particular requirements of a place where **authentic creative work** is really possible. As with other aspects of clinical style, individuals find their own ways to make even the most unlikely setting workable and inviting. Most art therapists work hard to create a peaceful and protected atmosphere, one where the spirit can safely soar.

Time and frequency are also important elements of the framework. Many kinds of art activities need adequate time as well as sufficient space, and some require continuity. While compromises are often necessary, the art therapist's understanding of the importance of all aspects of the physical and psychological framework is vital to her success.

DOING ART THERAPY: THE INTERFACE

Armed with a solid understanding of both art and therapy, the clinician is then prepared to put them together in the conduct of art therapy itself. As noted earlier, it is the interface between art and therapy that is the essence of the work. The chapters in the "Interface" section of *The Art of Art Therapy* (Rubin, 1984) deal with the need to accomplish a series of tasks—steps which include: setting the stage, evoking expression, facilitating expression, and looking at and learning from the art and the experience of creating.

Setting the Stage

The first task is to set the stage, in both larger and smaller arenas, as noted in the discussion of the necessary conditions for effective therapy. Art therapists are usually quite skilled in creating a studio space which is both orderly and inviting. Doing these well requires artistry as well as knowledge. A prepared environment, however, is rarely enough.

Figure 5–5 An Art Therapist Helps a Patient to Use Clay.

Evoking and Facilitating Expression

Art therapists work hard and thoughtfully at evoking expression. Stimulating often-resistant individuals to work creatively with materials requires skill and inventiveness. Once people have gotten started, the art therapist's job is to make sure they can work with the utmost freedom and success. There is an art to facilitating expression in a way that honors each person's creativity, yet provides assistance when needed (Fig. 5–5).

Looking at & Learning from the Art Process

One of the ways in which art therapy differs from other therapeutic uses of art is the frequency with which the clinician helps the patient to learn from the experience as well as the product. In addition to observing the creative process, art therapists help patients reflect on how it felt to use the materials or to express the ideas and feelings involved (Fig. 5–6).

Looking at and learning from art require skills that are highly developed among art therapists. **Art teachers** critique products in order to help students to improve, and **art historians** look at art work in order to understand a style or period. But those ways of looking at and learning from art are quite different from those that are crucial in art therapy (Fig. 5–7). The challenge facing **art therapists** is to find the best way to help each artist understand himself by relating meaningfully to what he has created. This can happen nonverbally, through gazing at the image, as well as verbally. And both can occur in a number of different ways.

Figure 5–6 An art therapist writes down a blind boy's story.

Working Artistically

Art therapists have a wide variety of approaches to all of the steps noted above, determined by personality as well as by theory. There are individual differences in every area of actual practice, from setting the stage, to evoking and facilitating expression, to looking at and learning from the art that has been produced. Most art therapists, regardless of personal style, see themselves as working **artistically.**

A principle which makes sense to me is to **intervene**—at all stages of the process—in the **least restrictive** and **most facilitating** fashion. Although this

Figure 5–7 Group members review a mural-making process.

may sound simple, it is a highly developed skill, best refined through practice. While relevant for all therapists, it is especially important in the specialized work of doing therapy through making and learning from art.

INDIRECT SERVICE

This refers to things art therapists do that do not involve patients or clients, such as teaching, supervision, consultation, and research. Many art therapists, like clinicians in other fields, have found themselves in the position of teaching, supervising, consulting, or conducting research with little or no formal preparation. However, the fundamental principles in each kind of indirect service are identical to those in direct service, and follow the same sort of sequence.

Basic Principles for Direct & Indirect Service

For example, it always helps to begin with some kind of **assessment** of the current situation. That means finding out where a patient is for therapy, where a student is for teaching or supervision, and where an institution or individual is for consultation. Even when doing research, it is important to know what has been done before, by reviewing the literature.

After assessing a situation by gathering relevant data, the next step is to set reasonable **goals,** and to decide how to **proceed** in order to achieve them. It is also necessary to form a respectful **alliance** with those being served, so that the work is truly cooperative; whether it is doing therapy, teaching, supervising, consulting, or conducting research. Ultimately, it is also necessary to **evaluate** whether the goals have been met.

Learning from the Source

Almost halfway through the writing of this text, I discovered that I needed to completely revise the outline I had originally made, although it had seemed fine when first planning the book. However, as I looked more closely at the **data**—what was actually happening in the field of art therapy—I realized I had to abandon the original organization. But that's how it is—not only in writing books, but also in life, in art, and in doing art therapy. You have to **let the source**—whether it's an image or a feeling or a patient—**speak to you.**

It's not mystical; it's simply a matter of responding honestly to whatever presents itself, whether it's a person or an artistic product. As with any creative process, you might have a general sense in advance of how it will turn out. But only when you fully, freely, and openly engage, can you discover how it's actually going to shape up, and what is required from you. This is true not only in creating art, but also in doing therapy, and for all kinds of indirect service as well.

APPLICATIONS

The final section of *The Art of Art Therapy* dealt with applications of art therapy to different **Populations,** in different **Settings,** and in different **Modes** (individual, family and group). The next five chapters in this book describe how art therapists think about their work, what they do, and how they do it—in diagnosis, in therapy, and with different kinds of people in a variety of places. Before getting into the **why,** the **what,** the **how,** the **who,** and the **where** of art therapy; this chapter would be incomplete without a brief look at some of the **basic reasons** why art therapy works.

WHY ART THERAPY?

Art Involves The Whole Person

Even though other modes of intervention can be very effective, and probably more so for certain problems, there are still many persuasive arguments for the special therapeutic value of art. Some are as old as the Greeks, Plato and Aristotle, and embody the notion that there is a unique way of being that only *Art as Experience* (Dewey) can provide. In truth, the art process offers one of the few ways we human beings have found to utilize and to synthesize **all of ourselves**—body, mind, and spirit. In the words of Saint Francis of Assisi: *"He who works with his hands is a laborer. He who works with his hands and his head is a craftsman. He who works with his hands and his head and his heart is an artist."*

The cognitive aspect of this idea is implicit in some of the recent studies on cerebral **hemispheric dominance.** They suggest that what Freud called the **"primary process"** is not inferior to **"secondary process"** thought; but that they are complementary modes of information-processing, each developing throughout our lives. These studies also support the idea that an integration of the two kinds of thinking represents an optimal cognitive state. Perhaps that is what psychiatrist Sylvano Arieti meant when he proposed that creativity utilizes a unique form of thought, which he called the **"tertiary process."** At a physiological level, while our understanding of cerebral functioning is relatively primitive, we do know that both the right and left hemispheres of the brain are involved when people are creating, and that they must interact effectively in order for art-making to occur.

Much of our Thinking is Visual

We have abundant evidence—from such normal phenomena as dreams and such abnormal ones as hallucinations—that much of what is encoded in the mind is in the form of images. In fact, there is no question that a great deal of human thought, at all levels of consciousness, is what psychologist Rudolf Arnheim called *"Visual Thinking."* Mardi Horowitz, a psychoanalyst and psychiatrist who did considerable research on imagery, used both art and mental imagery in therapy. He suggested that there are good neurological reasons why people can gain access to material not otherwise available by visual means. Psychiatrist Louis Tinnin also proposed several physiological explanations for the effectiveness of art therapy; citing the fundamental biological processes in nonverbal communication, mimicry, and the placebo effect (AJAT, 1990, p. 9; 1994, p. 75).

Memories May be Preverbal or Forbidden

A variety of conditions can be the outcome of a childhood environment full of painful experiences. Because their origins are so early, they are often more easily accessible through a nonverbal therapy. This is especially true for eating disorders, addictions, and severe narcissistic disturbances—in fact, most of what are commonly called "borderline" conditions, and many of the personality disorders. Since their development has been distorted and fixated at preverbal levels, such individuals respond well to art therapy, which often becomes the treatment of choice, since it can help them to express, to see, and to accept their tumultuous internal states.

Whether because we are dealing with memories from a period before the patient had words, or because there is an injunction that a traumatic memory must not be told, much of the anguish behind the dissociative disorders is most accessible through images. In *Bridging the Silence,* dance therapist Susan Simonds argued for the use of "nonverbal modalities in the treatment of adult survivors of childhood sexual abuse." She proposed that a combination of movement and art therapy was optimal, due to the inevitable body image distortions that are the residue of such painful assaults (Fig. 5–8). So it is no surprise that, as inhibitions about reporting have been overcome, more art therapists are working with people who have suffered abuse who may be unable to speak about their experiences, but who can use art as a way of *Telling Without Talking* (Cohen & Cox).

The Dark Side is More Easily Expressed in Art

In addition to the fact that the images at the root of the disorder may be inaccessible in other ways, there is another advantage of art therapy. Because art is symbolic and essentially **value-free,** it is an easier modality than words through which people can begin to express their **"dark side."** These disowned aspects of the self are sometimes called the **"shadow"** by Jungian therapists. Patients with delusions of demon possession, for example, have been successfully treated through art therapy (AP, 1979, p. 1). It is always hard to represent what has been rejected (Fig. 5–9). But if the unacceptable thoughts, feelings and impulses can be seen and accepted, the individual is then free to use otherwise-destructive energy for constructive aims.

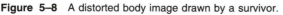

Figure 5–8   A distorted body image drawn by a survivor.

Art Helps in Facing Feared Aspects of Self: **Laurie**

Laurie, a woman in her late thirties, had seen four therapists prior to giving treatment one more chance. She announced from the beginning that if it didn't work, this was her last such effort; she would just have to accept the feared "fact" that she was incurable.

Art was a loaded issue from the first. Laurie was openly resistant, saying that she feared making a fool of herself, a common concern among adolescents and adults. Over time, we wondered if her negativism was a disguised form of oppositionalism—i.e., "You can't make me!"

In addition, we began to think that perhaps it was not so much that Laurie feared exposing her lack of skill; but rather that she feared what she would "see" inside of herself. Her anxieties about public speaking, doctor visits, and examinations—especially those which penetrate beneath the surface, like x-rays or mammograms—all seemed related to a fear of what was inside being made visible, of being "exposed."

This particular anxiety was clearly at work when she produced her first doodled drawing during the second year of treatment. Laurie was so self-conscious that I offered to leave the room, and did so briefly. After she had finished and showed the drawing to me, I was impressed by the skillful linear design she said was typical of her doodles (Fig. 5–10).

When she looked at it, however, and was asked if it reminded her of anything, she replied with shock that it looked like a **"Witch,"** and an evil one at that. She then confessed that she was sure that she was really

Figure 5–9 A disturbed adolsecent's "Ugly" self-portrait.

bad at the core, and that this frightening image, which she titled "It's My Fault," reflected that ugly truth. During the following years of therapy, there were many references to the witch inside, whose appearance had been vivid for Laurie; and who eventually was replaced by a more balanced sense of herself as both good and bad.

Figure 5–10   Laurie's doodle of a witch: "It's My Fault."

Art Offers Unique Possibilities for Expression

Art can do things which are impossible in words, like representing different times and places in the same pictorial space. These can be **simultaneous,** as in a **"Life Space"** picture, or **sequential,** as in a **"Life Line."** In a similar fashion, a single work of art can express and **synthesize** apparently incompatible affective states, such as love and hate. This is one reason why art is especially useful in the task of internal psychological **"integration,"** a major goal of most psychotherapy and self-development.

Art therapy is also especially valuable for any **group** in turmoil; whether living in a home (a family), an institution, or a community. Although people cannot talk simultaneously and still hear each other; different individuals can work on their art at the same time. Similarly, people cannot communicate with words unless they can take turns; whereas creating jointly in art can occur in a variety of ways.

The Art Product is a Helpful Presence

The presence of the art makes for a clinical situation which is very different from verbal psychotherapy. Even in individual art therapy, there is always a **"third party"** in the room. The art acts as a **bridge** between patient and therapist, and as a **transitional** or **transactional object** between the two. Paradoxically, the art serves both to **reduce self-consciousness** and to **enhance self-reflection,** just because of its **otherness.**

In group or family therapy, the presence of the art is also helpful. Whether responding to each other's creations, or working together and reflecting on the process, a jointly-made product, or both . . . looking at self, others, or the group is greatly facilitated by being able to see these in the art rather than in the person(s).

Art is Flexible & Versatile

Another of art therapy's greatest assets is its immense **versatility.** It can be used with people of any age, and can be adapted to almost any disability or setting. Art is also portable, so it can be offered to people who need to be seen at home, who are immobilized in hospital beds (Fig. 5–11), or who are stuck in shelters. Art is especially useful as therapy in crisis situations and settings, since many media permit rapid, easy expression, which is vital when trauma leaves someone speechless. Art is versatile in yet another fashion: It can be used in as many ways as there are theories of rehabilitation, treatment, education, and growth.

Art Normalizes Psychotherapy

Another significant asset is that, because art activities naturally occur in normal settings like schools, churches, and community centers, art therapy tends to be much less threatening to many people than verbal psychotherapy. In the seventies, the Pittsburgh Child Guidance Center was able to offer training in what we called **"Art-Awareness"** to people like youth group leaders and others working with teenagers. These trainees then worked under our supervision with adolescents in the community. We also held classes for art teachers in schools, colleges, and community centers, in order to sensitize them to do their job more therapeutically. So even when art as **psychotherapy** isn't indicated, the services of an art therapist as consultant, trainer, or supervisor of other caregivers can extend the therapeutic benefits of art to many individuals.

Figure 5–11 A hospitalized adult can still paint a picture.

The Creative Process is a Learning Experience

Many have pointed out parallels between psychotherapy and the creative process, another likely reason for the effectiveness of art therapy. Both involve the breaking down of old structures in order to give birth to new ones; as well as the confrontation of confusion and chaos within a containing framework. The creative process also offers an opportunity to experiment with new ways of seeing or being. As Edith Kramer so eloquently said: *"Art is a method of widening the range of human experiences by creating equivalents for such experiences. It is an area where experiences can be chosen, varied, and repeated at will"* (1958, p. 8). Even when one is helpless to change a painful reality, art can still help in the healing of a wounded soul, as in the following vignette.

Art as Solace at a Time of Sadness: **Marjorie**

Marjorie, a professional in her mid-forties, was reluctant to waste her valuable treatment time doing art. She had a pressing need to talk about the pain of acknowledging that her gifted son was showing signs of serious and possibly chronic mental illness. She wrote in a journal between her sessions too, mainly to deal with her internal anguish.

She was curious about art therapy, however, and wanted to try it out. So she began to experiment with materials at home, following my advice to "just fool around" with a medium and get to know it. After trying several media, Marjorie found one she preferred, and began to spend more and more of her spare time using it, surprised and delighted by how rewarding it was. Creating art took on a life of its own, and became a valued "fringe benefit" of her psychotherapy.

Marjorie was eager to share her artwork with me, but she was equally resistant to looking at her creative products with anything but an aesthetic eye. Analyzing was quickly dismissed as intrusive and possibly destructive. I was surprised at my own willingness to respect her wishes, and would have expected more inner regret. But in truth, her art developed so nicely and organically as she found not only her voice (the medium), but also her language (the style); that I didn't want to interfere in that process, for it had its own integrity and therapeutic benefit.

Her verbal therapy went well, allowing me to leave the art untouched by analysis with no sense of frustration. What I found most intriguing was that her tremendous pain, of which she spoke and wrote eloquently, was not visible in the artwork. Marjorie explained it by referring to Suzanne Langer, a philosopher whose work appealed to me long before I was a therapist. Langer's notion is that art is essentially "forms of human feeling"—not specific emotions, but a deeper emotional substrate.

Perhaps when someone is grappling with helplessness in the face of a human tragedy, he or she needs to get in touch with deeper forces in order to find some peace, to come to terms with an unwelcome reality. Marjorie's artistic creations, in addition to being highly original and beautiful, had a sense of harmony, of peace, of the quiet which finally follows even a raging storm. So far this woman, art became an unexpected by-product of her therapy, something she was able to keep and continue to develop as her own.

Art is a "Natural High" that Also Heals

We have barely scratched the surface of what is possible through art for our spiritual health, especially now that our society is going through an extremely painful period, hopefully one of transition. In a world where happiness is sought through mind-altering drugs and where pent-up rage erupts in senseless violence; making art is a means of safely sublimating otherwise destructive urges.

Moreover, creating art can offer, as Elinor Ulman said years ago, *"a momentary sample of living at its best."* The sensory and spiritual pleasures of art-making are profound, enriching lives already full, and brightening those still far too dim. Most art therapists see art, not just as a form of "symbolic speech" which augments verbal ways of knowing, but as a deeply healing activity. One reason was eloquently described by Ulman, who wrote that *"art is the meeting ground of the inner and outer world"* (in Jakab, 1971, p. 93). Ten years earlier she had said, also about art:

"Its motive power comes from within the personality: it is a way of bringing order out of chaos—chaotic feelings and impulses within, the bewildering mass of impressions from without. It is a means to discover both the self and the world, and to establish a relation between the two. In the complete creative process, inner and outer realities are fused into a new entity" (ATTP, p. 13).

In addition, because art is also sensory and kinesthetic; the very act of touching, shaping, and manipulating materials can be a source of deep pleasure. And, when the process has come to an end, viewing and showing the finished product(s) can be a wonderful source of pride.

Creating something unique with art media facilitates much more than a sense of accomplishment. Having an effect on even a small piece of material reality is a powerful antidote for feelings of shame and helplessness. Without a sense of efficacy, it is very hard—if not impossible—to feel hopeful about life. For those who are isolated or gravely impaired, making art can truly enhance the quality of life.

WHY ART?

When we ask **"Why Art Therapy?"** it implies another question, **"Why Art?"** It has been said that **"Art is a way of making ordinary experience extraordinary."** This idea returns to us to the roots of art therapy, which are deep and ancient, and to its branches, which seem able to flower in so many different ways.

I think the titles of two recent books by art therapists say it well: that *Art is a Way of Knowing* (Allen), and that artists and clinicians alike can make use of *Art as Medicine* (McNiff). If "therapy" means to heal, and hopefully to cure; then **art** may really be the **ideal medicine for the human soul,** the best way for the **spirit** to know and to actualize the **Self.**

There are many ways to think about why art is therapeutic. One was beautifully articulated by a psychologist named Ley: *"One cannot use a left hemispheric key to open a right hemispheric lock.**

Another was written by a psychiatrist named Jakab: *"The nonverbal aspect of art psychotherapy holds an important and unique position in the realm of mental health work, for it gives the clients an opportunity to listen with their eyes."* (1981).

A third was written by art therapist Edith Kramer: *"Since human society has existed the arts have helped man to reconcile the eternal conflict between the individual's instinctual urges and the demands of society. Thus, all art is therapeutic in the broadest sense of the word"* (1958, p. 6).

My favorite was said by a patient in a mental hospital to a British art therapist named Lyddiatt: *"In the Art Therapy room my sick self found my whole self and the therapist, by total, unquestioning acceptance of me and the things that I painted, encouraged me to believe in myself as a valid person"* (1971, p. 122).

*Ley, R. G. in Sheikh, A. A. & Shaffer, J. T. (Eds.) (1979) *The Potential of Fantasy and Imagination.* New York: Brandon House, pp. 955–956.

"Back to Basics"

The most recent trend in the field in the U.S. has been a return to the **art studio.**
The December 1995 issue of AATA's journal had a special section on **"Studio
Approaches to Art Therapy."** It included descriptions of an **"Art Studio"**
populated by people in wheelchairs and braces; an **Intern Studio Project** for
art therapy graduate students, and an **"Open Studio Project"** in an inner-
city neighborhood.

Having needed to prove our credentials as therapists in the early days of the
field of art therapy, we also ran the risk of **"clinification"** and of forgetting our
roots in art (AT, 1992, p. 22). The **"back to basics"** movement reaffirms that
which is unique to art therapy: **Art.** The challenge for the twenty-first century
is to demonstrate the art therapy can provide for human beings what is missing
in technology, to satisfy what many believe to be a **basic need to create**—in
order to feel and to be fully alive.

Chapter 6

Approaches

As a psychotherapist I found it particularly heartening that the use of art in therapy
seems to have the effect of reducing the differences between
Freudians, Jungians, Kleinians, and adherents of other schools . . .
Art not only bridges the gap between the inner and outer worlds
but also seems to span the gulf between different theoretical positions.
ANTHONY STORR

MULTIPLE PATHS: MULTIPLE PERSPECTIVES

The reader will recall that there were a number of individuals from different fields who, in one way or another, pioneered the use of art in therapy. Each of them had a primary identity in another discipline, whether it was art, education, or mental health. It was natural, therefore, that their ways of understanding art therapy were disparate, influenced as they were by their personal learning histories. Founding editor Ernest Harms expressed his concern about this variety in the second issue of *Art Psychotherapy*: "*What we find designated today as art therapy or art psychotherapy presents a* **conglomerate of undertakings** *with little coherence*" (p. i). Indeed, it would probably be accurate to say that there have always been as many different approaches as there are art therapists.

Nevertheless, it would be inaccurate to suggest that each one is completely idiosyncratic, having nothing in common but a shared basis in art and therapy. While every art therapist's way of working is stylistically unique, it is still possible to talk about different perspectives. Just like practitioners of verbal therapy, art therapists have grounded their work in a variety of theoretical frameworks.

In 1983, I invited some individuals who practiced art therapy from different points of view to write chapters on how they had translated a particular theory into technique. The book that resulted, *Approaches to Art Therapy* (1987), contains descriptions of a number of orientations. To grasp any one of them requires extensive study and close supervision by an experienced clinician. This chapter offers a broad overview of different ways to view, to understand, and to do art therapy. These multiple perspectives define the discipline as much as its common underpinnings.

PSYCHODYNAMIC APPROACHES TO ART THERAPY

Historically, art therapy's roots were in the then-dominant mode of understanding—psychoanalytic theory. Psychoanalysis is only one of many ways of trying to understand how and why people function as they do. But it is the oldest and most elaborate among modern therapeutic approaches, and has influenced all of the others, which are either modifications of or reactions to it.

Both **Freudian Psychoanalysis** and **Jungian Analytical Psychology** are based on an understanding of the dynamics of the patient's internal world. There are a variety of approaches to analysis and analytic psychotherapy. Many emphasize developmental and interpersonal phenomena, in addition to dealing with intrapsychic conflict. All assume that unresolved issues exert power, and that they are often unconscious.

Contrary to popular misconceptions, psychoanalytic therapy deals with the present as well as the past, has educational as well as cognitive components, relies heavily on empathy, and builds on strengths. Despite rumors of its demise, contemporary psychoanalysis is alive and well. In fact, it is extremely fertile, teeming with new ideas about both theory and technique, many of them relevant to art therapy.

Freudian Psychoanalysis

The two main pioneer art therapists each based their approach on the theory developed and modified by Sigmund Freud. Naumburg emphasized **insight**, uncovering unconscious forces through images and associations to them. Kramer focussed on **sublimation** through the creative process, a form of ego mastery. Many art therapists have followed in their footsteps, like myself in the Naumburg tradition or David Henley in the Kramer tradition.

Most art therapists who think analytically have emphasized one or another component of Freudian theory. Some examples are: Margaret Naumburg's stress on the **dynamic unconscious**, Edith Kramer's on **sublimation**, Laurie Wilson's on **symbolism**, Arthur Robbins' on **object relations**, Mildred Lachman-Chapin's on **self-psychology** and Myra Levick's on **defense mechanisms**. All analytically-based approaches value and foster free expression of the person's own imagery. Some emphasize spontaneity, while others stress the achievement of formed expression.

Psychoanalysts—both medical, like D. W. Winnicott and Nolan D. C. Lewis, and non-medical, like Madeleine Rambert and Marion Milner—were among the first to use drawing and painting, especially with regressed or resistant patients. Many other psychiatrists and psychologists were influenced by analytic thinking about the role of the unconscious in mental distress, and its tendency to speak in images. Several pioneered in doing such work, like Ainslie Meares in Australia, Ralph W. Pickford in Scotland, Irene Jakab in Hungary, and Mardi Horowitz in America.

Melanie Klein, who used drawing as one of many modalities in child analysis, was a disciple of Freud who developed her own unique ideas. Her theories have been applied to the discipline by British art therapist Felicity Weir, and are described in *Images of Art Therapy* (Dalley, Ed.). Analytic therapy, whether through art or words, relies on the method of **free association**, which is illustrated in the following vignette.

Free Association in Art Imagery: **Linda** (8)

Linda was a sad, inhibited eight-year-old who had come for several assessment sessions before she and her parents agreed to child analysis (four times per week). In her first analytic hour, she worked with soft colored wax, creating in rapid succession a series of three-dimensional images, which were later made into candles by the insertion of wicks.

Although Linda thought of making a Turkey for the first, she decided on an "Orange . . . because a turkey is too hard." She bragged that she would make "a whole bunch." She then pressed the round piece of wax on the table saying she had to make it "square," and talked about her older sister coming home from college for Thanksgiving tonight or tomorrow. She added dots to the square, and called it a "Dice." She then reiterated the concern she had voiced in the beginning of the hour, "I'm wondering if—if—who's your favorite person that goes with you?"

Linda's second product was a roundish piece of yellow clay on which she put "gold dust," calling it "A Gold Lump." Her third was a red "Apple," copied from a picture on a box. She complained about how hard it was to shape the wax, saying "I'm gettin' tired of it. I thought it was pretty at first sight, but I didn't know it was so much trouble!" She made a leaf for her apple, and told me that she was missing a party but didn't mind. She then joked about her friend's mother being "a wicked witch!"

Her next effort was called "An Eiffel Tower . . . very tall, one of the tallest!" Linda told a story about "a giant magnet and it was sucking everything up and it sucked the Eiffel Tower." She told me I was "a funny person." She then decided she would give away all her candles ("They're just candles") as gifts, saying "I love giving things. I really want the Eiffel Tower because it isn't so pretty . . . I think I'll keep that." In response to my questions about what she had created, Linda imagined that the dice belonged to "a famous game-player" and that the apple was owned by "the best person in the world—the King!"

What is striking is how very much Linda was able to tell about herself through free association with art media in this relatively brief segment from her first analytic hour—about her hunger for attention (supplies), her jealousy of siblings (my other patients), her difficulty with anger toward her mother (her friend's mother is a "wicked witch"), and her defense of reaction-formation . . . whereby this hungry, needy child who wants to suck up everything like a giant magnet, ends up deciding to give all of her creations to others as gifts. In a later version of this defense, Linda would

Figure 6–1 Linda welcoming the next patient.

welcome the next child analytic patient, of whom she was really quite jealous, by writing cheerful greetings on the floor (Fig. 6–1).

Jungian Analytic Therapy

Margaret Naumburg was analyzed not only by a Freudian, A. A. Brill, but also by a Jungian, Beatrice Hinkley—who analyzed her sister Florence Cane as well. Some of Jung's ideas about symbolism and imagery were incorporated into her formulation of what she called "**Dynamically-Oriented Art Therapy**." Jung's thinking has gradually become popular among American art therapists, in contrast to Great Britain—where one of the first books on art therapy was by a Jungian, E. M. Lyddiatt (1971).

Jung believed that all human beings shared a "**collective unconscious**," and that there were universal "**archetypes**" common to all cultures. The similarity of visual symbolism in widely separated artistic traditions was part of the evidence for this hypothesis. Jung's notions about **symbolism** were quite different from Freud's. Jung emphasized the capacity of symbols to **reveal** hidden ideas, while Freud stressed their ability to **conceal** unconscious feelings and fantasies.

Jung himself had found that building with natural materials and painting mandalas were helpful in his own self-analysis. Because he felt that there were messages to be "heard" in visual symbols, Jung's approach to mental and artistic imagery was respectful and intuitive—much less deductive than Freud's. He advocated the use of movement, drama, and visual imagery in the technique he called "**active imagination,**" which was a creative way of amplifying ideas and feelings in therapy. *"An emotional disturbance can also be dealt with in another way, not by clarifying it intellectually, but **by giving it visible shape**"* (Jung, 1916/1952).

Jungians are more likely than Freudians to promote art activity as part of analytic therapy, making Jungian analysis attractive to artists like Jackson Pollack (Wysuph) and Peter Birkhauser. Several analytical psychologists have published book-length case studies, including Adler, Baynes, Edinger, Harding, Ulanov, Wallace, and Weaver. Jungian analyst Edith Wallace also contributed a chapter to *Approaches.*

The arts played a central role at **Withymead Centre**, a unique therapeutic community run by a British Jungian analyst named H. Irene Champernowne (Stevens). Michael Edwards, one of the art therapists who worked there, later pursued Jungian training and contributed another Jungian chapter to *Approaches.* Joy Schaverien, also British, published *Analytical Art Psychotherapy in Theory & Practice* in 1992. In a later book, she extended her theoretical framework to include ideas from other non-Jungian psychoanalysts (Bion, Winnicott, and Lacan).

As a group, analytical psychologists are less likely to work with children, perhaps because Jung never articulated a fully developed theory of human development. A few, however, used art extensively, like Michael Fordham, John Allan and Carol Jeffrey. Gregg Furth, too, like his mentor Susan Bach, helped sick children through art. Dora Kalff was a Swiss Jungian analyst who was inspired by British psychologist Margaret Lowenfeld's idea of the "**World Technique**" to invent what she called "**Sandplay**," a technique used with patients of all ages.

Although her early training was in **Freudian object relations theory**, movement therapist Penny Lewis' latest book reflects her **Jungian** studies as well. Jungian psychiatrist David Rosen, like Lewis, has embraced a multimodality method in his treatment of depression. It is no accident that the word "transformation" is in the titles of both of their books. Jungian approaches often include a strong mystical and spiritual component.

Several art therapists have used Jung's thinking as one component of their conceptual foundations. Margaret Frings Keyes, for example, synthesized ideas from transactional analysis, Gestalt therapy, and analytical psychology. Her book was reprinted with a supplement, "**On Active Imagination**," by a Jungian analyst. Vija Lusebrink incorporated the idea of "**archetypes**" and the method of "**active imagination**" into her work. Joan Kellogg spent many years exploring the use of the **mandala** for both diagnosis and therapy, a technique embraced by others, like Suzanne Fincher.

Jerry Fryrear and Irene Corbit's book was subtitled *"A Jungian Perspective."* Lillian Rhinehart and Paula Englehorn integrated Jung's ideas with Gestalt and Native American teachings into their approach, which they called "The Art of the Sun Wheel" (CATT). And, as Jung's ideas have been "re-visioned" by contemporary analytical psychologist James Hillman, they have become even more attractive to art therapists.

HUMANISTIC APPROACHES

Another major group of therapies developed in reaction to the psychoanalytic focus on the past, on the unconscious, and on conflict. These are the Humanistic approaches, which emphasize the acceptance and development of individuals in the present. Such approaches were very popular in the sixties during the flowering of the "**human potential movement**." Humanistic psychology offered a "**wellness**" model of change, as opposed to a medical model of "**illness**." Josef Garai, who wrote that chapter in *Approaches*, also included "**Holistic**" in the title. "Holistic" ideas about healing are an outgrowth of humanistic ones, as are those in the growing area of "**Transpersonal**" psychology and psychotherapy.

Abraham Maslow, an early humanistic psychologist, emphasized "**self actualization**," or the fulfillment of the individual's innate potential for growth. He also described "**peak experiences**," a congenial way to think of creating art, which Elinor Ulman once called *"a momentary sample of living at its best."*

Person-Centered

This approach, developed by Carl Rogers, was originally called **Client-Centered**. It is based on the therapist's "**unconditional positive regard**" for the patient, and the powerful effect of "**empathy**" (feeling-into or feeling-with) as a way of fully responding to the person in pain. Carl Rogers' daughter, Natalie Rogers, was taught by Maslow. Though not an art therapist, she used art along with movement, music, and drama in what she called "**Person-Centered Expressive Therapy**." In Great Britain, Liesl Silverstone developed a training course: "*Art Therapy: The Person-Centred Way*," which was also based on Rogerian ideas.

Adlerian

Alfred Adler, a former colleague of Freud's who created "**Individual Psychology**," inspired several American art therapists. One was Rose Garlock, who led groups at an Adlerian "**Social Club**" in New York for many years and contributed a chapter to *Approaches*. Another was Sadie Dreikurs, wife of Adler's disciple Rudolf Dreikurs. She began her work in a Chicago hospital in 1962, and taught her approach in Adlerian Institutes.

Figure 6–2 Janie Rhyne teaching graduate students.

Gestalt

Like "Transactional Analysis," Gestalt Therapy also involved modifications of psychoanalytic theory and technique. Like Rogerian therapy, it emphasized **the here-and-now**. Unlike that approach, it required a more active role by the therapist. **Gestalt Therapy** was the creation of analytically-trained Fritz Perls, who integrated his dynamic understandings with the findings of **Gestalt Psychology**. The latter was an **experimental** approach which focussed on sensation and perception.

A major area of interest was visual perception, as in the work of Rudolf Arnheim, who has influenced many in art therapy. One art therapy pioneer trained by Perls also participated with him in the human potential movement. Janie Rhyne called her 1973 book *The Gestalt Art Experience*, and led workshops in that approach (Fig. 6–2). Joseph Zinker, a Gestalt therapist and sculptor, wrote about his multimodal use of expression. Violet Oaklander, another Gestalt therapist, described her use of art and other expressive modalities—with children, adolescents, and families.

Later in her career, Janie Rhyne became interested in George Kelly's "**Personal Construct**" theory of personality. She explored what she called "**mindstate drawings**" for her doctoral research. In a 1980 paper (AATA Conf.), Janie described her findings and their application in her clinical work, elaborating these ideas in her chapter for *Approaches*. Her later thinking is in the Foreword and Afterword to the 1996 reissue of her book, whose new subtitle—"Patterns that Connect"—reflected Janie's interest in both personal constructs and "**cybernetics**" (the study of feedback systems).

Ericksonian

Milton Erickson was a psychologist who created his own personal synthesis of various philosophies and techniques into a highly inventive approach. Like other humanistic therapists, he emphasized human potential, and advocated a collaborative vs. an authoritarian model of psychotherapy. He pioneered in many techniques, such as the clinical use of hypnosis and what he called "**creative reframing**."

In a 1940 case study with analyst Lawrence Kubie, Erickson described using "Automatic Drawing" to treat a case of "Acute Obsessional Depression"—an early instance of art therapy (?). Although art therapists have not been notably involved in Ericksonian therapy, both approaches rely heavily on **metaphor**, as in the use of art by Mills & Crowley.

Phenomenological

A strong current, with its roots in 19th century philosophy, also had a profound impact on 20th century psychology. Known as **Phenomenology**, the essence of the theory is the uniqueness of each individual's experience of reality at each moment in time. In psychotherapy, the clinician concentrates on helping the patient to focus keenly and intensely on each moment, to fully know the phenomenon of **being-in-the-world** (existing). Art therapy pioneer Mala Betensky developed an approach based mainly on Phenomenology, into which she integrated elements of Gestalt psychology as well. She wrote two books about her work (1973, 1995), and contributed a chapter to *Approaches*.

Existential

Existentialism also began in philosophy and was then embraced by a number of psychologists and psychiatrists. A strong element was the centrality of **meaning**, a key factor in art therapist Bruce Moon's work with adults, described in his book *Existential Art Therapy*. Although they were psychologists and not art therapists, both Clark Moustakas (children) and Rollo May (adults) described **existential therapy** in which **creativity** was synonymous with **mental health**.

All of the humanistic approaches emphasize man's capacity to take charge of his life, to exercise "**intentionality**," and to use **free will**. In contrast, psychoanalytic approaches stress unconscious dynamics and the power of the "**repetition compulsion**" to affect even "free" choices.

BEHAVIORAL & COGNITIVE APPROACHES

Behavioral

Experimental psychologists focus on what can be measured, i.e., overt behavior. They have enhanced our comprehension of how learning takes place. We know, for example, that if a behavior is reinforced or rewarded in some way, it will tend to be repeated. We also know that if a behavior is ignored or punished, it is less likely to recur, and that it will eventually "extinguish," i.e., disappear.

This understanding is the basis for techniques which have gained in popularity among clinicians during recent years. **Behavior Therapy** and **Behavior Modification** are approaches in which a systematic description of appropriate and inappropriate behaviors provides the basis for therapeutic intervention. All therapies provide reinforcement for some behaviors and not for others, but reinforcement is rarely the primary instrument of change.

These approaches have not been especially popular among art therapists, since at first glance they appear antithetical to a genuine creative process. They are not really incompatible, but require—as do all theories—a deep understanding in order to be able to be meaningfully integrated with art therapy.

Behavioral approaches have been used most often with the disabled, as in Ellen Roth's use of "**Reality-Shaping**" with emotionally disturbed retarded children (*Approaches*). They are also especially well-suited to treating specific anxiety symptoms, as in John DeFrancisco's "**Implosive Art Therapy**" with phobic children (1983 AATA Conf.).

Cognitive

Cognitive Therapies focus on habitual distorted thought processes which are thought to underlie maladaptive feelings and behaviors. The therapeutic approach is largely an **educational** one, in which the task is to identify the patterns of misperception or thought causing the persistence of symptoms. Patients are then taught new and more adaptive ways to think and to behave, using cognitive strategies. While there is an educational element in all therapies, teaching is not usually the primary mode of treatment.

One of the first to espouse a cognitive approach to therapy was psychologist Albert Ellis, who developed what he called "**Rational-Emotive Therapy**" (RET) in the sixties. At the 1982 Conference, art therapist Sondra Geller and a colleague described how they had "unblock[ed] the creative process" for students unable to complete theses. They felt that art therapy was enhanced when combined with the cognitive/behavioral strategies of RET.

Many art therapists of varied theoretical persuasion have considered the cognitive aspects of art activity to be **central** to its therapeutic power, including people as different in orientation as Edith Kramer and Janie Rhyne. Shaun McNiff developed his ideas about the therapeutic action of art in a series of books, paying tribute to his mentor, Rudolf Arnheim—the author of *Visual Thinking*. Other cognitive psychologists, like Howard Gardner and the Kreitlers (AP, 1978, p. 199), have also been appealing to art therapists, because they clarify and value the cognitive operations involved in making art (Cf. AP, 1979, p. 69).

Figure 6–3   Aina Nucho teaching an art therapy student.

Rawley Silver, who contributed a chapter to *Approaches*, called her book *Developing Cognitive and Creative Skills through Art*, applying the cognitive psychology of Jean Piaget and others to art therapy with the disabled. In 1987, Aina Nucho published her ***Psychocybernetic** Model of Art Therapy*, in which she synthesized cybernetic (feedback) theory with art therapy (Fig. 6–3). Nucho's most recent book is not about art, but rather about mental imagery, an active area in cognitive psychology for several decades. Vija Lusebrink is another art therapist whose work includes the use of imagery, reflecting her own application of such cognitive elements as **information processing** to art therapy.

All of these cognitively-based theories of art therapy are, however, quite different from what is currently known as **Cognitive Therapy**. Marcia Rosal (1996) has described a **Cognitive-Behavioral** approach which is more similar to current trends in treatment. There, she wrote about her use of George Kelly's cognitively-based **Personal Construct** theory in both assessment and therapy.

DEVELOPMENTAL & ADAPTIVE APPROACHES

Closely related to cognitive and behavioral approaches, and often a major component, are approaches which are based on an understanding of growth itself. **Developmental** approaches originated in the work of Viktor Lowenfeld, whose *Creative & Mental Growth* has been in print for over 50 years. Donald Uhlin, a student of Lowenfeld's, based his work in art therapy with disabled children on what he knew of normal development.

Developmental Therapy was invented by special educator Mary Wood, whose ideas were combined with those of art therapist Geraldine Williams in *Developmental Art Therapy*. Doing art therapy with children who were blind, deaf, and retarded, led Susan Aach-Feldman (Fig. 6–4) and Carole Kunkle-Miller to adopt a **developmental** orientation, as they described in their chapter in *Approaches*.

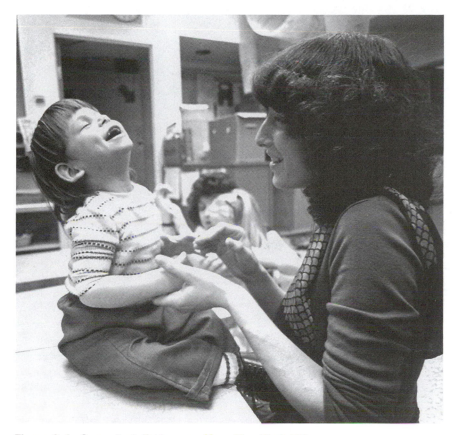

Figure 6–4 Susan Aach-Feldman working with a blind child.

The **Adaptive** approach, which works toward **normalization**, was first articulated by Lowenfeld, and has been amplified by Frances Anderson, an art therapist who has contributed several books on art therapy for individuals with
disabilities (Fig. 6–5). Robert Ault defined a similar orientation as "**Functional
Art Therapy**," where the focus is on achieving specific goals leading to better
and more adaptive functioning.

In contrast to psychoanalytic or humanistic approaches to art therapy,
those stemming from behavioral, cognitive, or developmental orientations are
more likely to offer **prescribed** art activities. While themes or tasks are also
used at times by psychodynamic or humanistic art therapists, they are even
more consistent with behavioral, cognitive, developmental, adaptive, and functional models of treatment. These approaches are also used more often in
the treatment of individuals with disabilities, who are more likely to require
a **remedial** approach.

Figure 6–5   Frances Anderson working with a client.

ART/IMAGE-BASED APPROACHES

All art therapists share the common ground of *art*. Some have conceptualized the effectiveness of art therapy from an **aesthetic** as well as a psychological point of view. We don't usually think of aestheticians as relevant theorists for clinicians, but there was one philosopher whose ideas were especially germane to art therapy. Susanne Langer published *Philosophy in a New Key* in 1942, and *Feeling and Form* in 1953. Her core idea, simple but profound, was that the arts have always existed because they are the **forms of human feeling**. She was not talking so much about specific emotions, but rather of a deeper emotional substrate. Gladys Agell has spelled out some implications of Langer's theories in "**Art Therapy in a 'New Key**'" (AJAT, 1989, p. 18). David Henley has also conceptualized an aesthetic basis for a theory of art therapy, by synthesizing Kramer's ideas on art therapy and artistic value with his on "outsider art" (AP, 1992, p. 153).

There are other approaches to art therapy which emphasize the **Art** or—as some prefer—the **Image**. Art-centered theories usually stress either the creative process, the visual imagery that results from it, or both. They are compatible with a wide variety of theoretical orientations, including Freudian (Robbins), Jungian (Wallace), Gestalt (Rhyne), Cognitive (Lusebrink), Phenomenological (Betensky), and Existential (Moon). Pat Allen focussed on the power of art to create meaning in *Art is a Way of Knowing*; Shaun McNiff stressed its healing potency in *Art as Medicine*.

A highly original theory, based on the formal elements of graphic style, was developed over the course of a long career by Rita Simon. Her first book was subtitled *"Art as Therapy,"* and her ideas are quite compatible with that orientation. Simon analyzed **Style** as **Archaic, Linear, Traditional** and **Massive**, suggesting a unique way to look at pictures, which served the author well in both diagnosis and in therapy. Equally idiosyncratic was the approach developed by Professor Tokuda in Japan, which he called **"Image Therapy."**

The most extensive original system, used with many patients at Hillside Hospital in Queens from 1943 to 1967, was **"Creative Analysis."** It was developed by psychologist Ernest Zierer and carried on by his wife, art therapist Edith Zierer. Although based on psychoanalytic ego psychology, it was unusual for an analytic approach in that it used many specific interventions. The art therapist chose, from among a number of possible artistic tasks, those considered most appropriate for each patient, for diagnosis as well as for therapy. Looking at the **form** rather than the **content** of oil paintings created in their studio, the Zierers assessed the degree of **"Color Integration"** in the art work. This was thought to reflect mental health, while its absence (**"Color Disintegration"**) was seen as reflecting mental disorganization or disturbance.

SPIRITUAL APPROACHES

A strong current in contemporary American art therapy has to do with the spiritual aspect of our work. This was reflected in the theme of the 1994 conference, **"Common Ground: The Arts, Therapy & Spirituality,"** where Shaun McNiff presented a paper on "Images as Angels." Jung, the son of a minister, valued the the spiritual elements in psychoanalysis; whereas Freud, the rationalist, was determined to prove the scientific nature of the new depth psychology.

Ironically, both polarities are more important in the mental health domain than ever before. **Psychobiological** approaches currently dominate the field of psychiatry; while **neuroscience** and **cognitive-behavioral therapy** dominate contemporary psychology. At the same time, in a technological world where human values seem to have been lost, the hunger for meaning has been intensified. One reflection of this longing is the popularity of spiritual approaches in mental health, as in the many kinds of treatment programs based upon the **"twelve-step"** method of overcoming addiction.

Art therapy, drawing as art has from time immemorial on the human spirit, offers a most appealing avenue for authentic expressions of the soul. Even the most rational among us knows of the deep inner well from which we draw when we express ourselves. While I have found a psychoanalytic orientation most useful in my work, it does not seem incompatible with the title I gave to a book I have been working on for several years: *"Soul Prints."*

Even though art therapists operate from a number of different perspectives, one that cuts across all of our theoretical differences is that of the human spirit, which is so essential to our creative capacity. The philosophy of **Anthroposophy** which underlies the work of Rudolf Steiner and his followers, while primarily expressed in the educational arena of the **Waldorf Schools**, has also spawned a somewhat mystical approach to **"color therapy"** (Collot d'Herbois) and **"painting therapy"** (Hauschka).

Spirituality is a strong element in Bruce Moon's work; in fact, his most recent book is entitled *Art & Soul.* Similarly, Ellen Horovitz-Darby has just published a book entitled *Spiritual Art Therapy.* Spirituality is also central in **Transpersonal** approaches to art therapy; as well as for many of those who work with multiple modalities, like "intermodal" expressive art therapist Paolo Knill, co-author of *Minstrels of Soul.*

FAMILY AND GROUP ART THERAPY

Although I had decided not to include Group or Family Art Therapy in *Approaches to Art Therapy*, some have argued that they should have been in that book. One reason for their omission was that there are many different theoretical orientations in both areas. Most early art therapists were influenced by the dominant psychodynamic thinking about groups, including families. Since then, however, the developing fields of **group dynamics**, **cybernetics**, and **systems theory** have spawned a whole new set of conceptualizations about people in plural. These ideas have greatly affected contemporary family and group art therapists.

Family Art Therapy

One of the most influential art therapists was Hanna Yaxa Kwiatkowska, who worked at the National Institutes of Mental Health (NIMH), where family therapy itself was being developed. Although other art therapists were seeing families too, Kwiatkowska was the undisputed pioneer of *Family Therapy and Evaluation Through Art.*

Many have followed in her footsteps, such as Helen Landgarten who described work with families in her first book, and later devoted an entire book to the topic. Barbara Sobol described her use of art in "Strategic Family Therapy" (AJAT, 1982, p.43). Shirley Riley, who had written about her "Structural" approach to family art therapy, later published a book on "Integrative Approaches" with Cathy Malchiodi. Sara Deco described her work with "structural

Figure 6–6   A pair in a mother-child art therapy group.

family art therapy'' at a Family Centre in Engand (WCAT). And Deborah Linesch edited a book which included a variety of approaches to *Art Therapy with Families in Crisis.*

As with behavioral and cognitive approaches to art therapy, it would appear that strategic and structural family therapy are not as incompatible with art therapy as they may look at first. What is essential is that—as with any approach to individual art therapy—the clinician needs to have thoroughly mastered the theory, in order to be true to it as well as to art.

Because of its versatility, art therapy has also been used with many of the possible variations on the family theme: **Couples**, **Multiple Family Groups**, **Mothers and Children** (Fig. 6–6), and **Siblings** (Fig. 6–7). Harriet Wadeson pioneered in work with couples and with ''Multi-Family Art Therapy'' (1980). Like Kwiatkowska, her early family work was at the National Institutes of Mental Health (NIMH).

Group Art Therapy

There is a similar variety of theories and techniques in Group Art Therapy, but no individual has so far emerged as dominant. This is somewhat ironic, because

Figure 6–7 Two brothers in art therapy.

it is likely that more patients experience art therapy in a group than in any other context. Although an ''**open studio**'' group was at first the most common format, the trend has been toward approaches which more consciously utilize the power of the group in conjunction with the power of art. As noted earlier, art therapy students often learn about **group dynamics** and **group process** through partici- pating in art groups themselves. Over time, many approaches to group art therapy have been described by different art therapists, working with both children (Fig. 6–8) and adults (Fig. 6–9).

Although Margaret Naumburg usually saw people individually, she once described how she helped a group of obese women to create ''spontaneous art.'' Their art work was then used by a psychiatrist in ''analytically oriented group therapy.'' Other early descriptions of group art therapy (in the fifties) included

Figure 6–8 Group art therapy with children.

a booklet by Emory Gondor on his work with children, two papers by Lucille Potts on her work with adults (*Int. J. Group Psychother.*), and a pamphlet by Dunn and Semple on their work with adolescents. In all of these groups, patients first created art individually, and then discussed it with the other members.

One of the first books on the topic, written by art therapist Cliff Joseph (Fig. 6–10) and psychiatrist Jay Harris, was *Murals of the Mind: Image of a Psychiatric Community*. Like other early publications, it was psychoanalytic in orientation. Because of the method (all patients working together on a mural), it offered a fascinating study of an inpatient group's development over the course of a year, by analyzing the form and content of **weekly murals**.

Though the practice of group art therapy gradually expanded during the growth of the field in the sixties and seventies, there were few publications. They

Figure 6–9 Group art therapy with adults.

more than doubled, however, between 1975 and 1980. Gestalt and humanistic approaches became increasingly common. Janie Rhyne's book devoted an entire section to work with groups, and several others wrote chapters on group art therapy (e.g., Landgarten, Rubin, and Wadeson). The group described by Xenia Lucas in her book was typical of analytically-based group art therapy. Though group process was acknowledged, the primary focus was on individuals and their artistic and psychological development.

When Kathleen Hanes compiled an annotated **bibliography**, *Art Therapy & Group Work*, in 1982, she noted that art was being offered in groups which ranged from unstructured "open studio" situations to theme-centered ones and those using interactional tasks. She also reported that the emphasis was intrapsychic as often as it was interpersonal; but that interventions based upon group dynamics were increasing (Fig. 6–11).

Figure 6–10 Cliff Joseph working with a group.

Meanwhile, our art therapy colleagues in Great Britain also found themselves often working with groups. In 1941 Dr. Joshua Bierer, who developed **Adlerian Social Clubs** in London, invited artist Rita Simon to work with his patients in groups, initiating her long career in art therapy. In 1986, Marian Liebmann published a survey of techniques used in group art therapy, which offered practical advice along with many exercises. The book provoked a debate regarding the wisdom of structured as opposed to unstructured approaches. The debate seems to have been especially heated, due to the importance in England of the "group analytic" tradition.

Figure 6–11 Group members compare pictures of the group.

Figure 6–12   One of Don's compulsive designs (marker).

Diane Waller recently described her model of *Group Interactive Art Therapy*, based on concepts deriving from group analysis, interpersonal group therapy, systems theory, and art therapy. "Interpersonal Group Therapy," as presented in the widely-used books by existential psychiatrist Irvin Yalom, has been popular in both countries. Many art therapists work with groups, but few have had formal training in group psychotherapy. Waller and several of her colleagues have been trained at the Institute of Group Analysis, enabling them to synthesize what they know about art therapy with what they know about analytic groups. Similarly, Mickie Rosen has applied Agazarian's "System-Centered" ("Group as a Whole") Method to group art therapy (AP, 1995, p. 133); (Cf. also Skaife & Huet).

The following vignette indicates how much even a brief art therapy group can help one of its members to begin to change and to grow.

Individual Growth in a Group: **Don** (9)

In the first few meetings of a summer art therapy group of latency-age boys, nine-year-old Don worked apart from the others, drawing compulsively tight abstract designs (Fig. 6–12). Gradually, however, he began to interact with the other boys. At first he sat closer, still silent. His designs became somewhat freer, and he began to use various kinds of paint, to explore color mixing, and to allow himself a greater range.

Stimulated by the other boys, Don then turned to the more tactile and regressive medium of clay. At first he made tame animals, like dogs and

Figure 6–13 "Somebody Who is Injured," by Don (painted clay).

cats. Then he made larger and more aggressive ones, like dinosaurs and lions. Eventually, he modeled a boy who had been violently wounded, painting red blood streaming out of his maimed body (Fig. 6–13).

Although Don wouldn't say who it was, the following week he whispered to me that he knew, but was afraid to tell the others. I asked if he could tell me, and he whispered, "My brother." I suggested that it might help the other boys in the group, many of whom had similar angry feelings and wishes toward siblings, to know they were not alone. During group discussion time at the end of the session, he tentatively whispered that it was "somebody younger," then "somebody I'd like to throw something at," and finally, "my brother." The others responded with relief, and an outpouring of their own impulses to hurt younger siblings, along with fears of their strength and destructiveness.

Don was delighted, and responded the following week by becoming uncharacteristically messy, smearing and mixing tempera paint colors with

Figure 6–14   Don's gift to his therapist at termination (paint).

another boy, for the first time allowing himself to interact playfully with other group members. His products for the next two weeks were not much to look at, but the process he engaged in was vital to his eventual recovery. He followed this aggressive/regressive phase with a freer kind of order in his work.

After the eight-week group had ended, Don continued in individual art therapy for several months. When he terminated treatment, he selected a tempera painting with movement, color mixing, and clear-but-not-rigid boundaries as a gift for his therapist (Fig. 6–14). It reflected the integration of freedom and order that he had been able to achieve internally as well.

THEORY, THECHNIQUE, & ART THERAPY

Art Therapists as Theorists

Art therapists are attracted to the field because they like both art and people; and they tend to be curious as well as compassionate and creative. For some, the curiosity extends beyond wanting to understand the people they see and the art that is created, to the creative process that seems to work so well in psychotherapy. This very combination can make theory-building endlessly fascinating. Since in many ways art therapy is "**a technique in search of a theory**," it has been fortunate for the field that these restless minds loved to explore new ideas in relation to art therapy.

Thus, Margaret Naumburg in her later years was busy reading **archeologist** Siegfried Gideon and applying his findings to art therapy. Edith Kramer has written extensively about the implications of Konrad Lorenz's work in **ethology** for art therapy. Joy Schaverien has used **anthropology** to amplify her understanding, offering us new ways to think about familiar phenomena, like the art as a "**talisman**" or a "**scapegoat**." All art therapists who have worked out ways of applying different theoretical constructs have done so by synthesizing what they knew about the therapeutic power of art with what they understood about one or more theories of psychotherapy.

The Unspoken Perspective

Theoretical ideas and the techniques that follow therefrom continually evolve and change in all forms of treatment, including art therapy. As with clinicians who help through words, the majority of art therapists don't think of themselves as following any particular theoretical model. Yet, like talk therapists, all art therapists have some notions of what is amiss and how to help people to get better. These ideas necessarily underlie what they do and the way they do it. Though it may be unarticulated, there is always some kind of unspoken theory behind any art therapist's technique.

Any clinician's preferred theoretical approach is likely to be chosen for largely personal reasons. These include those by whom she has been trained and with whom she has identified, as well as those with whom she works. In addition to experiential variables, temperament is another reason for choosing a preferred framework. The approach selected may be pure or mixed, rigid or flexible. Hopefully, it is both clear and consistent.

Selective Eclecticism

Although it is essential to have a solid grounding in some coherent notion of how people function and how to help them to get better, most clinicians are not purists. In fact, most art therapists are probably mainly **pragmatic**, selecting the approach that best fits the particular situation. Robert Ault has described four different approaches, each one to be utilized *depending on the needs of the patient(s)*. He called them **Analytic, Gestalt, Functional** and **Psycho-educational Art Therapy**. As Helen Landgarten said, "*The truth of the matter is that art therapy is not a discipline, it's . . . a modality. Art therapy is a way of getting there. It operates as a modality because **you can adapt it to any theory**"* (AJAT, 1995, p. 36).

In *Approaches*, two of the best chapters dealt honestly with the many determinants of theoretical positions and technical decisions. Harriet Wadeson described her **Eclectic** approach, how it evolved and how she has used it over the course of a long career. Elinor Ulman called her chapter "**Variations** on a Freudian Theme: Three Art Therapy Theorists." Both offer intelligent considerations of how to be open-minded without being sloppy.

Is Theory Really Necessary?

But what about the art therapist who rejects theory? Isn't it possible to simply be a sensitive person and to be a good therapist as well? There is a difference of opinion in art therapy, as in other clinical disciplines. An **intuitive** approach is probably more acceptable in art therapy, because artists pride themselves on their innate sensitivities, and tend to be anti-authoritarian and anti-theoretical. It seems a logical continuation of the romantic, bohemian tradition, which is appealing to creative people.

Art therapists, however, usually do their work not in artists' lofts, but in offices and institutions run by others. The art therapist is responsible for meeting the goals for which she is being paid, whether she is employed by educators, health professionals, or patients. For an art therapist in private practice, there is an even greater sense of responsibility; because, in truth, the patient's life is in her hands.

Art is a wonderful modality. It has the power to cut through defenses and to uncover unconscious material quite rapidly. It is also a very exciting modality, with the power to stimulate a regression which—in those whose defenses are too fragile—may need to be contained. An art therapist needs to know what she is doing, especially when people are in a vulnerable state. Most people who come to art therapy, even the "worried well" who are not grossly disturbed, can still be injured by naive or tactless work. Without some understanding of human frailties and the terrific complexity of mental functioning, as well as the delicacy of healing; I believe that even the most well-intentioned artist is in danger of violating the oath taken by physician healers, which is to **"do no harm."**

For this reason, art therapists in training are familiarized with many theories of psychology, psychopathology, and psychotherapy. And they are required to work under close supervision for a substantial period of time before being eligible for Registration, in order to be sure that they have assistance in the difficult task of translating theory into practice.

Theory is what enables any therapist to make sense of the data being received, and to be thoughtful about technique. Only with a coherent perspective on what she does can the art therapist make fully available the healing powers of art. In fact, it is only when she has truly mastered some theory of psychological functioning and of psychotherapy, when it is "**in her bones,**" that she can use her *intuition* in the most helpful way. Theory helps an art therapist to sharpen both her thinking and her clinical skills.

Since art therapy does have connections with other disciplines, it makes sense in theory, as elsewhere, to utilize any relevant insights to understand why and how art therapy works. It seems as unnecessary to throw the baby out with the bathwater, as it would be to reinvent the wheel. Just as those metaphors remind art therapists that they can learn from others, so the notion that "**a picture is worth a thousand words**" is one of the reasons art therapy works.

Effectively integrating the synthesis of art and therapy requires an internalized frame of reference.

The more extensive an art therapist's understanding of different approaches, the **more clinical lenses** she has with which to see. Like a stain on a microscopic slide, a theory can enable a therapist to literally see something that would otherwise be invisible. And if she can look at a problem from a different angle, she is often able to view possible solutions from a new perspective. It is a kind of "**reframing**" for the therapist, for whom a cup can look either half empty or half full, just as it can for the patient. That is probably why so many have struggled with the difficult questions of how to view, understand, and do art therapy—in order to help the people they serve as much as possible through art.

Chapter 7

Assessment

THE USE OF ANY COMBINATION *of verbal, written, and art tasks*
chosen by the professional art therapist to assess the individual's
level of functioning, problem areas, strengths, and treatment objectives.
                                AATA, GENERAL STANDARDS OF PRACTICE

Art and Diagnosis

It has already been noted that some of the threads which became part of the
fabric of art therapy came from wanting to understand people through their art
expression. The goal may be to identify exactly what is wrong, or to get to know
the person better in a more general way. Even when a diagnostic label is not
the purpose of an assessment, finding out where an individual is on any dimension relevant to treatment can be extremely helpful. Just as there are many
different ways of classifying the information obtained, so there are also multiple
methods of gathering data using visual means. This chapter will offer an overview of the many ways of understanding people through art as they have evolved
over time.

PROJECTIVE TECHNIQUES

As noted earlier, "**projective testing**"—both responsive and expressive—flowered in clinical psychology for several decades, beginning in the thirties. The assumption behind all such approaches is that the individual is revealing
important information which—because it is unconscious and therefore unknown—is not accessible in more direct ways. This is true whether a person is
responding to some kind of visual stimulus with his ideas, or is creating something himself using art materials.

Responding to Visual Stimuli

In some approaches, the individual is asked to give meaning to a series of stimuli.
They may be abstract, like the Rorschach inkblots or the molded shapes of
Twitchell-Allen's Three-Dimensional Apperception Test; or ambiguous, like the
color photographs in The Walker Visuals. They may also be more or less representational, like the drawings of people in Murray's Thematic Apperception

Test (TAT), or of animals in Bellak's version for children (CAT). More recent variations on this approach favor greater specificity, like Gardner's Adoption Story Cards or Howells' Family Relations Indicator.

Preference Tests

In these, the person chooses among visual stimuli. Some involve color, as in the Luscher Color Test. Others involve design, like the Barron-Welsh Figure Preference Test. Art therapist Joan Kellogg's studies of recurring patterns in mandala drawings were the basis for her selection procedure, the **MARI Card Test**, which involves both color and design. For her doctoral research, art therapist Doris Arrington created a **Visual Preference Test**, in which participants select and rank line drawings. Like images seen in inkblots or stories told about drawings, such choices are assumed to reflect fairly stable aspects of personality.

Copying & Completion

Used in art education for centuries, copying has also been helpful in the psychological assessment of organic impairment, as in the Bender Visual Motor Gestalt Test. Completion procedures are another popular approach. In the Kinget Drawing Completion Test, for example, each of the eight sections on the test blank contains a dot or a line, which the subject is invited to develop into a picture. This kind of standardized ambiguous stimulus is similar to the self-drawn stimuli suggested by some art therapists, and is used in treatment as well as in assessment.

The Scribble Drawing

At about the same time, a playful British analyst named Winnicott and an inspired American art teacher named Cane independently came up with the notion of using a scribble as a visual starter, i.e., developing a picture from a self-made scribble. For Winnicott, it provided a rapid and non-threatening way to get to know a child he was assessing; and because his interest was in communication rather than composition, a pencil and a small piece of paper suited his **Squiggle Game**. Cane, on the other hand, wanted to stimulate freedom and spontaneity in art expression; so her **Scribble** technique included preparatory breathing and movement exercises, and was done on large drawing paper with colored pastels.

Taught by her sister Margaret Naumburg, the scribble has been extremely popular among art therapists. It was incorporated into the first formally designed art therapy assessment batteries for both individuals (Ulman) and families (Kwiatkowska). Since young children have difficulty with the task, Ron Hays proposed a **Dot-to-Dot** drawing as an alternative for them (1979 Conf., p. 116).

Many other "visual starter" approaches are used in treatment as well as diagnosis, some of which are noted in Chapter 8.

Projective Drawings

The first individual to standardize procedures for using drawing tests with patients was a German psychiatrist named Fritz Mohr in 1906. Using children's drawings of a person to measure intellectual development was pioneered by a child psychologist named Florence Goodenough in 1926 as the **Draw a Man Test**. In 1931, a psychiatrist named Kenneth Appel described an extensive "drawing battery" he was using in his initial interviews with children, which included drawing human figures. Clinical psychologist Karen Machover noticed that many features of person drawings seemed to be dynamically significant, so she included the task in her assessments. In 1949 she published a book describing a number of "signs" and their meanings in her **Draw a Person Test**.

Psychologist John Buck also saw meanings in the drawings on IQ tests; and in 1948 introduced his **House-Tree-Person Test (H-T-P)**, in which all three topics were part of the task. His hypothesis was that the house and tree drawings were also self-projections, but less obvious and therefore potentially more revealing. Central to all projective drawing tests is the assumption that formal elements—like placement, line quality, or shading—are as significant as subject matter.

In 1958, another clinical psychologist named Emanuel Hammer edited a book, entitled *The Clinical Application of Projective Drawings*, with contributions by many individuals. One was Margaret Naumburg, who described the history of art therapy and presented a case study. She also noted some of the similarities and differences between prompted, standardized, projective drawings, and the spontaneous work created in art therapy.

Despite numerous research studies, in which most of the common assumptions about the meanings of various signs could not be validated, projective drawings have remained extremely popular among clinicians. This is probably due to their ease of administration, as well as the richness of material obtained. Many inventive ideas have been proposed by individual clinicians over the years (Hammer, 1958, 1997).

Some involved modifications or alterations of some sort. Rosenberg, for example, offered the freedom to change completed drawings (of a man and a woman) in any way, using a carbon copy for comparison. Caligor went even further with his Eight-Figure Redrawing Test, in which the person made a series of eight drawings of the human figure, each one based on the previous one—as seen through a sheet of onionskin. The instructions were: "Change it in any way you like."

Art therapist Harriet Wadeson used a similar technique with **couples**. She invited both members of the pair to draw a portrait of the other, after which each had an opportunity to modify their partner's picture as he or she wished.

Robert Ault also included such a task in his assessment battery for couples, to be described later.

Variations on drawing themes have been extensive. These include other self-representations, like a **Tree**, a **House**, or **Animals**. Sometimes the topic is designed to evaluate the person's ability to cope with stress, such as drawing **A Person in the Rain** or **The Most Unpleasant Concept Test**—"Draw the most unpleasant thing imaginable."

Though many other topics have been proposed, the drawing of the **Human Figure**—or its symbolic extension in the **House-Tree-Person**—remains most popular with the majority of clinicians, including many art therapists. The **H-T-P** is either done with a pencil (**achromatic**) or a set of eight crayons (**chromatic**). Along with the hypothesis that an individual projects core personality traits in drawing behavior; there is also the related assumption of an internal schema, the "**body image**." This idea, originated by psychiatrist Paul Schilder, is one reason for the continuing popularity of the person drawing.

Its only close competitor, clearly superior for getting a picture of the interpersonal situation, is the **Family Drawing**, described in 1931 by Appel (*Amer. J. Ortho.*, p. 129), and elaborated in 1952 by Hulse (*J. Proj. Tech.*, p. 66). Appel suggested adding activity, later popularized by Burns and Kaufman (1970) in the widely-used **Kinetic Family Drawing (KFD)**: "Draw a picture of everyone in your family, including you, doing something." Burns went on to suggest other ideas in subsequent books, like the **Kinetic House-Tree-Person Drawing**, the **Family-Centered Circle Drawing**, and the **Kinetic-Shop-Window-Drawing**. The latter was like guided imagery techniques: a setting is suggested by the clinician, and then "filled in" by the person.

One of the variations on the family drawing theme proposed in Burns' 1990 book was called the **Parents' Self-Centered Circle Drawing**. In 1970, art therapists Selwyn and Irene Dewdney asked some of their patients to draw a **Mother-and-Child** (ATV, p. 321). In 1994, Psychologist Jacqueline Gillespie suggested the diagnostic use of **Mother-and-Child Drawings**. In a temporal twist, a psychiatrist/pediatrician team created the **Prospective Kinetic Family Drawing**, in which a person draws the family "doing something after 5–10 years" (AJAT, 1992, p. 17).

Although the family is the first and most dynamically significant group, others become increasingly important in the course of normal development. In the forties, the inventor of psychodrama, Jacob Moreno, suggested making pictorial diagrams of interpersonal relationships, with names like **Social Atom** and **Sociogram**. The **Draw-a-Group Test** was suggested by the Hares in 1956 (*J. Genet. Psychol.*, p. 51) and **Draw a Member of a Minority Group** by Hammer in 1958.

In 1974, Prout and Phillips proposed a **Kinetic School Drawing (KSD)**, to be done following a KFD. Klepsch asked children to **Draw a Classroom** and to do portraits of authority figures—**Teacher, Doctor, Policeman**—to assess a youngster's sense of himself in relation to others. Following in the footsteps of

Wayne Dennis, who studied the subject, and wrote *Group Values through Children's Drawings*, Klepsch reviewed other such studies in a book with Logie.

Standardization in Drawing Tasks

Most projective drawing tasks developed by psychologists use standardized materials—such as 8″ × 11″ paper, a No. 2 pencil, and, when "chromatic," specific colors and types of crayons. Instructions for each of the drawings are also clearly specified, as are the guidelines for any post-drawing interrogation (PDI). Such standardization is needed to establish group norms, to which clinicians can then relate individual performance.

In 1995, for example, a new Human Figure Drawing (HFD) Test was published with adult norms for cognitive impairment, and scales to discriminate organic damage from thought disorder. Like norms, precise scoring methods are also needed. For example, another recent version of the Draw a Person Test used templates, in order to more objectively measure size and placement.

A systematic approach to test administration, clear identification of items to be scored, and the creation of rating manuals, are tedious but necessary steps on the road to **reliability**. One aspect is "test-retest reliability"—how consistent anyone's performance is on a particular instrument. The other is "inter-rater reliability"—how similar judgments are with any specific scale. Whether the instrument measures what it is supposed to—**validity**— is another heavily debated issue. It is the source of most criticism leveled at all projective techniques, especially drawings.

Nevertheless, despite negative findings in much of the research, projective drawings appeal to clinicians and researchers from many different disciplines. One of the most prolific writers in this area was a pediatrician named Joseph DiLeo, who published a series of books on children's drawings. DiLeo's goal was a differential diagnosis of "the unusual and the deviant" in the context of "the usual and the normative." His diagnostic battery included both copying tasks and specific topics.

Art & Psychopathology

In 1972 Schildkrout and her colleagues published *Human Figure Drawings in Adolescence*, using pictures collected at a medical clinic. The idea was that drawings could be an efficient **screening** device for potential psychiatric problems. Considerable attention was given to signs of emotional disturbance, of organicity, and of danger, i.e., "acting-out" of any sort, like suicide or homicide. The search for **warning signs** in artwork, whether in a prescribed task or in spontaneous products, can be critical, especially in acute psychiatric settings or in the criminal justice system. Art therapists and others have long sought to identify graphic clues to a variety of diagnostic puzzles.

Much of the early projective drawing literature—like art therapist Brown's *Psycho-Iconography* or psychologist McElhaney's book on HFDs—was an attempt to familiarize clinicians with typical drawing signs in patients with different disorders. ''Art as a Reflection of Mental Status'' was the title of psychiatrist Paul Fink's contribution to the first issue of *Art Psychotherapy*. In fact, there are many ways in which art products can help in differential diagnosis. But it is far from simple, as experienced art therapists, psychologists, and psychiatrists know.

Research attempts to validate the meanings of drawing ''signs''—like shading indicating anxiety—have found them to be less successful than global ratings. In fact, two psychologist/art therapist teams designed similar studies in the late sixties, independent of one another. Each asked the simple question of whether individuals could judge psychopathology from spontaneous art. Could they tell which picture was done by a patient and which was done by a nonpatient? The judges in a study using adult paintings (ATTP, p. 393) were more successful than those in one using child art products. (Rubin, 1978) Although in neither was success related to years of clinical experience (!), a subsequent study indicated that training art therapists could increase their accuracy (ATV, p.316).

Art therapist researchers have questioned most generalizations about patient art. Even though art therapists consult that literature, they tend to be nondogmatic, largely because of the impact of their direct experience. Harriet Wadeson, working at NIMH, designed a series of studies to identify the characteristics of pictures by people with various disorders, which she summarized in her first book. In addition to trying to be precise and descriptive, Wadeson sought a phenomenological understanding of a patient's experience. She asked for drawings such as: a self-portrait, what it was like to be depressed, to have delusions or hallucinations, or to be in a locked space (Fig. 7–1). Like many art therapists, she often included a free drawing in her assessment battery.

STUDIES OF ARTISTIC DEVELOPMENT

In the area of developmental psychology, there has been a gradual resurgence of interest in children's drawings over the last three decades. In 1963, Dale Harris revised and extended Goodenough's Draw a Man Test as a measure of ''intellectual maturity'' in children. In 1968, Elizabeth Koppitz refined procedures for the use of Human Figure Drawings (HFDs) of elementary school children to measure developmental level, as well as to assess adjustment via ''emotional indicators.'' She later wrote another book on evaluating HFDs of middle school pupils.

These researchers were able to build on the work of educators like Rhoda Kellogg, who published several books on the patterns she found in her large collection of art by normal preschoolers. Kellogg herself was familiar with the literature in early childhood education, including a classic investigation by Alschuler and Hattwick of the relationship between *Painting and Personality* in

Figure 7–1 "The Corridor of Loneliness" (a locked ward).

normal preschool youngsters (1947). The psychologist who invited me to do art therapy with schizophrenic children, Margaret McFarland, was one of the teachers participating in that study, probably contributing to her interest. Another study, *Understanding Children's Play* (1952), described the therapeutic benefits of clay, graphic materials, and finger paints. One of the authors was Lawrence Frank, who had written the first book on *Projective Methods* (1948).

During the forties, rating scales for spontaneous drawings and paintings were developed by Paula Elkisch and Trude Schmidl-Waehner, dynamic child psychologists. Peter Napoli's diagnostic use of finger painting (1946) was later used and amplified by others, like my college psychology professor, Thelma Alper. The Easel Age Scale (1955) was designed by psychologist Beatrice Lantz to study the growth and adjustment of normal young children through their spontaneous paintings. (Cf. Rubin, 1978 for complete references.)

Since the seventies, developmental psychologists have been busy once again studying children's art expression. This is due not to a fascination with art, but to an interest in the growth of cognition—and an awareness that drawing behavior is a useful index. The recent focus on the study of children's drawing behavior was inspired in part by the work of psychologist Rudolf Arnheim, an early supporter of art therapy.

One of Arnheim's students, Claire Golomb, has done some of the best research on the development of children's art. In 1974 she published inventive studies of young children's development in both sculpture and drawing. In 1992 she summarized further research, including two chapters of particular interest to art therapists: "Color, Affect, & Expression" and "Art, Personality, & Diagnostics." Though critical of poorly-designed studies and skeptical about finding group differences, Golomb is a believer in the overall diagnostic and therapeutic potential of art.

Other well-designed investigations by developmental psychologists of relevance to art therapists were done by Cox, Gardner, Goodnow, and Thomas & Silk. Some of the research they report seems to validate at least some common projective hypotheses, like the symbolic significance of size or color. Their observations on the diagnostic use of art, however, are useful reminders of the still-primitive state of this field of investigation.

During the child study movement at the turn of the century, drawing studies tended to be either collections of work done by large numbers of youngsters, or detailed longitudinal observations of an individual child, sometimes including the drawing process as well as the products. Some of the best recent investigations using naturalistic observation of creative behavior have come from an interdisciplinary series of studies done at Harvard called **Project Zero** (Cf. also Fein, Selfe). That project was the basis for Howard Gardner's work, and for Ellen Winner's book on the psychology of the arts—which has chapters on drawing development, brain damage, and mental illness, noting studies relevant to art therapy.

There is also a fine chapter by Dennie Wolf in Gardner's 1982 book about stylistic differences among preschoolers. It is reminiscent of what Viktor Lowenfeld discovered about perceptual styles in his work with blind and partially-sighted youngsters. The presence of such normal stylistic differences, and of intra-individual variability, make the diagnostic use of any single artwork or group of products exceedingly complicated. There are also a great many uncontrollable variables, like culture or hair style; making most diagnostic generalizations about art extremely uncertain.

ART THERAPISTS AS DIAGNOSTICIANS

Art Therapists and Projective Drawings

When art therapists seeing children were informally surveyed in 1991, it was found that they were almost as familiar with the DAP, H-T-P, and KFD, as they were with the art therapy techniques that were listed. Because of waning interest in projective drawings on the part of clinical psychologists, Klepsch and Logie concluded in 1982 that "people other than psychologists, professionals who work with children, should be prepared to acquaint themselves with what drawings have to say." It would appear that many art therapists are doing just that.

Art therapist Cay Drachnik's 1995 manual on the interpretation of children's drawings includes descriptions of the most common projective drawing tests, along with many traditional assumptions of the meaning of various aspects of both form and content. Although a recent book is called *A Therapist's Guide to Art Therapy Assessments* (Brooke, 1996), it actually contains more projective drawing tasks developed by clinical psychologists (6) than procedures devised by art therapists (5)! Art therapists do, however, sometimes use projective drawing tasks—like the Person and Self Portrait done by Jimmy in the following vignette.

Draw-a-Person & Self Portrait in Assessment: **Jimmy** (5)

Jimmy was a five-year-old boy who was a residential student at the Home for Crippled Children in 1967. He was first asked to "Draw a Person," and proceeded to produce a rather advanced picture of a Clown. (Fig. 7–2) He was then asked to make a picture of himself, and on the other side of the same paper drew a much younger version of a human figure—a crude enclosure with rough indications of limbs and features. (Fig. 7–3) When asked about his self-portrait, Jimmy explained: *"The legs got lost in the grass."* It was a poignant statement of how damaged he felt, for Jimmy's legs were lifeless: he was able to move only in a wheelchair.

His picture of the Clown, on the other hand, showed how bright he was, since it was a superior human figure drawing for a child his age. The massive difference in the developmental level of his self-portrait indicated not only Jimmy's "body image," but also his rage and helplessness about his disorganized physical state. The Self drawing is particularly poignant

Figure 7–2   Jimmy's drawing of a Person: "A Clown."

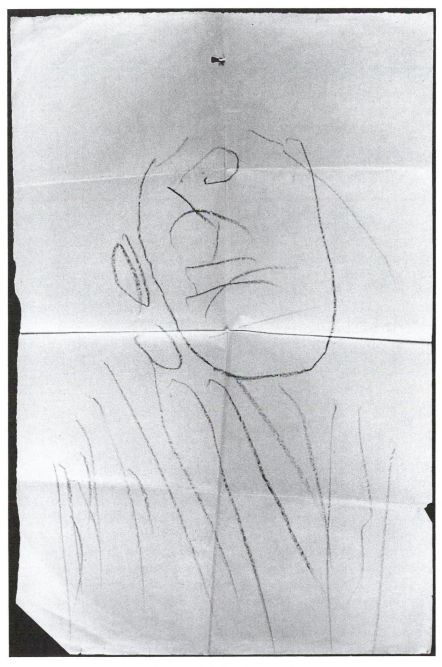

Figure 7–3 Jimmy's Self Portrait: "Legs lost in the grass."

in contrast to his choice of a Clown, who can not only walk, but who can also jump and hop—and perhaps even "fly" on a trapeze.

Applications of Developmental Studies

As noted earlier, many art therapists entered the field through the pathway of art education, bringing with them some familiarity with the many attempts in that discipline to understand the development and the meaning of child art. Some have looked at the implications of this literature for art therapists, like Sandra Packard who taught "A Workshop for Sensitive Analysis of Children's Art Products" at the 1977 AATA Conference; or Betty Jo Troeger, who wrote about the "Application of Child Art Theories to the Interpretation of Children's Art" (AT, 1992, p. 30).

For her 1981 doctoral dissertation, Dr. Troeger also created an **Art Skills Assessment for Special Education Students**, using a developmental scale to rate behaviors while using art materials (drawing, painting, cutting paper, using clay). When Fugaro adapted the **Silver Drawing Test** for assessment with neurologically and emotionally impaired children, he included many behavioral measures as well as the drawing scales of the original instrument. Similarly, I once designed a scale which rated behaviors and attitudes during the artistic process, and in relation to other people—used in a study described in Chapter 11. This approach evolved in the late sixties when behavioral objectives became popular in education. It now characterizes most evaluations in mental health and rehabilitation, and is used by art therapists to assess patient progress in a variety of settings.

ART THERAPY ASSESSMENTS

Linda Gantt's chapter in *A Guide to Conducting Art Therapy Research* (Wadeson, Ed.) is an excellent "description and history of art therapy assessment." The next two chapters in that book describe a number of drawing batteries and art-based assessment procedures and instruments, including unpublished materials.

There is no standardized or commonly-accepted approach to diagnostic art interviews, any more than there is a universally-accepted way of doing art therapy. A great many different and varied approaches are used by art therapists today. In the responses to a 1991 survey of those who work with children, many different art assessment tasks and batteries were described, in addition to the nine that were listed. It seemed that art therapists at all levels of experience had *"modified existing techniques and created new ones, rather than relying on published tools"* (AT, 1991, p.11). Perhaps because of this inventiveness, art therapists have typically contributed their own ideas to the diagnostic problem-solving so critical to effective treatment.

Rating Scales

Art therapists working in research settings have often collaborated with other professionals in developing more sensitive rating scales for spontaneous and directed art. The most extensive early studies were done by Hanna Kwiatkowska and Harriet Wadeson at NIMH, where they were able to construct imaginative tasks to study patient art (Cf. Wadeson, 1980, 1992). With the help of colleagues in psychiatry and psychology, they also developed scoring methods and rating manuals, the most elaborate one being the **Dent-Kwiatkowska Rating Manual** (Cf. Kwiatkowska, 1978, Appendix IV). In "Art and Madness: Can the Interface be Quantified?" two art therapists described using the **Sheppard Pratt Art Rating Scale** to measure "pictorial integration" (AJAT, 1993, p. 81).

Beginning in the eighties and continuing with her doctoral research, Linda Gantt has worked to identify the graphic equivalents of specific syndromes in the *Diagnostic and Statistical Manual of Mental Disorders* (DSM-IV). She has been working on the **Formal Elements Art Therapy Scale** (1990), designed to measure variables in patients' drawings of **A Person Picking an Apple from a Tree**—a topic used in teaching by Viktor Lowenfeld. Gantt and Carmello Tabone have recently created a **Rating Manual**, which includes 13 formal categories and 12 content areas (Cf. AJAT, 1996, p. 15).

Unstructured Approaches

Some approaches to art therapy assessment are **unstructured**, like my own **free choice procedure**, for which I have also described ways of "decoding symbolic messages" in art and behavior (1978). Edith Kramer and Jill Scherr suggested a **series of art activities**: drawing, painting, and working with clay, the sequence of which can be varied. They too outlined "observational consideration." (AJAT, 1983, p. 3). Neither of these interviews specifies subject matter. In Bruce Moon's chapter on "The Role of Assessment" in his 1992 book, he proposed a wide range of choices of media and topic. He also noted the importance of attending closely to the individual's mode of working with the art materials.

I recently came across my original proposal for an art evaluation (April, 1969). Although I had first suggested that a free choice be followed by offering a different art medium (like Kramer) and—if time permitted, requesting a self or family portrait (like many assessment batteries)—I ended up finding the open-ended approach to be most fruitful. The following vignettes illustrate its power . . . For Evelyn, free art expression was possible, and sufficient to supply evidence not available elsewhere. Tim needed the help of a "Scribble" drawing to be able to create an image, from which he and I were then able to learn a good deal.

Art Assessment Reveals Pathology: **Evelyn** (16)

Sometimes an art interview is a peculiarly sensitive instrument where others are not. Evelyn, a painfully shy adolescent of sixteen, was thought to be "mildly inhibited" but not "grossly disturbed."

Her first production in a diagnostic art evaluation, however, was a painting of a stark purple "Tree" (Fig. 7–4). Asked what sort of place it was in, she said it was "nice" and that she would like to be there, right next to the tree. Evelyn then shifted and said she might be the tree itself. Her next drawing was a bizarre figure named "Fred" (Fig. 7–5), who she described as "an eighteen-year-old girl." "Fred" was called "crazy" by the kids, and talked to herself because it was better than talking to others.

Although the referring psychiatrist remarked that the girl's art looked "sicker" than anything else, it was her subsequent suicide attempt which validated the confusion and withdrawal evident in her artwork and her verbal associations to the imagery.

She was able to be treated through adjunctive art therapy while hospitalized, which was especially helpful during a time when she refused to speak. Retrospectively, the glove on Fred's hand and the denial of the body in that drawing, as well as the vaginal "split" in the tree, were clues not only to the depth—but also to the nature—of her pathology, which became more apparent in her therapy over time.

A Scribble Unblocks a Tense Teenager: **Tim** (16)

Tim, a boy of sixteen, was acutely uncomfortable about drawing freely, since he felt inadequate as an artist. He agreeably made and developed a Scribble, however, and described it as the head of "A Person" who was sad and crying, a teardrop coming from his eye (Fig. 7–6). "Maybe he lost something, like a friend . . . the friend might have died, might have been the same age."

In a spontaneous insight, Tim exclaimed, "Hey! I just thought of something! I'm talking about myself!" He then told of his friend who had died from drugs two years ago, and how "the exact same thing almost happened" earlier in the week to his girlfriend, about whom he felt responsible, having introduced her to drugs himself.

Tim's capacity for self-awareness in his first art interview, despite a long history of resistance to court-mandated therapy, was a hopeful sign that he might be able to face and to know himself. Indeed, he did come for two years to an Art-Drama therapy group and made significant changes, helped not only by the modalities and the therapists, but also by his peers.

Structured Approaches: Themes

Other art assessments specify subject matter, like the drawing of a **Bridge** suggested by Ron Hays (AP, 1981, p. 207). Like the human figure or the family, such topics are not chosen at random, but rather because they are assumed to

Figure 7–4 Evelyn's Painting of a Tree.

Figure 7–5 Evelyn's drawing of "Fred, a Teenage Girl."

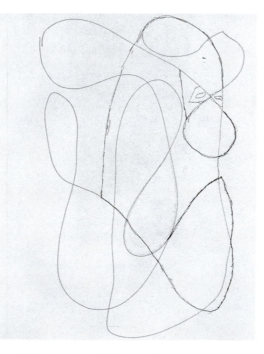

Figure 7–6 Tim's scribble drawing of "A Person."

tap significant symbolic issues. A bridge, for example, can represent connections and transitions. The added instructions to indicate the direction of travel by an Arrow, and to show where the artist might be with a Dot, further amplify the information.

Many clever projective themes have been proposed by art therapists—like a **Rainbow** (Shoemaker), a **Rosebush** (Allan), a **Doorway** (Vogel, 1996 Conf.), a **Bird's Nest** (AP, 1996, p. 333), an **Amusement Park** (AT, 1996, p. 261), or a **Road** (Hanes, 1997)—each with a rationale. Noting that abused children often drew inclement weather, Trudy Manning theorized that drawing **A Favorite Kind of Day** (**AFKD**) would reflect how a child viewed his interpersonal environment. She also designed and validated rating scales—using measures of weather, size, and movement (AP, 1987, p. 15).

Creative Analysis was an elaborate system developed by psychologist Ernest Zierer and his art therapist wife Edith, which was practiced at Hillside Hospital from 1943 to 1967. For assessment, they used **"a battery of therapeutic painting tests** which are structured but not explicitly directive of the patient's painting activity"** (AT, 1987, p. 114). The sequence was flexible and determined by each individual's needs. The initial diagnosis was arrived at by making a record of specific elements in the artwork, and creating what they called a **"Psychogram."** They devised a similarly visual way to represent progress over time, measuring the degree of "color integration" in a patient's artwork, and then recording their observations in what they called an **"Integration Graph."**

Art Assessment Batteries: Individuals

A battery—a series of tasks in a prescribed order—is the norm for diagnostic interviews in psychology. Hammer, the most vocal proponent of projective drawings, recommends a drawing battery. Experienced clinicians agree that a single product—like a single act or thought—cannot possibly be a valid sample for anyone being assessed, whether the focus is on problems or potentials.

Thus, both structured and unstructured assessment batteries designed by art therapists usually encourage or specify multiple products. The first was proposed by Elinor Ulman in 1965 (ATTP, p. 361), and is now known as the **Ulman Personality Assessment Procedure** (**UPAP**) (Fig. 7–7). The sequence of four chalk drawings on 18″ × 24″ paper is: (1) Free Drawing; (2) Draw Movements (following directed "drawing" in the air); (3) Rhythmic Scribble; and (4) Choice: Free or Scribble Drawing. Gladys Agell has developed revised instructions for the UPAP, which can be used with all but the very young.

In 1988 art therapist Barry Cohen designed a three picture tool, the **Diagnostic Drawing Series** (**DDS**). The DDS is reported, on the basis of fairly extensive trials, to be both reliable and valid—rare for any projective device, especially one using art. The pictures, to be done on 18″ × 24″ white drawing paper with 12 pastels, are: (1) Free Drawing; (2) Tree Drawing; and (3) Feeling Drawing (lines, shapes, colors). Modifications for children have also been developed.

Figure 7–7   Elinor Ulman conducting a "UPAP."

Many art therapists have contributed data to ongoing studies of the DDS, coordinated by Ann Mills (AT, 1994, p. 105).

Mala Betensky (Fig. 7–8), an art therapist also trained in clinical psychology, designed several different combinations of tasks as **Art Therapy Diagnostics** for different age groups, which she described in her 1995 book:

For ages 3–6: (1) Exploring Materials; (2) Free Drawing & Painting; (3) Clay; (4) Dollhouse Play & Story; and (5) Family Drawing (crayons).

For ages 7–10: (1) Free Media Experimentation; (2) Free Picture; (3) Scribble Drawing; (4) Family Picture; (5a) Work with Pipe Cleaners; (5b) Free Clay Modelling; (6) H-T-P (pencil & crayons); and (7) 'Grouping Game.'

For Pre-Adolescents, Adolescents & Adults: (1) Color-Form Blocks; (2) Poster Paints; (3) Free Picture; (4) Free Clay Sculpture; (5) H-T-P (pencil & crayons); (6) 'Self-in-the-World' Scribble; (7a) Adolescent Window Triptych; (7b) Family (realistic); (8) Family (abstract); (9) Colored Sociogram (You & Your Friends); and (10) Free Picture.

Though Betensky incorporated projective drawing tasks, her modifications are those of an art therapist; like large paper for family drawings, or using color for a Sociogram. She also designed original tasks, like the **Adolescent Window Triptych** (pictures of Past, Present, and Future). Her directions are detailed, and the rationale for doing and assessing each task is clear.

Figure 7–8 Mala Betensky conducting an art evaluation.

Myra Levick's doctoral work on defense mechanisms in children's drawings (based on Piaget and ego psychology) led to the development of the **Levick Emotional & Cognitive Art Therapy Evaluation & Assessment (LECATA)** (1989). The six tasks, done on 12" × 18" paper with 16 oil crayons are: (1) Free; (2) Self; (3) Scribble; (4) Developed Scribble; (5) Place; and (6) Family. The scoring is based on cognitive stages in graphic development, as well as emotional stages in the use of defense mechanisms.

Art Assessments for Specific Purposes

Just as certain approaches might be especially appropriate for different age groups, so particular sets of tasks may be used for specific purposes or populations. In order to assess **the extent of stroke damage**, for example, art therapist Drew Conger described using six tasks at the 1978 AATA Conference: (1) Build with Blocks; (2) Draw Around a Block; (3) Copy the Shape of a Block; (4) Draw a Clock; (5) Draw a House and a Tree; and (6) Match Colors Using Chalk (p. 26).

Patricia St. John described a similarly well-designed task battery for **children with neurological impairment**, which included copying, drawing from memory, a Human-Figure-in-Action Drawing (someone doing something), a Story-Sequence Drawing (draw a story with a beginning, a middle, and an end), and a

Clay Human or Animal (AT, 1992, p. 67). Both Conger and St. John articulated the rationale for each task.

Child custody evaluations are another arena in which art therapy can be helpful. Sherry Lyons described her preferred battery of drawing tasks for this purpose: (l) Free Drawing; (2) KFD; (3) Joint Family Drawing; and (4) Dot-to-Dot Drawing (AP, 1993, p. 153).

With the emphasis on shortening hospital stays and using time efficiently, art therapists can contribute a good deal to **triage** (screening) for psychiatric emergencies. Dale Smith, trained in both art therapy and clinical psychology, described an evaluation which included such projective drawings as the H-T-P, the DAP, the KFD, and an artistic task—a **Self-Expresssion Collage** (AP, 1983, p. 151).

Recent pressures to gather diagnostic data as rapidly as possible have resulted in further creative ideas by art therapists, like Nancy Gerber's **Brief Art Therapy Screening Evaluation (BATSE)** (1996 Conf.). The patient is asked to draw "A Picture of Two People Doing Something in a Place" in five minutes on small white paper using 8 fine-tip colored markers without using stick figures. As in psychologist-designed projective drawing tasks, Gerber specifies the questions to ask and what to look for. Since it is so efficient and rich, it is now a routine part of the intake process at Friends Hospital. This has often happened with art therapy evaluations, even those which take more than the 30 minutes of the BATSE, because a wealth of information can be gleaned in a very short time.

Assessing Abuse through Art

Art therapists have played an important role in assessing possible molestation, but we are still looking for the answer to the question that pioneer Clara Jo Stember asked at the 1977 Conf. about art therapy and child abuse: "Are there Graphic Clues?" Others who have studied patterns in the drawings and paintings of abused children include: Marge Howard, Don Uhlin, Felice Cohen, Cathy Malchiodi, Trudy Manning, Nancy Sidun, Bobbie Kaufman, and Cay Drachnik. Recent studies have also used other materials in assessment, like Sandplay and Anatomical Dolls (AP, December, 1995).

Literature reviews have concluded: "current information demands a healthy skepticism" (AJAT, 1994, p. 51); and "it has been consistently demonstrated that drawings alone cannot be used as evidence that sexual abuse has occurred" (AT, 1994, p. 41). "Overall, findings from empirical literature to support the presence of sexual abuse graphic indicators are limited" (AP, 1995, p. 485). Nevertheless, one art therapist specializing in this area has contributed a "Composite List of Indicators" in childrens' drawings (AP, December, 1995); as well as thoughtful advice for art therapists on how to be an expert witness in child sexual abuse litigation (AT, 1994, p. 260).

As noted earlier, Trudy Manning requests "A Favorite Kind of Day" drawing. Cathy Malchiodi requests a chromatic H-T-P along with other options (Free

Drawing, AFKD, KFD). In 1996, "a quantitative scoring system for the H-T-P as a measure of abuse in children" was developed. In 1997, Peterson and Hardin published guidelines for administering and scoring drawings to screen "children in distress" . . . the search goes on.

As for adults, Dee Spring collected her observations about graphic signs of sexual trauma in art by **abused women** in *Shattered Images*. She also described her **Art Therapy Assessment With Rape Victims:** (l) This is Me, I Am; (2) My Space; (3) My Life's Road; and (4) My Family and Me.

Assessing Spiritual Development through Art

Ellen Horovitz-Darby—who had earlier contributed a format for conducting and reporting an art-based evaluation with deaf children (AT, 1987, p. 127)—recently published a book in which she described the **Belief Art Therapy Assessment (BATA)**. Offered a choice of media and surfaces for drawing, painting, or sculpting; the person is asked (1) "If you . . . have a belief in God . . . draw, paint, or sculpt . . . what God means to you," and (2) "If you believe there is an opposite force . . . draw, paint or sculpt the meaning of that" (p. 32–33). She also suggests how to ask questions and what to observe in the person's attitude and artwork. The goal is not to assess cognitive or emotional states, but rather spiritual development or "**stage of faith.**"

Art Assessment Batteries: Families

In 1967, Hanna Kwiatkowska (Fig. 7–9), inspired by family art therapy and by Elinor Ulman's **UPAP** series, designed a **Family Art Evaluation** (ATV, p. 297) with six tasks: (l) Free Picture; (2) Picture of Your Family; (3) Abstract Family Portrait; (4) Scribble Drawing; (5) Joint Family Scribble; and (6) Free.

In 1974 Rubin & Magnussen (Rubin, 1978) adapted the idea to an outpatient clinic with younger children, using three tasks: (1) Scribble Drawings (Fig. 7–10); (2) Family Portraits—abstract or realistic, choice of media and location (Fig. 7–11); (3) Family Mural (Fig. 7–12). In l987, Helen Landgarten developed her **Family Art Diagnostic**: (1) Nonverbal Team Art Task (pairs of family members, each using one marker color on the same paper); (2) Nonverbal Family Art Task (whole family working on the same paper); and (3) Verbal Family Art Task (deciding and working together).

A three-dimensional procedure was proposed in 1974 by Margaret Frings Keyes—the **Family Clay Sculpture**. Many inventive, unpublished family art diagnostics probably exist, like the **Interactional Dynamics Game**, presented at the 1996 Conference, in which family members use assemblage, collage, and found objects to construct a personalized game.

Figure 7–9 Kwiatkowska doing a family art evaluation.

Figure 7–10 A child describes his scribble to the therapist.

Figure 7–11 Members view & discuss family drawings.

Art Assessment Batteries: Couples

In 1971 Harriet Wadeson developed an **Art Evaluation Battery for Couples** as part of a research project at NIMH. She used four tasks: (1) Family Portrait; (2) Abstract Picture of the Marital Relationship; (3) Joint Scribble; and (4) Self-Portrait Given to Spouse—to "do anything you want to him or her" (AJAT, 1973, p. 147).

In 1984 the *Menninger Perspective* described Robert Ault's diagnostic drawing series for couples: (1) Free; (2) Family; (3) Joint Picture of Doing Something

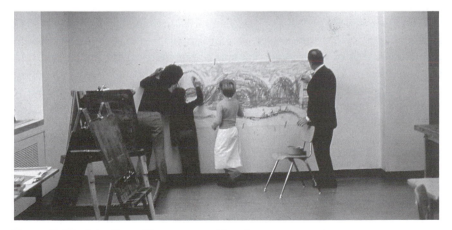

Figure 7–12 A family working on a mural together.

Together; (4) Individual Abstracts of the Marital Relationship; and (5) Self-Portrait Given to Spouse.

Just as Kwiatkowska was inspired by Ulman, so Ault borrowed from Wadeson. There is much **cross-fertilization** in the still relatively small field of art therapy. In fact, a survey of assessment in art therapy with children commented on the apparent existence of "**an oral tradition**," in which techniques were passed on to students (AT, 1991, p. 12). Such creative pollenizations occur elsewhere too, as in child psychiatrist Stewart Gabel's **Draw a Story Game** (AP, 1984, p. 187)—a synthesis of Winnicott's **Squiggle Game** and Richard Gardner's **Mutual Storytelling Technique**.

Selection/Creation Art Assessment Batteries

One of the most unusual approaches to assessment in art therapy grew out of research by Rawley Silver. Inspired by her discovery in their art of untapped capacities in deaf children, she looked for ways to assess competencies through art. Silver used her own artistry to create the 50 pictorial "**Stimulus Drawing**" cards that serve as stimuli for the **Silver Drawing Test**. There are three tasks: (1) Draw from Imagination; (2) Draw from Observation; and (3) Predictive Drawing. The first involves selecting two images from the cards and combining them in a drawing that tells a story. In the years since the test was first developed, it has been continually revised, and has been used with a wide range of people, including elderly stroke victims and delinquent adolescents (AP, 1995, p. 339).

Although the test was originally designed to measure "cognitive and creative skills," like the psychologists who saw more in person drawings than IQ scores, Silver soon realized that feelings were being expressed too. She therefore published the **Draw-A-Story** test, using the first task of the battery, to screen "for depression and emotional needs." The three–task battery is now called the **Silver Drawing Test of Cognition & Emotion**.

The **Magazine Photo Collage** was elaborated by Helen Landgarten in a 1993 book. Pointing out that the technique is relatively unthreatening and accessible to people of any ethnic background, she outlined an **Assessment Protocol**. Given a box of People Pictures and one of Miscellaneous Items, the client is asked to do the following:

(1) Select pictures that catch your attention, paste them on paper, and write or tell what comes to mind.

(2) Pick out four to six pictures of people, paste on another paper, and write or tell what you imagine each person is THINKING and what he/she is SAYING.

(3) Pick out four to six Pictures that stand for something GOOD and something BAD, paste down and tell what they mean.

(4) Pick out ONE picture from the People Box, paste down, and write or tell what is HAPPENING to that person. Ask, "Do you think the situation

will CHANGE?'' If the answer is YES, then ask client to find a picture illustrating the change or tell WHAT will make it change.

The rationale for the series, as well as for each task, is clearly delineated. A major advantage of the approach is that people of all cultures can easily find photographic images with which they can identify.

CONCLUDING THOUGHTS

By now it should be clear to the reader that many varied approaches to understanding human beings through their art are alive and well in art therapy of the nineties. While art therapists continue to probe and to work to refine their **third eye** in becoming even more sensitized to graphic language, they are also striving to be **more objective**. There has been a consistent attempt over time to be **more systematic**, in the presentation of tasks as well as in the evaluation of data.

Although art therapists are sometimes the only clinicians with whom a regressed patient can ''speak,'' the language of color and form is, like poetry, very difficult to quantify. And, even if that can be accomplished, the whole is still greater, deeper, and much more meaningful than the sum of its graphic parts. Messages contained in artwork are received in the context of all associative behavior—before, during, after, and in response to images. Despite the popular myth that art therapists can ''see through'' people by looking at their creations, the majority view the artist as the most knowledgeable expert about his own symbols.

Most art therapists question formula approaches to understanding, and resist the temptation to be clever interpreters. They see patients as complex human beings, and many have trouble with the kind of labelling involved in psychiatric diagnosis. Nevertheless, art therapists are often called upon to assist in such tasks, and do have some unique tools.

Any time an art therapist can tell something from artwork that is not available in other ways, it is potentially useful. For example, Rawley Silver saw a gifted artist in a deaf boy called Charlie (1978, p. 69). Edith Kramer found artistic talent in a delinquent named Angel (ATV, p. 253). I discovered that Claire was not profoundly retarded (Chapter 3). Similarly, the DDS, the latest art therapy drawing battery, can help to predict treatment course—like identifying the prefusion of ''alters'' in multiple personality disorder (Mills & Cohen in Kluft, 1993).

As part of developing a **Certification Examination**, the Art Therapy Credentials Board surveyed Registered art therapists. While agreement about most knowledge areas was impressive, there was so little consensus about **Assessment** that a separate commentary was published in the journal:

''Although the general public often views art therapy as dealing with the use of drawings in a diagnostic manner . . . within the field of art therapy little consensus has developed over the years as to what types of assessments are legitimate and

which ones (if any) should be taught to students of art therapy. There was much disagreement and ambiguity in the findings of the Art Therapy Practice Analysis Survey regarding this area" (AT, 1994, p. 151).

There is no question that the use of art for the purpose of assessment and diagnosis is extremely complex, reflected in the title of a panel of experienced art therapists at the 1995 Conference: "Art-Based Diagnosis: Fact or Fantasy?" (AJAT, 1996, p. 9). Despite the discomfort of art therapists with simplistic approaches to the topic, current trends in mental health and special education require that serious attention be paid to this area.

The assessment of individuals and families through art can contribute a great deal to such diverse areas as: differential diagnosis, clarifying family dynamics, the evaluation of medication effects, or the prediction of dangerous behavior. Moreover, art can enable people to reveal both hidden conflicts and potential capacities. Art is very rapid and extremely rich, both of which are relevant in times of shrinking resources. A sophisticated art therapist is aware of the hazards as well as the potential in understanding others through their creative work. Used with respect as well as restraint, art can be a powerful tool in diagnosis and assessment.

"We attempt to confirm, moderate and predict the outcome of our treatment process through the fervent study of client artwork. Yet we must do so cautiously and in reverence to the artwork, which tells us so much more than we can describe" (Henley, AT, 1987, p. 57).

Most important, the art made in therapy is not only a source of information for the therapist; it is also a **mirror** for the artist himself, as Edith Kramer wrote in a 1959 article

*"Paintings are valuable not so much because they can tell the adult something about the child, but also because the very act of creating helps the child to learn something new about himself. **This process of self-discovery and self-acceptance through art is the core of art therapy"*** (School Arts, 1959(58), p. 5).

Chapter 8

Technique(s)

THE ONLY TECHNIQUE OF ART THERAPY
*is the technique of **relating to a patient through art.***

                                        HANNA KWIATKOWSKA

*We experience it [a dream] predominantly in **visual images**;*
feelings may be present too, and thoughts interwoven in it as well;
the other senses may also experience something,
but nonetheless it is predominantly a question of images.

Part of the difficulty of giving an account of dreams
is due to our having to translate these images into words.
*"**I could draw it**," a dreamer often says to us, "but I don't know how to say it."*

                                        SIGMUND FREUD

INTRODUCTION

As Margaret Naumburg often pointed out, "Although Freud made the modern world aware that the unconscious speaks in images, he did not follow the suggestion of his patients that they be permitted to draw their dreams rather than to tell them. Art therapy, however, encourages just such an expression of inner experience" (1966, p. 2). This was the basis for Naumburg's conception of dynamic art therapy, i.e., promoting the release of spontaneous imagery. But it is not the only way to proceed. In fact, one of the most pleasurable aspects of art therapy is the creative challenge of deciding what to do and how to do it.

As you have seen, there are many different ways of using art to achieve some kind of diagnostic understanding. Similarly, there are many different ways of using art as a therapeutic modality. The specific approach chosen depends upon the goals of the particular intervention, the context in which it occurs, and the range of what is possible. Art is used **in**, **as**, and **for** therapy in a variety of ways.

Regardless of what is done, there are a series of necessary steps noted earlier. They begin with setting the stage, a major element in promoting expression in art therapy. A well-prepared environment can inspire creativity, whereas a confusing or uncomfortable one can have a most inhibiting effect. Introducing the task, whether free or specified, is also critical, since instructions need to be

Figure 8–1   Mickie Rosen explaining the task to the group.

both clear and inviting (Fig. 8–1). This is all part of the art therapist's special area of expertise: evoking expression. Another element central to art therapy is facilitating that expression once it has begun, which requires sensitivity as well as skill.

After the work is completed, the art therapist turns her energies to helping the artist to learn from expression . . . from the process of creating and from the art product that is made. At each step of the process, art therapists use what they know about art and therapy to make the experience as helpful as possible for the person(s) involved (Fig. 8–2).

This work, like all therapy, is most effective when it is done **artistically**, with tact, sensitivity, and a well-integrated **technique**. Although I added the optional "(s)" to this chapter title, I have been concerned, as was Hanna Kwiatkowska who is quoted above, about the apparently insatiable hunger among beginners for lists of "techniques." I suspect Kwiatkowska would have agreed with dancer Rudolf Nureyev, who said *"the reason for technique is to have*

Figure 8–2 Helping children to look at their art work.

something to fall back on when you lose your inspiration.'' Despite those insecure practitioners who want to be told what to do, most art therapists value
individual creativity.

Evolution of Art Therapy Technique

Because of its historic roots in psychoanalysis, free art, like free association,
was initially the most common method. Although some of us still feel most

comfortable with that approach; there is much to be said for a thoughtful consideration and selection of specific tasks, especially under circumstances such as time-limited therapy or work with certain groups.

Ernest Harms long ago called for art therapists to *"design specific art interventions to address specific psychopathology"* (AP, 1973). Honig and Hanes, who worked with hospitalized psychotic patients, listed a variety of art activities used to treat specific dysfunctions (AP, 1982, p. 269). They noted their indebtedness to Linda Gantt, who had articulated the need for structure for patients with fragmented egos in "The Other Side of Art Therapy" (AJAT, 1979, p. 63).

Aina Nucho's book contained a thoughtful discussion about what an art therapist might do during each phase of the therapeutic process. The names she coined are useful too: **Unfreezing**, **Doing**, **Dialoguing**, **Ending**, and **Integrating**. Dr. Nucho articulated many of the considerations that go into decisions about what to offer, how to offer it, and how to behave during each phase of a session and of a course of art therapy. This chapter will offer just a sampling of the many ways art therapists work.

EVOKING EXPRESSION

Warming Up

Aina Nucho gave considerable attention to the idea of **Unfreezing**. Overcoming natural resistances and blocks to creativity is sometimes called **Warming Up**. All art therapists are concerned with helping individuals of any age who are uneasy about using art media. From Florence Cane's use of rhythmic body movements before a scribble drawing, to the recent popularity of guided imagery, art therapists have always looked for methods of releasing the creative stream. For they are confident that such a force flows in all human beings, even though it may be temporarily dammed up and therefore inaccessible.

Several popular techniques for loosening inhibitions use some kind of **stimulus**, like music, stories, or fantasy. It may be active and focussed, as in Barry Cohen's planned sequence of alternate art and movement activities with an inpatient therapy group (AP, 1983, p. 229). Or it may be background and subliminal, as in the soft lighting and music provided by art therapist Bernard Stone to enhance the dreamy atmosphere of his hospital studio, a place I visited 20 years ago but have never forgotten. I have found that modifying the light—by using candles, flashlights, or projectors and shadows—can also promote an altered state of mind.

Pictorial Stimuli

Stimulus Drawings were originally created by art therapist Rawley Silver for assessment (Fig. 8–3). Although her initial purpose was diagnostic, she and others have reported that the set of 50 line drawings can be helpful in art therapy

Figure 8–3 Rawley Silver working with a deaf child.

with people who have cognitive impairment, such as chronic schizophrenics or stroke patients. They are also useful in overcoming resistances, as with suspicious adolescents. First, the pictures—of people, animals, places, and things—are presented. Next, the person chooses some, imagines something happening, and shows it in a drawing.

Another easily-available and frequently-used source of visual stimulation are **Photographs**, which can become all or part of the final product, as in Helen Landgarten's *Magazine Photo Collage*. Many art therapists have used **Art Reproductions** in varying forms—from postcards that can be handled and sorted, to slides that are projected and magnified. For example, one used small art reproductions to motivate hospitalized adults, another used surrealistic paintings to inspire adolescents, and yet another used art and museum visits with a variety of groups.

Visual Starters

These are especially popular with art therapists of all persuasions, since they act as a stimulus for the person's own creative ideas. Both Prinzhorn and Cane referred to the Renaissance painter, Leonardo da Vinci. His sources of inspiration were ambiguous visual forms, such as the variegated colors and cracks on stones and walls, or on wet, crumpled up paper. The **Scribble** is the most widely used ''visual prompt'' in art therapy, and there are many variations on the theme.

Aina Nucho described several examples of what she called **The Free Flow Technique**. Art therapist Evelyn Virshup invited her patients to drag a kite string soaked in ink across the paper, then to develop the abstraction into an image. I have often suggested "fooling around" with paints on wet paper as a way of getting ideas for pictures. Walter Brown "drew out" schizophrenic patients by placing a **Dot** on the paper, and Ron Hays used a **Dot-to-Dot** exercise with children too young to use a Scribble.

Drawing on the Right Side of the Brain

There are other kinds of "loosening up" or "unfreezing" techniques, which are thought to depend on accessing the nondominant hemisphere of the brain. One involves drawing with the opposite of the preferred hand; another requires copying a picture viewed upside down. These and many others have been suggested by art educator Betty Edwards, in two books which have been popular with art therapists as well.

Rapidly executed **Gesture Drawings** were first suggested by Kimon Nicolaides in *The Natural Way to Draw*. Another of his ideas, **Contour Drawing**, was instrumental in curing Elizabeth "Grandma" Layton's lifelong depression. Art therapist Robert Ault has reported that doing regular contour drawings actually seems to have an antidepressant effect.

Stimulating Materials & Methods

Another way of relaxing inhibitions is to use contact media, like clay or fingerpaint (Fig. 8–4). Elaine (Chapter 1) had found that she could represent her memories of child abuse only when using fingerpaint. Clay has also been recommended for many different groups, ranging from encopretic children to geriatric patients and those with dissociative disorders.

Adding the element of speed, psychiatrist Wilhelm Luthe, suggested a structured approach based on "autogenics." His *Creativity Mobilization Technique* consisted of producing a series of 15 painting exercises in a 30–minute period—four times a week for six weeks. Art therapist Roberta Pashley has described her adaptations of Luthe's ideas, such as the "No Thought Mess" or "Contained-Secret" Techniques (Bejjani, p. 103).

Sometimes stimulating media are used deliberately, as in the treatment of Gloria, a young widow in her thirties who came for weekly art therapy.

Regressive Media Help with Shame: **Gloria**

Gloria had vocally expressed her disgust at the fingerpaints, always noticing but never using them. I had asked if she could describe her feeling of revulsion, but she found it hard to define. I then wondered if we might not find out more if she were to try the paints, despite her negative response. She was willing to do so in an openly experimental way; and it was quite a powerful session, referred to many times in succeeding months.

She began by feeling and expressing disgust, but gradually got more and more into it, exclaiming with glee, "Ooh! What a pretty mess!" After

Figure 8–4 A tense boy unwinds at the potter's wheel.

a tentative beginning, she took large gobs of paint, and eventually used both hands and fingers with a high degree of freedom. Her unexpected discovery was that she liked it, that it was not unpleasant as she had anticipated, but that it was actually fun. She related this surprise to her initial anxiety about getting her daughter out of school for morning appointments, and her discovery that it was neither uncomfortable nor harmful as she had feared.

Her associations to the first painting were that it was a series of "Roads" which led to various places, and that she had to decide where she was going, a fairly accurate description of where she was in her life at that time. The second, she described as "Like Hell, a Storm with Light-ning and Turmoil," and ended up talking about her own feelings of sin-fulness and guilt over sleeping with a man to whom she was not married. The shame she felt about being "dirty" was stimulated by the medium itself, as well as by the images she saw in her abstract fingerpaintings.

Mental Imagery

The evocation of visual imagery has been used by many clinicians, beginning with Freud, to stimulate memory, fantasy, and awareness of feelings. It has also been used to facilitate art activity. I became interested in spontaneous mental imagery during my psychoanalytic training, and began reading the rapidly-mush-rooming literature on the topic.

As with studies of drawing development, imagery was long dormant in psy-chology, largely because it is so introspective and hard to quantify. Due to its frequent use in behavior therapy techniques like desensitization, however, the study of mental imagery has once again become a lively arena (Cf. Watkins, 1976). This interest is reflected in the existence of the International Imagery Association (*Journal of Mental Imagery*) and the American Association for the Study of Mental Imagery (*Imagery*). Other clinicians who use mental imagery in therapy, such as psychiatrist Mardi Horowitz, sometimes invite people to draw. Vija Lusebrink and Aina Nucho have both discussed the relationship between art therapy and mental imagery.

Series of Images

Making a series of images is another evocative technique, one used by art therapists in a variety of ways. Bernard Stone, who worked with hospitalized adults, reported on a **Sequential Graphic Gestalt**, where the client was asked to rapidly draw a series of pictures in response to his own painting (Jakab, 1975). Psychiatrist Mardi Horowitz also invited patients to do a series of (six) drawings, beginning each time by staring at a dot in the middle of the page until they had an image.

Stimulated by my analytic training, I experimented with a similar idea using various media, called **Free Association in Art Imagery** (1981 Conf., p. 3). These approaches using art materials resemble free association in mental imag-ery. They also resemble **Active Imagination** as practiced by Jungian analysts, who encourage not only mental imagery, but also art, movement, and drama as ways to enhance the associative process.

A **series of cartoon drawings** was proposed by Crowley and Mills, Erickson-ian child therapists. Using children's natural fascination with cartoon characters, they published *Cartoon Magic*. The exercises in the book are primarily designed for parents, as ways to help children deal creatively with stressful situations.

FACILITATING EXPRESSION

Motivational Techniques

Although young children are less likely to be inhibited about using art materials than adolescents or adults, they may still have difficulty creating authentically. Edith Kramer has proposed a classification of ways of using art materials which is relevant for all age levels: (1) Precursory Activities; (2) Chaotic Discharge; (3) Art in the Service of Defense (stereotypes or copying); (4) Pictographs; and (5) Formed Expression.

Such an analysis is useful not only in understanding what is produced, but also in thinking of ways to motivate people to achieve a higher level of artistic expression. Stereotyped work, for example, is common during what Viktor Lowenfeld called the "schematic" stage in normal artistic development, for which he suggested various motivational techniques.

One of his central ideas was the importance of what he called the child's **"self-identification"** with whatever was being represented. Lowenfeld recommended that children not only **imagine** doing the activity to be drawn (like brushing teeth), but **enact** it as well, thus activating the child's sensory awareness. He also proposed the intuitively respectful notion of **"extending the frame of reference"**—working within and with the child's imagery, rather than trying to suppress even bizarre ideas.

Artistic Interventions

Another set of Lowenfeld techniques involved the use of the worker's auxiliary ego to assist the child when his own resources are not sufficient to function autonomously. That is one way to think about **"closure,"** which means starting a clay modelling or drawing for the child to finish. David Henley has described the use of Lowenfeld's ideas in art therapy. He also noted that pictorial interventions—which Edith Kramer called "using the art therapist's **third hand"**—are compatible, as long as they do not distort.

One clinician who used his own drawing and associative processes in order to relate to children was British analyst D. W. Winnicott, who took turns making and developing pencil squiggles into pictures. Although playful, the technique penetrates deeply, and requires considerable expertise on the part of the therapist. It is particularly effective where time is of the essence, as it often was for Winnicott, who might have only one consultation with a child brought to see him from a great distance.

Like any other activity by the therapist, doing art can be harmful as well as helpful to the patient. Frances Kaplan's **"Drawing Together: Therapeutic Use of the Wish to Merge"** is a thoughtful discussion of working along with a patient in art; noting those for whom it is beneficial, as well as those for whom it might be disruptive (AJAT, 1983, p. 79).

Another use of the art therapist's artist-self is to **draw a portrait of a patient**, perhaps while he is creating. Many of us have done this, as in my own experience of painting Ellen, an elective mute, when she was acting especially hostile. This same girl also stimulated me to invite her to work together on a **joint nonverbal drawing** (Chapter 9). Other clinicians have reported doing this with withdrawn patients of all ages, like Horowitz, who drew and painted with regressed schizophrenics. **Drawing Dialogues** have also been used as a way of "breaking the ice" (Landgarten, 1981).

Many of us have found ourselves **drawing "on demand"** with the patient giving instructions, like Irene Rosner did for a quadriplegic who told her what and how to create (AJAT, 1982, p. 115). Having developed a **Boss-Slave game** to deal with authority issues in work with mothers and children, I have found it useful at times to "follow orders" with patients of all ages. In one of the activities proposed in *Advances* as "Starting Points in Art Therapy with Children," the child acts as **Graphic Secretary** for the therapist. In another, the therapist acts as Graphic Secretary for the child. A similarly playful approach to getting started with youngsters is described in the same book: the traditional **Fold-Over** drawing game.

Although the use of one's artist-self is probably quite common in the work of art therapists, there may be reticence in reporting it because of the obvious countertransference hazards. It is indeed possible that an art therapist's own exhibitionism, competitiveness, or lack of sensitivity to the patient's defenses might cause such an experience to be disruptive. Another reason for the selective use of this tool is that it can absorb too much of the artist-clinician's attention. Nevertheless, most art therapists have worked with materials alongside patients in a variety of ways, and for a great many possible reasons. One is to model behavior, as in the "Pied Piper" effect I described in Chapter 5; another is to defuse anxiety about using materials and being observed. Yet another is to convey an idea graphically, a useful form of **interpretation**.

An original method of mutual communication has been described by art therapist Mildred Lachman-Chapin (AJAT, 1984, p. 13). After first talking with the patient about current concerns, both draw simultaneously, neither one seeing the other's image (Fig. 8–5). After creating the drawings, both parties share their pictures and thoughts about each of them. In my opinion, this very powerful technique is appropriate—like Winnicott's—only for experienced practitioners.

An art therapist might use her artist-self either **simultaneously** or **in turn**. Her creation might be a reflection **of** or **to** the patient. The art therapist's ability to use visual language expands her clinical repertoire, just as art enlarges expressive possibilities for the individual(s) hoping to grow through treatment.

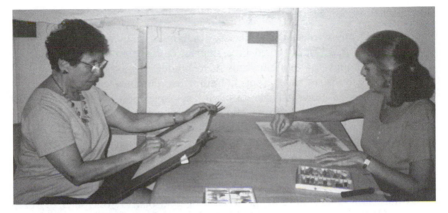

Figure 8–5 Mildred Lachman-Chapin draws with a woman.

Drawing Workbooks & Guides

Like fairy tales and art in therapy, the cartoon story drawings proposed by Crowley and Mills in *Cartoon Magic* offer both disguise and distance, enabling loaded themes to be dealt with more comfortably. The popularity of such **self-help materials**, for both adults and children, has not been lost on art therapists.

Some have developed **creative workbooks** which suggest various drawing and writing activities. The pioneer in this area was Lucia Capacchione, whose *Creative Journal* was the first of her many drawing workbooks. Barry Cohen and his colleagues have recently published a creative workbook for those suffering from post-traumatic stress syndrome; Sandra Graves has created one for those who have been bereaved; and Nichols and Garrett wrote one for those who are depressed.

Marge Heegaard's series of workbooks for children—and her guide for facilitators—deal with specific problems, like death or divorce. Over twenty years ago, I tried out a variety of **drawing books** with children, including one on reality testing (*Make-Believe Drawing Book*), one on self-concept (*My Book About Me*), and a *Hospital Drawing Book* for children in a medical hospital. My young subjects' responses were uniformly positive, confirming the need for such tools.

Closely related to drawing workbooks are books which encourage readers to explore their own creativity. Art therapists have contributed to this literature, which also includes work by artists and art teachers like Betty Edwards. Janie Rhyne, an art therapist who began her work in the human potential movement, devoted a large part of her book to helping readers gain access to their own creativity. Several recent books by art therapists also invite the reader to create with art media, and give clear directions for doing so, like those by Pat Allen, Shaun McNiff (1998b), and Suzanne Fincher (Cf. also D. Brown; Gold & Oumano).

Classifications of Art Activities

When James Denny wrote "Techniques for Individual and Group Art Therapy" in 1972 (ATTP, p. 132), he noted little interest or research on "the effects of particular techniques and combinations of techniques on a variety of groups." Observing that the early art therapy literature had emphasized "catharsis and the release of unconscious material through free expression," Denny suggested that "[art] therapists must choose techniques in the light of a deep appreciation of their effects and of patients' readiness to make use of them" (p. 132). His classification of tasks which might be chosen for different purposes is still a useful one, and focusses on the main variable to be considered in selecting art activities—the goal:

Exploration: liberation and the release of controls: (1) Scribble; (2) Free Drawing; (3) Blob on Wet Paper; (4) Media Exploration; (5) Color Exploration; or (6) Drawing Completion.

Rapport-Building: (1) Conversational Drawing; (2) Other ways of Working in Pairs; (3) Painting Completion by a Group; or (4) Painting with an Observer.

Expression of Inner Feelings: (1) Feeling-Laden Words; (2) Recurrent Problems or Feelings; (3) Mood of the Moment; (4) Dreams or Fantasies; or (5) Three Wishes, or (6) The First Memory (noting that Relaxation Exercises, Music, Poetry and Expressive Movement also promote emotional imagery).

Self Perception: the pictorial or sculptural representation of immediate states, like: (1) I Am; (2) I Feel; (3) I Have or Do; (4) Drawing of a Man; (5) Drawing of a Person; or (6) A Self-Portrait (which could be phenomenal, ideal, real, as an animal, or done with a time limit).

Interpersonal Relations: (1) Pictures of Group Members; (2) Portraits by Pairs; (3) Portraits by Combined Effort; (4) Drawing the Family; (5) The Family Doing Something (KFD); (6) A Group Portrait; or (7) A Group Mural.

The Individual's Place in his World: (1) H-T-P; (2) The Elements Picture Series based on Wittgenstein (Earth, Air, Fire and Water), as well as (3) techniques like Collage and Assemblage.

Denny's proposed classification was just one of many possible ways to slice the pie of therapeutic art activities. A few years later a **survey of art therapy techniques** was conducted by Linda Beth Sibley (Robbins, 1976/1995). She too grouped the activities she listed according to their goals: **Building Out** (focus on self and self-and-other(s)), **Revealing and Discovering the Self** (focus on the person's inner world), and **Integration**.

In 1979, Carol Beighley Paraskevas published a book in which she described how and why she had modified her initial unstructured approach to group art therapy, and included an extensive list of possible activities. In 1986, Marian Liebmann surveyed other British art therapists, and collected many ideas in her *Handbook of Themes, Games, & Exercises*.

Deciding What to Offer and Why

The advantages and disadvantages of directive and non-directive approaches have yet to be evaluated in a systematic fashion. What seems evident is that the more non-directive approaches are more likely to be successful with high functioning clients. In contrast, the more impaired recipients of art therapists' services often seem to require more structured approaches. As Diane Waller noted in her book on group art therapy, even those favoring open approaches have needed to modify them for patients who function better with clear external structure; like psychotics, retarded individuals, or children with attention deficit disorder.

In *Advances*, Harriet Wadeson described one art therapist's work with two retarded young people, who required different approaches because of their different levels of functioning. In that same book, another art therapist found that a non-directive approach with hospitalized depressed patients resulted in defensively cheerful images; whereas specific themes, like "Barrier Drawings," helped patients to express the pain and anguish they were actually feeling (p. 357). Conversely, a British art therapist reported how he had *"abandoned the directive approach in favor of the non-directive"* with an outpatient art therapy group (AP, 1983, p. 211).

In her book, art therapist Vija Lusebrink elaborated the **Expressive Therapies Continuum (ETC)** model she had first conceptualized with Sandra Kagin in 1978. ETC postulates four levels of image formation and information processing, in a developmental sequence from **Kinesthetic/Sensory (K/S)** to **Perceptual/Affective (P/A)** to **Cognitive/Symbolic (CS)**. The **Creative level (CR)** can be present at any of the previous ones, and may also be a synthesis of all of them. This model offers a way to think about media and activities according to specific objectives for people at different levels of functioning. Lusebrink gives a number of examples of how to use the model in decision-making.

Being inventive, art therapists have come up with a great variety of intriguing and idiosyncratic ways of working. While most are not as conceptual or abstract in their thinking as Lusebrink or Nucho; there is usually some kind of systematic deliberation behind *choice of media, degree of task structure, and the nature of the task itself.*

What is evident in reviewing the literature is the creativity in the field. An experienced art therapist is familiar with a wide variety of media and processes. She also has in her armamentarium many different ways to offer materials, and knows tasks which range from unstructured to highly specific. The following vignette describes using a task in family art therapy.

A Specific Task Helps a Family to "See" the Problem

In family art therapy, initiated because of the persistence of six-year old Tim's stuttering, my cotherapist and I became increasingly frustrated by how effectively this family could rationalize. One day we suggested that they try to draw on the same sheet of paper without talking, a helpful task for verbal families (Fig. 8–6). They worked on the drawing for 45 minutes, mother "taking over" almost half of the space, even adding to the others' pictures.

Figure 8–6 A family works together without talking.

Tim began by drawing a house in the center, but soon gave up and left to work alone with clay at another table. He tried to get his father to join him, and his dad did so for a while, but then went back to the table where his wife and daughter were still at work on the group drawing.

When all were seated, it was safe for Tim to go up and add some more details to his house. For the first time, mother understood what the others had been trying to tell her. The picture and the process it recalled was used by the family as a dramatic reminder for a long time. It was a visual record of some of the interaction patterns causing stress in the family system.

Selecting the best option(s) for any particular therapeutic situation is not that difficult—as long as the clinician's imagination is unclogged, her repertoire is broad, and the purpose is clear. A critical variable in effective therapy is the worker's ability to be open-minded and flexible. For art therapists, this means being sympathetic to a wide range of approaches and materials. The most common modalities in art therapy are the fine arts of drawing, painting, modelling, and constructing—in both two and three dimensions. Since these are well-known, the rest of this chapter is devoted to descriptions of several of the many possible variations on the visual arts.

VARIATIONS ON THE VISUAL ARTS

Sandplay

For generations, children have played with *miniature life toys*, and people of all ages have built castles in the sand. Since I have always had a sand table in my playroom, Dora Kalff's (1980) idea of *Sandplay* seemed natural. And, although the majority of sand tray devotees are Jungian analysts, the technique itself is used by a variety of practitioners. (Cf. Amman, Bradway & McCoard, Jung, Mitchell and Friedman, Ryce-Menuhin). Terri Zweig (in Kluft, Ed.) and Betsy Caprio, author of *"The Sand Tray and Art Therapy"* (CATT, p. 306) are two of the many art therapists who have found this method to be a useful adjunct to their work.

Hypnosis & Guided Imagery

One aspect of Sandplay is that doing it usually creates a dreamy state of mind. Like most art therapists, I am not trained in clinical hypnosis. But reading the fascinating work of Australian psychiatrist Ainslie Meares about painting and modeling while hypnotized, long ago impressed me with the potential value of creating in an altered state of consciousness. In 1992, psychologist John Watkins devoted a book chapter to what he called **Hypnography** and **Sensory Hypnoplasty**. Approaches to art therapy which use meditation, relaxation, or imagery are closely related, such as the **Guided Imagery in Music (GIM)** technique developed by music therapist Helen Bonny and art therapist Joan Kellogg.

Phototherapy, Videotherapy, & Computers

Hypnosis is as primal as hypnagogic states, which are as old as mankind. Using modern technology, the visual worlds of **Phototherapy** and **Videotherapy** are extensions of the artist's eye, with the camera as the medium. As photographer Alfred Eisenstadt said in a televised interview, "I'd have liked to paint, but I can't paint. I have to paint with my camera!"

Many clinicians have asked patients to bring in *family photographs*, both historical and current, as described by psychiatrist Robert Akeret. And therapists of all sorts have used *"published pictures as psychotherapeutic tools"* (AP, 1985, p. 245). Another psychiatrist's use of "ambiguous artistic images for enhancing self-awareness in psychotherapy" (AP, 1986, p. 241) has recently been published as a projective test, the "Walker Visuals." The unclear images function as projective stimuli, like a Rorschach inkblot.

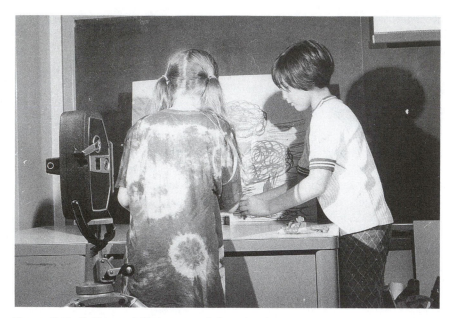

Figure 8–7   Setting up & filming art work for animation.

Art therapist Jane Teller once published a paper on "Using **Slides** of Patients' Work in Art Therapy" (AJAT, 1972, p. 29). In the same journal issue, two Swiss psychiatrists wrote about the **animated cartoons** that had been made for the last ten years by patients in their clinic using a 16 mm. camera. During the seventies, I became fascinated with **simple animation** techniques, and tried them out with several individual children in art therapy at a clinic, as well as with some youngsters who were in "Art-Awareness" groups in schools (Fig. 8–7).

At about the same time, Robert Wolf introduced the incorporation of **Polaroid photography** in art therapy, publishing several papers about his work with adolescents (AP, 1976, p. 197; 1978, p. 81). Canadian art therapist Judy Weiser wrote about using personal snapshots and family albums. Jerry Fryrear and Irene Corbit have published two books on **Photo-Art Therapy**—the use of photography in art therapy. From the brief existence of the **International Phototherapy Association** and its *Newsletter*, one might conclude that this visual treatment modality is a form of art therapy, since many of its practitioners ended up settling in AATA.

Shaun McNiff, who wrote the Foreword to Fryrear and Corbit's book, was one of the first art therapists to explore the usefulness of **videotaping** group art therapy sessions and playing them back to the group (AP, 1975, p. 55). He pointed out that *The Arts in Therapy*, which Fryrear wrote with Fleshman in 1981, included a chapter on **media arts**—audiotape, video, photography, and film; and that Fryrear had also co-edited publications on **videotherapy** (1981)

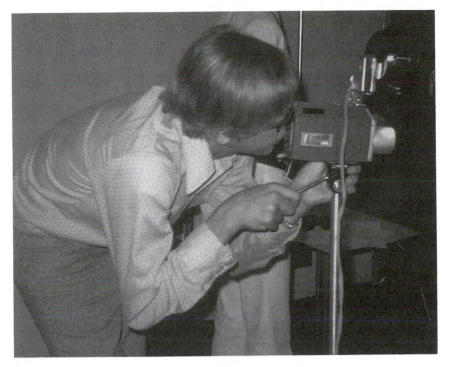

Figure 8–8 A boy films a scene in an art-drama group.

and **phototherapy** (1983). Like Jung, whose theory they embrace, the authors favor multimodal "active imagination."

As with viewing the art, photography is another way for a person to gain both aesthetic and psychological distance. In **art-drama therapy** groups at PCGC, Ellie Irwin and I often used **slides and films** taken by ourselves or the members as a way to re-view and reconsider. A film about an adolescent group, *"The Green Creature Within"* was composed of such photographic records. They were also used in the therapy, viewed and discussed like the art, and film was especially useful for recording dramas (Fig. 8–8). But the film needed to be developed, so the visual feedback was necessarily delayed for a week.

Video technology, on the other hand, allows instant replay, and is helpful for training and supervision as well as therapy. A combination of **Art and Video Therapy** is indeed remarkably powerful, as Irene Jakab and I discovered when we conducted some video-art therapy family evaluations in the eighties at WPIC. Recent papers and presentations describe using the medium not only for recording and playback, but also as an expressive tool; as in David Henley's use of **video art therapy** with individuals who are developmentally disabled (AP, 1991, p. 441). For a boy named Isaac, both art and film were central to his therapy as a young child, as an adolescent, as a young adult, and eventually to his life.

Figure 8–9 Isaac enacting a drama with clay creatures.

Art & Film Therapy Help a Boy Grow Up: **Isaac**

I had seen Isaac for five years in child analysis. He was a sad and preoccupied little boy, but took to the use of expressive media with enthusiasm. Art and drama were his prime modes of comunication throughout his treatment. One of his favorite activities was the making of animated films using clay, where the stories he often enacted with his artwork could come alive (Fig. 8–9). He made slow and steady progress, but had a hard time ending therapy and saying goodbye.

Three years later, Isaac returned for two months of art therapy, saying that he was depressed because he felt rejected by other kids. When he began to express suicidal thoughts, I referred him to a psychiatrist, and we all agreed on hospitalization and a trial of medication. After leaving the hospital, he enrolled in a creative arts high school, where he did a lot of acting and began to make films and videos.

Toward the end of his senior year, Isaac returned once more for art therapy. Deeply discouraged, he had been rejected from all of the colleges to which he had applied. Although he blamed his guidance counselor, he had not applied to a "safety school" as he had been advised. I thought he was probably having a hard time leaving his parents, who were not only angry at him, but also loving and very needy.

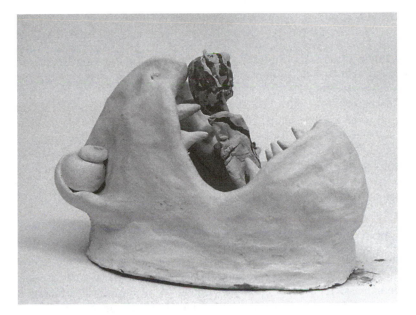

Figure 8–10   Isaac's Hungry Head with Victim in Mouth.

Since Isaac was still attached to me as a parental figure, I suggested that he see an art therapy intern I was supervising at the time. With her assistance, Isaac was able to overcome his lethargy, find a job, and apply to schools where he had a reasonable chance of being accepted. His dream of becoming a filmmaker helped him to manage the stresses of working and waiting. He also took courses in filmmaking, and began to feel generally more hopeful.

Having made progress in dealing with the outside world, Isaac was then able to use art therapy to deal with his inner world. In his twice-weekly sessions, he was able to get in touch with more of the rage that he had repressed when he was younger. This rage, turned on himself, had been a significant factor in his depression and feelings of worthlessness.

Isaac spent many months working on what he called his "statement." He first sculpted a massive clay head, then covered it with gesso, so it was literally "whitewashed." He displayed it, along with sculptures by other patients, on a round table in my office. Its most outstanding feature was a wide open mouth, full of carefully sharpened teeth. At one point, he picked up a bloody-looking sculpture by another patient, and placed it inside the devouring mouth, instantly creating a drama (Fig. 8–10).

The head was an eloquent symbol of the fears Isaac needed to work through in order to separate and become a truly autonomous young adult. He left it as a memento for both of his art therapists, and has kept in touch as he has made his way through college as a filmmaking major. His most recent request was for reactions to a film.

While it wasn't explicitly autobiographical, Isaac was aware that the story reflected continuing work on his own wishes and fears. Parts of the film used clay animation, reminding me of his earlier dramas. It seems clear that the arts—in one form or another—will always be Isaac's mode of coping with and contributing to the world.

Computers, like video, are also extremely versatile. They have the ability to do all sorts of creative and colorful things with all kinds of visual elements, both still and in motion. If my experience with a computer-literate intern is any indication, the future holds exciting possibilities for expression; as described in a chapter in *Advances* (p. 296). A recent article told how images created on the computer were less disruptive to borderline psychotic patients than those made with paint (AP, 1997, p. 367).

Multimodality Approaches

The notion that individuals need to find the materials that suit them best is one to which many art therapists subscribe. The related idea—that some media serve certain expressive purposes better than others—is also one with which most art therapists would agree. Since film, video, and animation involve action as well as imagery, they are excellent for the telling of stories. Because they can incorporate art, movement, music, and drama, they lend themselves well to "expressive therapy."

Although there are some practitioners who are fluent in several modalities, most art therapists aren't equally facile in other art forms. A few have been trained in two expressive therapies, like Jean Peterson, whose chapter on "The Marriage of **Art Therapy & Psychodrama**" in *Advances* (p. 317) represents a genuine integration. Art therapist Suzanne Lovell found deep compatibility between art therapy and the kind of dance therapy called "Authentic Movement." Lovell's sense of conviction was especially strong, since a combination of the two helped her to successfully combat her own illness (CATT, p. 291). Gong Shu, who had already integrated Chinese meditation techniques with art therapy (1980 Conf.), later reported on the successful addition of psychodrama (1996 Conf.).

Sometimes two expressive therapists work together, like Norwegian art therapist Ase Minde and British drama therapist Sue Jennings, whose book, *Art Therapy & Dramatherapy*, reflects respectful collaboration. Although one motivation is the practitioners' interest in learning from one another; it also seems as if more than one modality can sometimes better meet patient needs. Ellie Irwin and I have collaborated on art-drama groups, parent play groups, and a study comparing responses of the same individuals to art and drama diagnostic interviews (Rubin and Irwin in Jakab, 1975, p. 193). In that research, we found that some themes were more easily expressed in art, and some were more easily expressed in drama—another asset of a multimodal approach.

Just as it seems to help patients when art therapists are open to collaborating with other clinicians, it also helps when therapists are open-minded, albeit not naively so. Fads and techniques come and go rapidly in the lively world of psychotherapy. All therapists need to examine new and potentially helpful adjuncts, especially if they have primary responsibility for treatment. Linda Cohn's combination of "Art Psychotherapy and Eye Movement Desensitization" (EMDR) is one such example (CATT, p. 275). Art therapists seem less rigid and doctrinaire as a group than others, perhaps because of the openness which is necessary for a genuine creative process.

I once had the fascinating experience of putting together what I know about art therapy with what Louis Tinnin was finding out about using video in what he calls "Time Limited Trauma Therapy." Tinnin, a psychiatrist who is also a believer in art therapy, was using videotaped feedback with clients who have multiple personality disorder.

Thanks to his generous sharing of ideas and procedures, I was able to help one of my patients to get to know a number of her "alters" who had so far eluded "co-consciousness." She first viewed a videotape of herself in each personality state, made while she was in the hospital. Since she was also taped while watching the first video, she was then able to watch the second tape as well. When we later videotaped the "alters" drawing and painting as well as talking, the recognition and acceptance of her "parts" was greatly accelerated for the patient. This was a truly multimodal approach, most useful for this hard-to-treat condition.

CONCLUDING THOUGHTS

I could go on and on, and that in and of itself is the most wonderful thing about technique(s) in art therapy. There are so many different ways of using art to help people. Sometimes they offer possibilities which would be impossible in any other way. For example, time can be collapsed. A **Life Line** of colors and shapes can tell a person's story, and a **Life Space** picture can show how things are at any moment in time. A Journal can be kept in color and line as well as in words, as in a **Doodle Diary**. Relationships can be depicted in three dimensions, as in a **Family Sculpture**. And, because you can move three-dimensional forms in space, their dramatized action can further enhance awareness. There is probably no limit to what can be explored and expressed through the rich, wordless medium of art.

And there is similarly no limit to what can be imagined as an approach to helping people through art by the therapist. The source of artistic technique, as noted earlier, is for the art therapist to have digested and assimilated a theory so well that she is then able to respond with disciplined spontaneity. Similarly, the more media and technique(s) about which she knows; the greater the menu from which she can choose, as she seeks to provide the most nourishing and most digestible treatment for those she serves. Deciding how to go about either assessing or treating through art requires a thorough familiarity with artistic resources, as well as with ways of understanding and helping people in pain.

The specific fashion in which any art therapist puts them together is the artistry of this work—a source of deep pleasure and continual satisfaction.

Robert Ault has cited a metaphoric image proposed by art therapist Virginia Austin. It is of an "**ice skater** . . . one skate representing art understanding and involvement, the other . . . representing psychological understanding as well as interpersonal skills." In order to get anywhere, you have to *shift your weight* from one to the other, sometimes pushing off with one and sometimes gliding with both. As Bob said,"the skill of the therapist is in the timing, and knowing when to use one or both" (1983 ms.).

I have thought of **sailing** as a good metaphor for doing art therapy, since the clinician needs to "catch the wind" when it comes up, often with little notice. There may be long periods of waiting for breezes and tides to shift, so that the course of the art therapy voyage can be a safe one. It takes alertness to sense when the patient is ready to move in a new direction—whether in the creative process or in self-understanding. An art therapist tunes in to multiple frequencies for evidence of readiness to go deeper: artwork, dreams, mood, attitude, and behavior in and out of the sessions. As is true when sailing, there are inevitably rough as well as smooth periods, during which the therapist must hold firm to the rudder, in order to keep the boat of treatment as steady as possible.

Whether the art therapist is seeing an individual, a couple, a family, or a group, whether the goal is assessment or treatment, whatever the age and wherever the setting, the creative challenge of this work consists in deciding what to offer and how to do it. The artistry of the work lies in helping people to become engaged in the creative process in ways that enhance their personal growth.

A good art therapist is selective and sensitive, trying to accomplish the goals of any particular intervention within whatever constraints are present. This may involve using one or another technical approach, but always doing so with the deepest respect for both the materials and the human being(s) involved. Effective and thoughtful art therapy is at least as much an art as it is a science. As in other art forms, only practice can help the practitioner to develop both skill and spontaneity.

As with knowing theory, well-developed "technique" is not so much a collection of ideas, as it is deeply ingrained and easily available. Elinor Ulman made this point in 1966, when she wrote that *"a little learning may be worse than none. Our understanding must be well digested if it is to inform lightning decisions"* (ATTP, p.28). A good art therapist—like the psychoanalyst Donald Winnicott or the psychiatrist Milton Erickson—has both theory and technique "in her bones."

Chapter 9

People we Serve

WHEREVER THERE IS A SPARK OF HUMAN SPIRIT--*no matter how dim it may be—it is our sacred responsibility as humans, teachers, and [therapists] to fan it into whatever flame it conceivably may develop . . .*

We are all by nature more or less endowed with intrinsic qualities, and no one has the right to draw a demarcation line which divides human beings into those who should receive all possible attention in their development and those who are not worth all our efforts.
One of these intrinsic qualities is that every human being is endowed with a creative spirit.

VIKTOR LOWENFELD

Just as art therapy can be done in an endless variety of ways for the purpose of diagnosis or treatment; so there seems to be no limit to those who can be served. Art therapy can indeed be helpful to people of any age level, and with any degree of health or handicap. Its uniqueness, however, lies in its ability to reach people who are not accessible to other forms of help. Whether the condition is temporary, extended, or permanent; there are times when art expression seems to best fill a need.

ART THERAPY IS ESPECIALLY GOOD FOR . . .

Those Who Have No Words

Art may be the only communicative channel for those who cannot speak, whether because of autism, deafness, retardation, brain damage, or dementia. Claire, the deaf-mute in Chapter 4, could only talk through her drawings. Individuals who do not know the therapist's language—like recent immigrants—can still speak the universal language of color and form.

One of the roots of art therapy, you may recall, was the spontaneous art done by people with incurable mental disorders, whose paintings and drawings were sometimes their only intelligible communications. Those suffering from chronic mental illness are still well-served by art therapy, though they are now more likely to be seen in partial or day treatment programs than in long-term psychiatric settings (Cf. Shaverien & Killick). As artist Marilyn McKeown told interviewer Susan Spaniol, *"art is all the feelings trapped inside"* (AT, 1995, p. 227).

Even highly verbal people of all ages find that they have no words for certain experiences, especially those that elicit overwhelming feelings. Like Mrs. Lord who was in such a state of "shock" that she could not talk (Chapter 1), there are many times when creating visual imagery is far more effective than anything a person might say.

Those Who are Resistant

Those who are able to talk, but are resistant to verbal therapy, may be more easily accessible through art, especially if other avenues have been tried and have failed. Despite the anxiety of most adolescents and adults about their artistic abilities, even wary and hostile patients can become engaged if the art activity is presented in a nonthreatening way. Those who are suspicious of verbal therapy, who fear that a therapist will "play with their minds," may be more willing to use paint or clay than to talk. Like all elective mutes, Ellen refused to speak; but art was an open avenue.

Art Therapy with an Elective Mute: **Ellen** (11)

Ellen had seemed quite normal until the day she got mad at her deaf older sister and stopped talking to her. Shortly after that, she stopped talking to her alcoholic mother, then her father, and then her best friends. By the time she was admitted to Children's Hospital for a month of observation, her selective silences had been going on for almost two years. When Ellen refused to return home, she was sent to live with her grandmother, one of the few people she still spoke to, on the condition that she come to the Child Guidance Center for psychotherapy.

She had refused to enter the building or to talk to the child psychiatrist assigned to her case, even when he went to her grandmother's car. Ellen was therefore referred for the only nonverbal treatment available—art therapy. I was relieved that she was willing to come to my office, to use some clay (albeit with her back to me), and to draw, facing me as she did so. But when I requested, at the end of her first session, that she leave her picture on a shelf reserved for her, like the others in art therapy, Ellen got very upset. When I asked if we could photocopy it before she left the clinic, she refused, angrily blurting out, "You didn't *tell* me!" She walked out rapidly, clutching the drawing tightly to her chest.

Despite this uncomfortable beginning, Ellen seemed to loosen up a bit during the next four sessions. She was interested in my portraits of her doing art work, and was willing to engage in a "drawing dialogue" which became fairly intense. She even whispered responses to some of my questions about her drawings. I thought we were getting somewhere.

After a six-week interruption—due to vacations and scheduling problems in the Fall—Ellen returned, and created the first versions of what eventually became a rigidly repetitive visual theme. She began her marker drawing with several tight, geometric, linear designs, then continued on the same paper with a fishbowl, a horse's head, a tree, a geometric flower pot, and finally three creatures in the center, the last with an angry tongue sticking out of a twisted mouth (Fig. 9–1). I noted with relief that her posture was more relaxed while she was drawing the creatures.

In response to my questions, she told me that all three were female. The one on the left was older, the one in the middle was younger, and

Figure 9–1 Ellen's first drawing of her strange creature.

the one on the right was very angry. Asked who *she* might be in the drawing, Ellen pointed to the fish bowl, then to the horse. I was thrilled that her repressed anger—which is usually behind the stubborn symptom of "elective mutism"—had finally emerged.

Ellen spent the following session drawing an enlargement of her odd cephalod (head-foot) creature, while I drew a sad-angry girl with a long nose and prominent eyes, similar to but different from Ellen's creation. She said that the girl in her drawing was both happy and sad (Fig. 9–2). The girl in my drawing, Ellen said, was "sick because she's going to the doctor [who will make her] worse and sicker." She was clearly afraid of this process we had begun, but how fearful I had yet to discover.

From then on, Ellen was stuck on her theme, drawing only variations of it and turning her back to me more and more. Her whispered answers stopped, replaced by head-nodding, then silence. As the same creature

Figure 9–2   A later drawing by Ellen of her creature.

was drawn week after week, month after month, Ellen seemed more and more frozen. Having unsuccessfully tried music, silence, and other maneuvers throughout the Fall and Winter, in mid-February I began to wonder aloud about what was going on, empathizing with her anger and anxiety.

In mid-March, though her therapy-hour behavior was unchanged, her grandmother brought in a book Ellen had made, entitled *"From Isolation to Involvement."* With photographs and poetic text, it seemed a statement of intent. It also included many of the things I had said in our one-way communication system, leading me to hope that perhaps I was getting through after all. Nevertheless, Ellen continued to face me with her back, and to draw the same rigid creature for five more sessions, avoiding eye contact more than ever.

The last session in late April began like all the others, but at one point in her drawing Ellen stopped as if immobilized, seeming more openly fearful than usual. I first spoke of, then acted on, an impulse to put my hand on her shoulder. It was close to the end of the hour; Ellen did not respond. She remained tense and frozen, went on with the picture, and walked out, more rapidly than usual. She went back to her grandmother's and, for the first time in almost a year, telephoned her mother. The purpose of the call was to tell her that she didn't want to come to the clinic any more "because I don't like Mrs. Rubin."

Although she never opened the note I sent her, and returned no more, Ellen gradually proceeded to go home—first for weekends, and in a few months for good. When I called her mother two and a half years later to follow up, she told me that Ellen had come home warmer and more open than ever in the past, and had done well in school. Most delightful was the fact that this teenager, who had been so frightened of how dangerous her words might be, had become a high school **cheerleader** (!).

ABOUT THIS CHAPTER

Unfortunately, space does not permit examples of clinical work with each group of people, although the vignettes in the first and subsequent chapters are cited where relevant. It would be impossible to write about every population that is served by art therapy. Instead, I have presented a general overview of work with different ages and the disabled, as well as a few examples of some of the many specific conditions we treat.

Like most art therapists, I have had more experience with some groups than with others. So, rather than being encyclopedic, this chapter inevitably reflects both the loves and the limitations of my personal journey. Fortunately, there are other writings, which convey much better than I could, the essence of work with different kinds of people.

I have identified those with which I am familiar for the reader who desires a deeper understanding of work with any particular group. A thorough discussion would require an extensive literature review, which is, regrettably, beyond the scope this book. My apologies, therefore, for the omission of many people who are served by art therapy, as well as for my ignorance of any pertinent resources about those included.

ART THERAPY FOR ALL AGES

Children

There is a widespread notion that art therapy must be used mostly with children, since older clients have more verbal facility and can discuss what's bothering them (Fig. 9–3). There is, of course, some truth in the title of Myra Levick's book, *They Could not Talk and So They Drew*. Although more art therapists actually see adolescents and adults than youngsters, many do work with children—from preschool to puberty.

Art comes naturally to little ones of all ages, and can be helpful in therapy even before a child can work representationally . . .

Art and Sandplay Help a Grieving Toddler: **Billy** (2)

Two-year-old Billy, whose dad had committed suicide, would paint a blob of color, then angrily cover it over—compulsively repeating this ritual for many weeks. He next turned his attention to the sand table, first playing with water and sand, then having plastic animals engage in fierce battles. This was followed by play with people figures—a boy and a man. They too would fight, and Billy would furiously bury the father figure in the sand, while I would talk about how angry he was at his dad for leaving him and his mom so suddenly. After several months of this drama—which was interspersed with quiet times of painting shapes that were no longer obliterated—Billy's mother reported that he was no longer oppositional or clingy, but was his old cheerful, agreeable, self.

Art therapy can be helpful at all stages of development; both Alan (Chapter 1) and Isaac (Chapter 8) were able to use it in early childhood and come back to it later. Paradoxically, art therapy seems to be especially helpful to children at each extreme of the behavioral continuum (Fig. 9–4). A tightly constricted child like Linda (Chapter 6) can become freer; and a chaotic child like Dorothy (Chapter 4) can become more organized. An oppositional child like Jack (Chapter 1) can sublimate his aggression in clay; and a timid child like Don (Chapter 6), can explore free behavior by using fluid media, then by safely expressing his ''scary mad wishes'' in sculptures which cannot hurt.

Many different kinds of children can be helped, because the process of creating with art materials requires both spontaneity and control. Thus, children who are treated with art therapy not only span a wide age range, but also an even wider range of problems. A boy with a developmental or cognitive disorder like Randy (Chapter 1) can use art to organize his thoughts, as well as to express them. An anxious child like Carla (Chapter 2) can picture her fears and end her

Figure 9–3 A preschool child working with art materials.

Figure 9–4   A latency age child painting a picture.

nightmares. A depressed child like Lori (Chapter 1) can work through her feelings about loss through art and play. Parents and children who are having problems can see interaction patterns more easily on a piece of paper than in words,
like the family in Chapter 8.

Many different approaches are used in art therapy with children, as described
by Marcia Rosal. There are a number of articles and a few books that deal
mainly with child art therapy—like Margaret Naumburg's first one, my first
book, and those by Edith Kramer, Mala Betensky and John Allan. Some focus
on a particular group, like those by Anderson (1992, 1994), Henley, Malchiodi
(1997), and Silver (1978); while others focus on work in a particular setting,
like schools (Bush). In addition to an edited book by Case and Dalley (1990),
there are chapters about work with children in many other books on art therapy.

Adolescents

Teenagers, who are normally narcissistic, tend to be extremely interested in themselves and, by extension, their creations. Although it is usually necessary to deal with their anxieties about performance and about the therapist ''seeing through'' them, art therapy is a fine avenue for the developmental task of identity formation (Fig. 9–5).

Art is one way to make relatively uncensored self-statements, since every creation is a self-representation, even when it is not so identified. Exploring media, finding out what you like and what you don't, what is comfortable and what is not, are all fairly nonthreatening forms of self-definition (Fig. 9–6). Developing a personal ''style,'' so important to adolescents in dress and grooming, can be explored without embarrassment in the area of artistic style, as with Lucy (Chapter 1).

Normal adolescence is also a period of rapid physiological change, creating confusion and concern about body image. Overwhelming and sometimes disorganizing feelings, along with sudden mood shifts, are also characteristic of this hormonally fluid period of life. Art offers a safe way to deal with such transformations, as was true for Betty Jane (Chapter 1).

Defining the self in relation to the peer group is another major developmental task. Creating alongside other teenagers about common themes like friends, or working together on art projects like murals, are some of the many ways to deal with relationships through art therapy. Adolescence is also a time to redefine one's role in the family; and family art therapy can help all members adjust to the changing equilibrium. Vignettes about adolescents include those of Lucy, Betty Jane, and Melanie in Chapter 1, Evelyn and Tim in Chapter 7, Isaac in Chapter 8, and Lila in Chapter 9.

Most of the books noted above about art therapy with children also include work with preadolescent and adolescent youngsters. Adolescent art therapy per se has been addressed by some, with one book by Deborah Linesch devoted exclusively to that topic. Vija Lusebrink has a chapter on ''Daydreaming & Adolescent Depression'' in hers. There are a few detailed case studies, like Margaret Naumburg's work with Harriet (1950) or Helen Landgarten's with Lori (1981). Landgarten also published a case study of her work with the family of an acting-out adolescent (1987).

Shirley Riley has written a good deal about this age group, including ''Treating the Adolescent Family'' (1994) and ''Rethinking Outpatient Adolescent Art Therapy Treatment'' (CATT, p. 1). As is also true for young children, adolescents seen in art therapy suffer from a wide variety of disorders, including depression, phobias, eating disorders, addictions, other problems with impulse control, and conflicts with authority.

Figure 9–5 Self-portrait by the author in adolescence.

Figure 9–6   A Cerebral Palsied Adolescent Doing Rug Hooking.

Adults

While most adults are reluctant to use art materials at first, many can be helped to do so when the activity is explained as yet another way to work on their problems, and one which may speed up the process (Fig. 9–7). Art therapy is also appealing to normal adults who want to improve the quality of their lives, whose goal is not so much symptom relief as it is creative personal growth (Fig. 9–8). Identity formation is a task that continues as people go through the life cycle; as in the vignettes about Hannah in Chapter 1, Marjorie in Chapter 5, and Gloria in Chapter 8.

Using art materials, parents can draw about their children, and couples can deal with their relationships—like Mr. and Mrs. T. in Chapter 1. In fact, people can represent practically anything in art—from abstract ideas like freedom to feeling-states like panic. As noted in Chapter 5, on ''Why Art Therapy Works,''

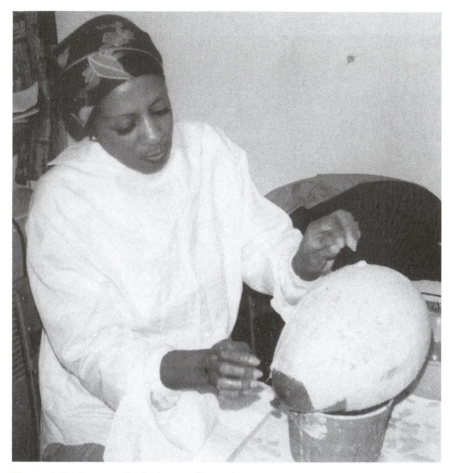

Figure 9–7 A woman beginning a self-portrait.

there are many good reasons for its success in the treatment of adults with all sorts of problems, including cognitive disorders like schizophrenia and affective disorders like depression (Cf. Sally & Elaine in Chapter 1). Art therapists treat adults with a wide range of problems, including psychoses and disorders of personality, adjustment, and anxiety. Because images can bypass verbal censorship, art therapy is especially helpful to those who use words defensively, like Evelyn in Chapter 5 and the family in Chapter 8.

While the majority of art therapists see grownups, and most of the literature describes work with people in the middle phase of life; only one book deals specifically with adult art therapy (Landgarten & Lubbers). Pioneer Margaret Naumburg's seminal books, *Schizophrenic Art*, *Psychoneurotic Art*, and *Dynamically Oriented Art Therapy*, all include detailed case studies of individuals in

Figure 9–8 A man beginning to work with clay.

Figure 9–9 An Elderly Woman Painting in a Nursing Home.

both young and middle adulthood. Although many also contain work with children and adolescents, the treatment of adults is the major topic of most general books on art therapy.

The focus of most art therapy literature about work with adults is not on developmental issues, but on specific conditions, like psychosis (Killick & Schaverien). Conversely, art therapy with the elderly, an area which has grown in recent years, tends to focus on aspects of aging per se—a normal but progressively handicapping condition for all human beings, even the most fit among us.

The Elderly

People are living longer lives. But aging carries with it inevitable and painful losses—of people, position, role, resources, and faculties (Fig. 9–9). Depression is common; and art therapy is a powerful modality for *Railing Against the Rush of Years* (Ridker & Savage).

Elizabeth ''Grandma'' Layton's story shows that it is never too late to learn art, and that it can have amazing healing powers. This Kansas housewife overcame a lifelong depression at age 68 by making contour drawings of herself and her concerns—a technique she learned in an art class (Fig. 9–10). The 82 year-old artist (Cf. Fig. 11–1) testified at Senate Hearings on the **Older Americans Act** in 1992, while her drawings were on exhibit at the Smithsonian Museum (Cf. Ault; Lambert; Nichols & Garrett). Her story was also told at the hearings by art therapist Robert Ault, and art therapy was included as a supportive service. Four years later, successful lobbying led to the inclusion of the arts therapies in the regulations for **Day Treatment Programs**, which often serve the elderly.

When I first consulted to nursing homes in the sixties, if there was any art at all for their elderly occupants it was limited to such impersonal tasks as making pot-holders or filling in paint-by-number pictures. Like the long-term state hospital patients who I watched pouring clay into molds, the elderly were

Figure 9–10   "I'm Into Art Therapy," by Grandma Layton.

thought to be incapable of creating personally meaningful art. Although pre-formed approaches may indeed guarantee ''successful'' products, they do so at the expense of personal expression. Worse, they do not permit an authentic experience of mastery, which is especially vital when so many formerly-intact faculties are ebbing (Fig. 9–11).

Although some prejudices still exist, they have been successfully challenged by those art educators and therapists who have seen beyond the limitations of older adults to their capacity for genuinely creative work. Whether to touch the past in ''life review,'' or as a way to find order in the changing present—art can be a veritable lifeline for those whose world has shrunk, and whose days have become heavy with empty time. The sensory aspects of art materials provide pleasure in contact. There is also a sense of pride in having formed something new and beautiful. Art is one way to fill the need for ''vital involvement in old age'' (Erikson et al., 1986).

Art can help in assessment too, since drawings may show the extent and nature of organic impairment (Cf. Figs. 10–5 and 10–6). A recent issue of *Art Therapy* devoted to the topic of the elderly described several programs. It also included a research study, which demonstrated that making pottery on a wheel led to an increase in self-esteem and a decrease in both depression and anxiety in a group of older patients (1997, p. 163).

A few art educators pioneered in bringing art to the elderly, like Pearl Greenberg and Donald Hoffmann. Art therapy pioneers with this population

Figure 9–11   An Older Man Painting in a Day Treatment Center.

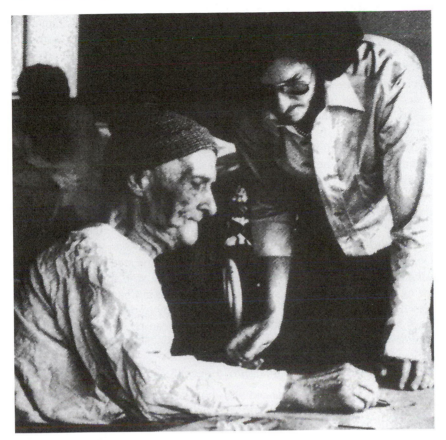

Figure 9–12 Jules Weiss working with an elderly gentleman.

included Irene Dewdney (ATTP, p. 126) and Betty Zeiger, who used the technique of Life Review (ATV, p. 187). Jules Weiss (pictured in Fig. 9–12) published an eloquent pictorial essay, and later a book. Georgianna Jungels described her work on film and in writing. Judith Wald has also written about her work with those suffering organic impairment (*Advances* pp. 181, 204; AT, 1993, p. 88); and Madeline Rugh and Francine Ringold have published a self-directed guide to drawing and writing for older adults (Cf. also Fausek). In addition, AATA distributes *Aging Artfully: Health Benefits of Art & Dance* (Proceedings of Hearings on the Older Americans' Act—PL 102–375) and *Applying for Funds from your Area Agency on Aging.*

ART THERAPY FOR THE DISABLED

Introduction

Art therapy cannot give a blind person sight, a retarded person comprehension, or a crippled person mobility. But it can and does give him a stimulating and pleasurable way to enjoy and to explore the sensory world. It gives him a way to be in charge in a limited sphere, to master tools and processes within his reach, and to savor the pleasure of skills honed through practice. It gives him a way to safely smear and pound, and to symbolically express feelings like anger—which is especially hard to do, because he is necessarily dependent on others—like Jane in Chapter 1.

Art gives a disabled person a way to "map out" a confusing sense of his body or his world. It gives him a way to define himself through choices and decisions, and creations which are uniquely his. It gives him a way to create products of which he can be proud, which can add beauty to the world and meaning to his life. Through art, a handicapped person can both escape symbolically, and come to grips with his feelings—especially those about his disability, as in Jimmy's Person and Self images (Figs. 7–2 and 7–3).

While these benefits are available to all human beings, they have special value to the disabled, for whom—like the elderly—there are many more problems and many fewer avenues of expression. The same medical progress which extends more lives now saves more premature babies, who are at greater risk for having multiply-handicapping conditions, like Claire in Chapter 4. The following story demonstrates the use of art and drama therapy to master traumatic experiences, and to come to terms with the blindness caused by Barry's congenital glaucoma.

Expressive Therapy Helps a Blind Boy: **Barry** (8)

Barry was an eight-year-old who had everybody worried about him. He looked and acted "crazy," and was always threatening to smash things or people. Sometimes he withdrew into a private world where he would sit in a closet and make up stories, playing all the characters using different voices. He was finally brought to a clinic for therapy, because the teachers and houseparents at his residential school were unwilling to let him remain there without some kind of treatment. His parents reluctantly agreed to try the Pittsburgh Child Guidance Center.

So Barry came to the clinic for weekly individual therapy, while his parents saw a (blind) social worker. Although it may seem strange that a boy with two artificial eyes was referred for art therapy, he enjoyed the sensory pleasure of squeaky markers and smooth wet clay. At first, Barry made clay "rockets" (Fig. 9–13), in which he imagined himself as an astronaut who would explore outer space. The playroom was a safe "closet," where he could share his fantasies with an accepting adult.

Art materials often became props in his dramas, and these stories helped us to figure out why he was acting so "crazy" or—as he would say—"mental." Many of his early stories were about a a boy getting lost, sometimes on a clay "planet." Then, for almost a year, he played and replayed scenes of doctor/dentist/nurse and patient. Though I was often assigned a role, sometimes he was both doctor and patient, doing things like examining himself or giving himself a shot (Fig. 9–14).

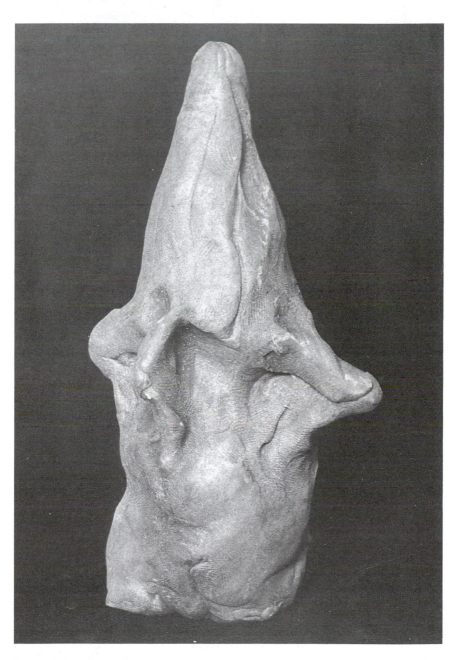

Figure 9–13 One of Barry's clay rockets.

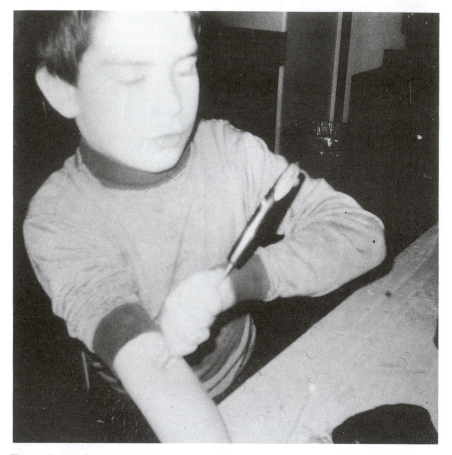

Figure 9–14 Barry playing doctor and patient.

In fact, Barry had been hospitalized fifty times for congenital glaucoma before his eyes had been removed at age five. To make matters worse, he had been jealous of his baby sister; and she had died of cystic fibrosis just before the operation. His repeated dramas were related not only to the trauma itself, but also to his unconscious guilt about his sister's death: He thought his blindness was a punishment for his badness.

With his dramatic flair, usually using art materials as props, Barry went on to create a series of dramas about a "Good Barry" and a "Bad Barry." He played both parts, and I was myself/parent/teacher. The struggle went on for many months, but finally the "Good Barry" was victorious. He ended up taming the "Bad Barry" so he could stay at the School for the Blind, where the real Barry was starting to make friends and to enjoy learning. He left after several years of therapy, announcing his "resignation" from the Child Guidance Center. He had come out of his closet of fantasy, and was warmly regarded by others.

Figure 9–15   Individuals working at "Creative Growth".

Fifteen years after he terminated, I ran into Barry on the street. He recognized my voice immediately, and greeted me warmly. He told me proudly about the life he had made for himself: his friends, his job at the Guild for the Blind, and his performances at a local Comedy Club (he had always done wonderful vocal imitations). He recalled our times together fondly, and grinned as he announced that he was no longer "mental!"

Evolution

When I began working with Barry in 1969, blind adults were making brooms, not expressing themselves. Like the elderly, disabled individuals were most often seen as incapable of genuinely creative work. In 1967, when I started an art program at the **Home for Crippled Children** (now the Children's Institute), I found only one project which promoted authentic work with severely disabled individuals. A New York artist had started a program in 1958 with cerebral palsied adults. He had noticed something I had also observed, which looked miraculous . . . that when a person with involuntary muscle spasms is absorbed in a painting process, like mixing colors, he sometimes achieves a degree of relaxation that allows him to actually control the brush (!) (*Bulletin*, 1964, p.66).

Although promoting genuine creativity was rare, there were notable exceptions, like **Creative Growth**, a sheltered workshop developed by art teacher Florence Ludins-Katz and psychologist Elias Katz in 1974 (Fig. 9–15). This environment—in which each person was carefully nurtured—was a model of respect, as was a textile workshop in Montreal run by Louise Annett (AJAT, 1977, p. 145). In such an atmosphere, individual talent could blossom, like that of artist Dwight Mackintosh: *"The Boy That Time Forgot"* (MacGregor, 1992).

In the spirit of the early pioneers—Viktor Lowenfeld and Henry Schaeffer-Simmern—there were individual art teachers who had faith in the creativity of the disabled, and who tried to dispel negative stereotypes in their books; like Zaidee Lindsay in England, Shiro Fukurai in Japan, Charles Gaitskell in Canada, Angel Schechtman in New Jersey, and Yasha Lisenco in New York. Several described their therapeutic teaching of art to retarded children in the *Bulletin* during the sixties (ATTP, pp. 181, 191, 213). A few college professors, like Caroline Allrutz, began to train students in this specialty.

In 1967, Sally Smith founded a school for learning disabled children which took advantage of the remedial potential of art activities through an arts-centered curriculum. In 1979 she published *No Easy Answers*, and in the Fall of 1995 the school was profiled on national television—as a model of the power of the arts to bypass linguistic difficulties (Cf. also Rees). The Waldorf Schools have long stressed the therapeutic benefits of art for mentally retarded individuals of all ages (Kirchner). In 1977, Virginia Minar reported on a three–year pilot study of art therapy with special education students in the schools of West Allis, Wisconsin (AATA Conf., p. 142). Since 1979, the Dade County, Florida, schools have had a large Art Education Therapy Program, serving many children (Bush).

The handicapped are also helped through art therapy in psychiatric settings. At a 1992 Congress on Arts & Medicine an art therapy program for mentally ill deaf adults was described. The program itself had been in existence at St. Elizabeth's Hospital in Washington since 1963 (Bejjani, p. 63) (Cf. also Kagin in Jakab, 1968; Roth in Rubin, 1987).

Viktor Lowenfeld's goal was to help children adjust to the emotional or "subjective handicap" caused by having an "objective handicap" (1957). Frances Anderson emphasized the need for the art-giver to adapt whatever is offered to the abilities of a disabled child. Rawley Silver's demonstration project with deaf children in 1967 led to travelling museum exhibits—*Shout in Silence* (1976/Metropolitan) and *Art as Language for the Handicapped* (1979/Smithsonian). With her Drawing Tests and her book (1978), Silver has contributed greatly to this area, and a curriculum based on her ideas was developed by Rocco Fugaro.

Donald Uhlin, like Silver who had a hearing loss, was handicapped himself—by polio. Uhlin first published his studies of neurologically handicapped children and art in 1969 (in Jakab) and his textbook in 1972. Other art therapists who have contributed to our understanding of work with the disabled include Edith Kramer, Susan Gonick-Barris (ATV, p. 197), and Laurie Wilson (ATV, p. 47). The ideas of Viktor Lowenfeld and Edith Kramer have been synthesized into a therapeutic approach to art with the handicapped by David Henley (Fig. 9–16). Like most books, his is addressed to both art educators and art therapists who serve the disabled (Cf. Kunkle-Miller) (Cf. also Caprio-Orsini).

Figure 9–16 David Henley working with a disabled child.

As with the elderly, there are still misconceptions about art with this group. But the tide has been turning, due partly to a landmark piece of legislation: **PL 94–142**, the **Education of All Handicapped Children Act** of 1975–updated in 1990 as the **Individuals with Disabilities Education Act**, IDEA-PL 101–476. For the first time, the public schools were required to deliver the best possible education to all with disabilities. And successful lobbying enabled **art therapy** to be mentioned as a **related service**.

1975 also saw the birth of the **National Committee * Arts for the Handicapped** (now **Very Special Arts**). Based in Washington, D.C., the organization has supported ''Very Special Arts Festivals'' and model programs in every state involving artists, educators and therapists. It has also funded studies, publications, and conferences like the one on ''Art in the Lives of Persons with Special Needs'' described in Chapter 4.

The Family of the Disabled Individual

The 1974 Conference on Arts for the Mentally Retarded which gave birth to NCAH was funded by the Joseph P. Kennedy Jr. Foundation. The Kennedys were energized by their distress over the empty life of their retarded sister Rosemary, who was institutionalized after a lobotomy. Sally Smith's failed efforts to educate her learning disabled son led her to start her school. And those who provided the force behind PL 94–142 were frustrated parents. The grief and confusion of the family is inevitable, for a disability affects everybody. And the others need as much help in coming to terms with their lot as the disabled individual himself.

Thus, a **family art evaluation** enabled the older brother of a multiply-handicapped blind child to express his rage in his family representation, in which his wood scrap shape was shooting missiles at the shapes of all of the others. For the first time, this teenager was able to show and then to talk about how displaced he felt by his parents' constant involvement with his sister's overwhelming needs.

In a **mother-child art group** at the school for the blind, Barry's mom asked him to paint with her, only afterward realizing how impossible it was for a boy with artificial eyes to meaningfully use this medium (Fig. 9–17). She was then able to discuss with the other mothers her denial of his blindness, which made it hard for Barry to give up his own wishful fantasy that he was "the only kid at the blind school who could see."

In addition to joining with their children on occasion, the **mothers' groups** at the school for the blind sometimes used art activities as a way to explore their own feelings and fantasies about their blind child. Some of the more highly motivated mothers went on to run **support groups** for other mothers, with training and consultation about the use of creative activities to facilitate the groups. Shirley Riley has also done **multifamily group art therapy** with families who have a disabled member.

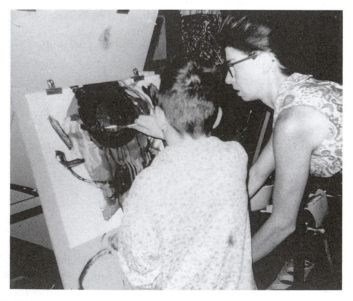

Figure 9–17 Barry and his mom in a mother-child group.

Parents and siblings of disabled individuals suffer greatly from their own confused feelings, like guilt over their role in causing the handicap, or shame about feeling resentment or envy. A group of mothers of disabled children was formed at their request, after accidentally meeting in my waiting room. They met for many years after their children's therapy had ended, supporting each other in their lifelong struggles.

Whether a disability is temporary, permanent, or unpredictable, it affects a person's self-concept, mood, and outlook on life. Although the disabled individual may not be in treatment specifically for emotional problems, art can become a powerful tool for understanding, for self-expression, and sometimes even for healing itself. A drama therapist and I once helped a group of teenagers born with cleft palates to make a film. The movie was designed to tell their families and friends what it feels like to have such a painfully visible condition, a most creative way to cope.

SOME PROBLEMS HELPED BY ART THERAPY

I have not written in detail about each of the many conditions which can be treated through art therapy, for that would be not only lengthy, but also beyond my expertise. Although art therapists see people of all ages, with every kind of psychiatric problem and every type of disability, most are not singled out below. Since art therapy seems to be uniquely helpful for certain disorders, however, I have chosen to highlight just a few of them; as examples of the much larger group of people we serve.

Eating Disorders

Art and other expressive therapies are very effective in the treatment of **anorexia**, **bulimia**, and **compulsive overeating**. People who are obsessed with their weight, who frantically pursue "magical control of the body" (Levens), are usually not in touch with the powerful feelings and fantasies they are working so desperately to master. Because what is repressed can be expressed in imagery more easily than in words, art therapy is a way to get in touch with the ideas behind their symptoms (Fig. 9–18). And using art materials can satisfy the intense need of these patients to be in control.

Since those with eating disorders tend to deal with their problems through action, the energy involved in creating makes art congenial. For these patients, who are indeed "starving" for affection, art therapy offers a way to be "fed," by "gobbling up" luscious supplies—and a way to "feed" the self and others, by "cooking up" delicious creations. It is thus not surprising that the first hospital to specialize in treating eating disorders—the **Renfrew Center**—made extensive use of art and other creative therapies. For Lila, art therapy was her self-selected "treatment of choice."

Figure 9–18   A statement of body hunger by an anorexic.

Figure 9–19 An Anguished, Starving Person by Lila.

Art Therapy for an Adolescent with Anorexia: **Lila** (17)

I had met Lila during her junior year of high school when she was hospitalized for a life-threatening weight loss. She was referred because of her artistic talent, as well as her tendency to hide feelings in defenses like intellectualization and rationalization. She attended an art therapy group I led on the adolescent unit, but preferred her individual sessions. After Lila was discharged and I'd left the hospital for private practice, she asked to continue in art therapy. We met twice a week for about a year.

Like many patients with eating disorders, Lila had found that her old symptoms began to return as soon as she left the controlled environment of the hospital. Unlike some, however, she was eager to overcome them. She expressed her feeling of emptiness and her longing for nurturance in a series of agonized and eloquent drawings and paintings (Fig. 9–19).

Despite Lila's excellent intellect, she could articulate her pain in pictures far better than in words. Using her own images as springboards for associations, she began to name her vague feelings. An intense family art evaluation session enabled both of us to better grasp the source of her problems, as they related to her painfully enmeshed family (Fig. 9–20).

Meanwhile, determined to increase her appetite and to maintain a normal weight, Lila got an after-school job in a homemade ice cream parlor. During her senior year, she also concentrated on building her portfolio, and was able to win a full scholarship to a prestigious art school in New York. She was then able to manage college without a recurrence of her disabling symptoms, a significant achievement.

Shortly after she had graduated, Lila called from New York to tell me that she liked her design job, and that she was enjoying a deeply satisfying

Figure 9–20   People struggling to break free by Lila.

love relationship. Ten years later, I heard indirectly that she was still finding constructive ways to nourish herself, and had been able to maintain a healthy distance from her family while sustaining warm connections.

Several art therapists have discussed why and how these patients are especially well-suited to art therapy, including Barbara Sobol and Mari Fleming in *Experiential Therapies for Eating Disorders* (Hornyak & Baker, Eds.); Joy Schaverien in *Arts Therapies & Clients with Eating Disorders* (Dokter, Ed.); and Mary Levens in her book. A number of other books on art therapy include chapters about work with eating disorders, like the one by Darcy Lubbers in *Adult Art Psychotherapy*.

Substance Abuse

Some patients with eating disorders also suffer from the similarly oral and addictive problem of **substance abuse**. From the days of Elinor Ulman's pioneering work at the **Alcohol Rehabilitation Unit** of the District of Columbia in 1951, art therapy has been used extensively with such patients (Cf. AP, 1983, p. 251). It seems to be appealing for many reasons, like the fact that it is both concrete and gratifying. Many forms of art therapy have been used in the effort to help addicts—from individual, to family, to group, to the multi-family group art therapy employed with mothers and children in a recovery program (Linesch; Cf. also Chickerneo; Waller & Mahoney).

Figure 9–21   Some of Amelia's Swans (Plasticene).

The women I saw in one drug rehabilitation program were initially distrustful and wary, skeptical that group art therapy could really help. Like children, they delighted in being "fed" beautiful materials, "hungrily" but constructively using them to create personal statements. They were surprised at their own creativity and enhanced self-esteem. There is no question that an addiction to creating is a lot healthier than being hooked on cocaine.

Art Therapy Helps a Recovering Addict: **Amelia**

Amelia created a series of pictures, paintings, and sculptures of graceful **swans** (Fig. 9–21). She spoke to the group with feeling about how she had discovered that she herself was not an **ugly duckling** after all, but rather a swan—and that her little swans had grown as she had grown (Fig. 9–22). She hoped to continue studying art after finishing the program.

A Prisoner Finds a Healing Craft: **Raymond M.**

On December 11, 1994, an article in the *New York Times* described the embroidered pictures created in prison by a former drug addict named Raymond Materson. A year after he was imprisoned, said Materson, he "became 'desperate for something to do' and remembered his grandmother absorbed in her sewing as she sat for hours in her rocking chair." By the time the article was published, Mr. Materson was being shown by the American Primitive Gallery, where his work was selling for prices as high as $2,500. Like Amelia, he had found a healthier addiction.

Victims of Sexual Abuse

Whether the abuse happens in childhood or adulthood, it is often repressed and unavailable to both patient and therapist. Even if he might remember, the victim has usually been threatened with reprisal if he tells anyone what happened. So whether the traumatic events are unconscious or supressed out of fear, art is an excellent avenue for "telling without talking" (Cohen & Cox). Art offers a way

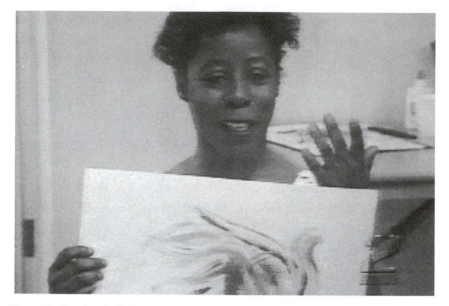

Figure 9–22   Amelia Talking about a Swan Painting.

for a person of any age to utter "silent screams and hidden cries" (Kaufman & Wohl). As society becomes more comfortable with the truth, art therapists are helping more people in an ever-expanding array of settings, from shelters to hospitals. Although other modalities are helpful as well (Simonds, 1994); most of the articles in two issues of *The Arts in Psychotherapy* devoted entirely to the treatment of sexual abuse (1987 & 1995) were about **art** therapy.

Pioneer Clara Jo Stember literally carried art therapy to abused children in her **Artmobile** (AJAT, 1976, p. 83). Art therapist Connie Naitove contributed a chapter to the *Handbook of Clinical Intervention in Child Sexual Abuse* (1980). Art therapist Bobbie Kaufman and social worker Agnes Wohl wrote two books on drawings by abused children. There is also a fine chapter on the topic in WCAT, and a vividly written article in AJAT—"Trauma, Children & Art" (1990, p. 48).

Since abuse is usually perpetrated by a family member, the therapy often involves the **family** (Cf. Landgarten, 1987). *Adult Art Therapy* contains a description of **group art therapy** with the **mothers of incestuously abused children**. Linesch's book on work with families in crisis (1993) includes a report of group art therapy for **young sexually abused children and their mothers**.

By the time adult survivors of abuse seek treatment, they usually have problems in many areas, and often carry multiple psychiatric diagnoses. They sometimes discover repressed memories of sexual abuse in the course of therapy, which has stimulated serious questions about the accuracy of such "memories" (Cf. AJAT, 1995, p. 9).

Elaine, whose story was told in Chapter 1, actually came to art therapy because, when she started to recall her own abuse, she could not talk about it in words, but could only "say" it in fingerpaint. In art therapy, work with both clay and paint slowly brought forth even more memories (Cf. Orleman). Despite many years of intensive psychotherapy, analyst Alice Miller did not uncover her own abuse until she started painting the images in *Pictures of a Childhood*. Similarly, artist Pat Harris didn't find her buried images of trauma until she was drawing the pictures for her book, *A Child's Story* (Cf. A. Brown). "Exploring the links between creativity and healing" was the mission of a short-lived but moving journal, *Creative Lifelines for Survivors* (1995–1996).

Advances included a chapter on work with incest survivors (p. 114), and CATT contained one on art therapy with "survivors of sexual violence." Frances Anderson led ceramics groups for incest survivors, described in "**Courage! Together We Heal**" (Cf. AP, 1995, p. 413). Carolyn Waller also conducted an art therapy group with adult incest survivors (AT, 1992, p. 135). And Stephanie Brooke used art therapy with a group of abused adult women to raise self-esteem (AP, 1995, p. 447; Cf. Brooke, 1997). Dee Spring, one of the first art therapists to specialize in working with abused patients, described her methods in *Shattered Images*. And dance therapist Susan Simonds proposed a combination of **art and movement therapy** to address the body image disturbances that are almost always present.

Dissociative Identity Disorder (DID)

Formerly known as **Multiple Personality Disorder** (**MPD**), this painful condition is caused by severe early trauma, usually some kind of sexual, physical, and/or psychological abuse. Elaine (Chapter 1), who had been repeatedly abused, was in treatment for chronic depression for many years before her DID was discovered, a common story. Since her "alters" were split-off (dissociated) at different ages, making art was an excellent way for each one to "speak" at her own level and in her own style. Elaine is the person for whom a combination of art and videotherapy was helpful in getting to know "parts" of which she was consciously unaware (Chapter 8).

Readers and viewers of *Sybil* (Schreiber) may recall the drawings by her alters of different ages and personalities. Christine Sizemore, whose story was told in the film *All About Eve*, spoke at the 1980 AATA Conference on how her own painting had been helpful to her (AT, p. 125). And art therapist Don Jones worked with the man described in *The Minds of Billy Milligan* (Keyes).

Of the 16 chapters in a book on expressive therapies in the treatment of MPD (Kluft, Ed.), six are by art therapists. CATT includes chapters on art therapy in the treatment of both children (p. 84) and adults (p. 117) with DID. And art therapists Barry Cohen and Carol Cox have published a book on *Art as a Window into the World of Multiple Personality*.

Is Art Therapy Dangerous for Some People?

This question is often asked by other professionals who worry that art therapy may put their patients at risk. The fear is that people whose controls or reality-testing are already weak might be overstimulated by the materials or over-whelmed by what emerges, and go "over the edge" mentally or behaviorally. This anxiety is shared by some art therapists, who issue such warnings as: "Never use red paint with psychotic patients" or "Avoid clay with children who have conduct disorders."

Certainly, if profoundly retarded children put art materials in their mouths, then it is best to "fingerpaint" with chocolate pudding or to "model" with edible dough. Or, if patients are agitated and potentially violent, it is common sense not to provide dangerous tools like scissors. And of course one must set limits on destructive uses of materials, like throwing clay at other people or pouring paint on the floor.

Nevertheless, it has been my experience over the last 35 years, in my own work—and that of the many therapists I have supervised in the use of art with a wide range of patients—that there is no one for whom art therapy is necessarily hazardous, although it is naturally more helpful to some than to others. I believe that those dangers that exist are due not to problems inherent in art, but to an inadequately-prepared clinician.

That is why art therapists in training are required to have many hours of close supervision, in order to be able to utilize themselves and their modality safely as well as creatively. In my experience, when patients are given a choice of materials and themes, even those who are acutely disturbed tend to select media and ideas they can handle. There may be more of a risk when the art therapist decides what is best for a patient or group, and that assignment turns out to be unmanageable.

Neverthless, if an art therapist is imaginative and knows a broad repertoire of possibilities, and if she can provide structure and help when needed, most patients can be enabled to have a safe and satisfying art experience most of the time. A good clinician knows when it is best to modify or modulate the art experience, so that it is not frightening for the patient. In other words, if the art therapist is skilled, potentially disruptive art experiences are less likely to occur. And if they do, it is usually possible to transform them into events which are not traumatic.

Art Therapy for Artists

You might wonder whether art is an especially appropriate form of therapy for artists. Most artists feel that their own art has been therapeutic for them, espe-cially at times of stress (Cf. Birkhauser, Sherman, Spencer). Many individuals have decided to become art therapists because making art helped them to get through some serious crisis in their lives.

Some artists fear that any kind of psychotherapy will rob them of inspiration, but the evidence is to the contrary (Kubie, 1958). **Jackson Pollock's** drawings and paintings were used extensively in his analysis, and seem to have accelerated the treatment (Wysuph, 1970). Many art therapists have treated artists through art, like Josef Garai who helped a painter to resolve "identity conflicts" (ATTP, P. 311). Dissolving creative workblocks, a subject often mentioned by Margaret Naumburg, is sometimes the goal of art therapy (Landgarten, 1981). There is a thoughtful discussion of treating artists in AJAT (1978, p. 123).

CONCLUDING THOUGHTS

As Lowenfeld said so eloquently in the quotation that began this chapter, art therapists know that "every human being is endowed with a creative spirit." That conviction, along with a belief in the power of art—to liberate, to enliven, and to heal—fuels the effort to reach people of all ages with all kinds of psychological and physical problems. With the energy born of this faith, art therapists have been able to fan the creative spark inside many who had given up. From the very young to the very old; from those who are mute to those whose words camouflage feelings; from those who live in mental pain to those who seek self-development; art therapy can help artists and nonartists alike.

Many different approaches to assessment and treatment are used in art therapy, and there is no single agreed-upon method for work with any particular group. What is clear from reading the literature is that art therapists take responsibility for learning about the special needs of the particular people they are trying to help. Whether patients are psychotic, neurotic, or learning disabled, art therapists attempt to fully understand their problems in order to help them with art in a safe and sensitive way.

Since there is such a wide range of people who can be served, art therapists can sometimes choose to work with those with whom they are most comfortable. The practice of art therapy with different groups of people naturally varies considerably. Doing art therapy with an autistic four-year-old, for example, is radically different from helping rebellious adolescents, paranoid adults, or withdrawn elders. In order to be most effective, art therapists get to know the group in general as well as the individuals—who are always unique.

In a similar fashion, the role of the art therapist in diverse settings varies considerably. In order to be most effective, art therapists learn about the institution in which they work. Whether its mission is psychiatric, rehabilitative, or educational; an art therapist learns about the type of place as well as the particular hospital, clinic, or special school in which she finds herself. The next chapter will deal with the widening range of places, the people within them, and the ever-expanding purposes being served in the developing world of art therapy.

Chapter   10

Places we Practice

Art is Man's Most Passionate Rebellion against his Fate

ANDRE MALRAUX

INTRODUCTION

An analyst once wrote: "Man creates, as it were, out of his mortal wounds." Most of the situations in this chapter concern problems which are not primarily psychiatric. Instead, they have to do with stressful things that can happen to ordinary people—like illness, bereavement, violence, dislocation, or discrimination. In order to be available to those who are facing crises of all sorts, art therapy has migrated into new places—like general hospitals, hospices, shelters, and schools.

These are all forms of "secondary prevention"—helping those who are at increased risk for psychological problems—because of acute crises like war, as well as chronic conditions like poverty. If society paid as much attention to the prevention of emotional distress as to its treatment; the economic and social savings would be tremendous. And because art is a normal part of everyday life, art therapy is an especially good way to promote mental health. For that reason, it is an extremely compatible modality for "primary prevention"—facilitating "wellness."

Although its origins were in diverse settings, the developing discipline of art therapy grew up mainly within psychiatry, in hospitals and clinics. At the 1978 AATA Conference, Bernard Levy with his usual flair for drama, proposed "*A slogan to live by ... Out of the Hospitals and Into the World!*" (p. 122). In the twenty years since then, the extension of art therapy into the community has progressed steadily. Its river continues to flow in even more directions, reaching new people in new places.

Some of these widening streams will be described in this chapter, although it is far from encyclopedic. Inevitably, my personal experiences have colored what I have chosen to highlight. The resources noted in each area, therefore, are representative examples I have come across in my own journey, and are not meant to be inclusive.

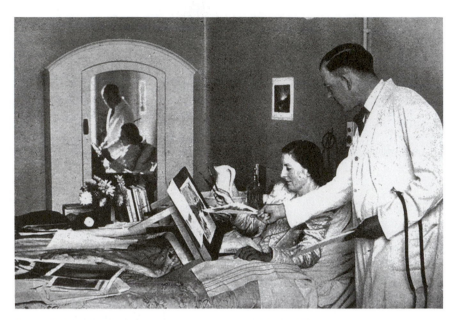

Figure 10–1   The doctor studies the patient's art (Adrian Hill).

MEDICAL ART THERAPY

The idea that art can promote physical healing is ancient. Images in their tombs show Egyptians painting on barges in the Nile River, taking excursions as part of their medical treatment. The idea that art can color otherwise-dreary times of enforced inactivity is also not new. Adrian Hill, who coined the term "art therapy" in 1942, painted his way through a tedious convalescence in a tuberculosis sanatorium (Fig. 10–1). That art can give meaning to a life twisted by trauma was eloquently demonstrated in the work of painter Frida Kahlo (Fig. 10–2). Her spine and pelvis were crushed in a bus accident at age 18, leaving her with chronic pain and the constant threat of illness. As she told her biographer, Hayden Herrera, *"The only thing I know is **that I paint because I need to"*** (pp. xi-xii).

Since making art comes naturally to suffering artists, it makes sense that more and more patients dealing with illness and injury are receiving art therapy as part of their treatment. A head trauma patient admitted to MetroHealth Center in Cleveland might be referred to the **Art Studio**, where he will be helped to cope through creating (Fig. 10–3; AT, 1995, p. 167). A child with severe **burns** entering San Francisco General Hospital may be enabled to deal with his pain through art therapy (Fig. 10–4; AT, 1993, p. 71). A stroke victim who has lost the ability to talk might now have an opportunity to "speak" by making art (AT, 1996, p. 265).

In 1985 a medical school held a conference on **Art & Medicine**. As the only art therapist among the speakers, I knew very little about the area. After

Figure 10–2   A portrait of her pain, by Frida Kahlo.

some time in the library, I was impressed by how much interesting work had been
done—especially since most art therapists don't write, and what is published is
only the tip of the iceberg of actual practice. In 1993 an entire issue of *Art
Therapy* was devoted to **Medical Art Therapy** (Vol. 10, no. 2), defined by
editor Cathy Malchiodi as: *"the . . . use of art therapy with individuals who are*

Figure 10–3   Mickie McGraw helps a patient in the Art Studio.

physically ill, experiencing trauma to the body, or undergoing aggressive medical treatment such as surgery or chemo-therapy'' (AT, editorial). Her editorial contains a good review of the literature on the topic, about which she is currently preparing a two-volume edited book (1998c, 1999).

As in psychiatric settings, medical art therapists usually work as part of a team. The difference is that the major problem for which the person is being treated is not psychiatric but physical (Cf. AJAT, 1987, p. 5; and AJAT, 1993, p. 2 for discussions of the role of the art therapist with hospitalized children). But being sick, being treated, or having surgery—like being old or blind—has powerful effects on mind, mood, and self-concept; and art therapy can help to facilitate medical care in a variety of ways.

Art in Medical Assessment

A patient's art work can provide a much-needed window on the mind for the others involved in his treatment. For example, the social skills of Susie, a woman with Alzheimer's, masked the cognitive deterioration that became dramatically evident to her art therapist, Judith Wald in her drawings (Figs. 10–5, p. 270,

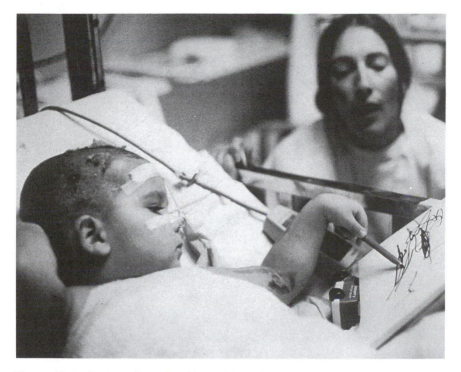

Figure 10–4 Art therapist works with a child in a burn unit.

and 10–6, p. 271; AP, 1984, p. 165). Art is often used to identify the extent and nature of organic impairment.

Art can also sensitize medical professionals to a patient's feeling about his illness and treatment. For example, a psychologist asked children with serious diseases to draw pictures about some of the procedures they had to have—like dialysis or blood transfusions (Fig. 10–7, p. 272). The drawings helped their doctors to be more empathic and more effective (AP, 1980, p. 165).

In a study funded by the **American Nurses Foundation**, we invited children to tell stories and draw pictures before and after surgery. **Body image distortions** in the drawings showed how **anxious** each child was, allowing parents and professionals to better prepare them for their operations. Similarly, drawings by transplant patients and their families reflected how much **stress** they were feeling about cardiac catheterization, helping the medical team in case management (Jakab, 1984 ISPE Conf.).

Sometimes drawings have been used as clues to **disease processes**, and in determining a person's possible **prognosis**. Susan Bach, a Jungian analyst who studied the prognostic value of pictures in the mid-fifties, spelled them out in *Life Paints its own Span*. Her student, Gregg Furth, elaborated them in *The Secret World of Pictures*.

Figure 10–5   Human figure drawing early in Alzheimer's.

Figure 10–6   Human figures later in the disease process.

Art Therapy for Psychosomatic Conditions

Art therapy seems to be particularly useful for these ailments, which are physically very real, but in which stress can exacerbate symptoms. The mind-body connection is especially visible when anxiety triggers a tension headache or a bout of diarrhea. Since these symptoms are so good at expressing repressed emotional states, art—which bypasses defenses—can help such patients to **feel what they fear** (Cf. Fleming & Cox in *Advances*, p. 169).

At a center for respiratory medicine, the art therapist developed an interview in which a patient makes a series of drawings—**about his asthma**. The drawings help to identify aspects of patients' coping styles which need to be addressed in order to promote a good recovery (AT, 1988, p. 59). Similarly, asking **stutterers** to draw the stuttering episode helped a speech therapist to formulate a more effective treatment plan (Bar in Jakab, 1969).

Although it is not a psychosomatic disorder, stuttering also tends to run in families, probably reflecting an inherited vulnerability. Just as its occurrence can be triggered by stress, it can disappear with relaxation. I have noticed that stutterers are often **fluent** while they are using "contact media," like clay or fingerpaint (Fig. 10–8). An art therapist serving people with **rheumatoid arthritis** wrote: "*all my patients reported at least partial abatement of physical pain when painting or sculpting*" (AJAT, 1991, p. 117).

The sensorimotor aspects of working in art are indeed relaxing, as is the focus on creating; one of many reasons why art therapy is often used for children

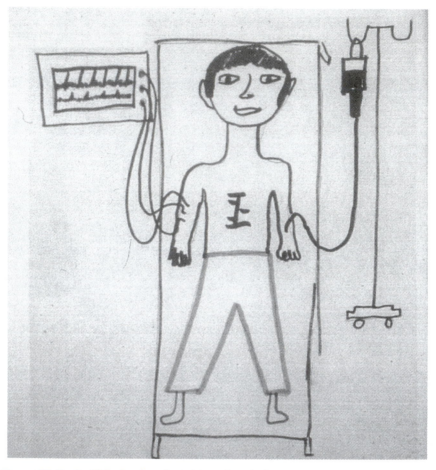

Figure 10–7   A child's drawing of receiving a transfusion.

with **enuresis** or **encopresis** like Amy, Alan, and Randy in Chapter 1. Art offers a way to "let loose" for people of all ages with many types of intestinal motility problems, from **chronic constipation** to **irritable bowel syndrome**. The subtitle of a chapter on art therapy with such young people was "Control, Uncontrol, Order, and Chaos" (WCAT, p.72), all aspects of working with art media as well. Since family life is greatly affected by these disorders, **family art therapy** may be the treatment of choice, as in Helen Landgarten's work with the family of an encopretic child (1987).

Art Therapy in Trauma & Rehabilitation

Even when a person has just suffered a physical trauma, whether accidental injury or surgery, making art can help. A massive shock to the system elicits

Figure 10–8 A stutterer regresses safely with fingerpaint.

powerful feelings for which words are weak, but for which art can be a release. Art helps both to express and to contain otherwise-overwhelming emotions. In one hospital where burn patients have had art therapy for over 20 years (Fig. 10–4), a **protocol** (a detailed guide) was developed for **art therapy in** [all] **medical trauma settings** (AT, 1993, p. 71).

Traumatic injuries, like severe burns or car accidents, are usually followed by long periods of anguish, pain, disability, and treatment, often with uncertain outcome. Art therapy can be helpful at every stage, from the shock of the initial trauma to the long and often discouraging process of rehabilitation. In modern medical hospitals and rehabilitation institutes there are now more **Art Studios** like the one in Cleveland noted earlier (AT, 1995, p. 167). This program was started in 1967 by art therapist Mickie McGraw—whose own life in a wheelchair since polio in adolescence inspired her to bring the healing powers of art to others (Fig. 10–3).

Sometimes making art is self-initiated, as in the work of Frida Kahlo, whose pain was transmuted by the injured artist into haunting self-portraits (Fig. 10–2). Ophir, a 5–year-old Israeli boy, had never been interested in art before, but after an accident which left him "temporarily handicapped," drawing became his chief form of "self-rehabilitation" (AP, 1985, p. 81). Since normal anxieties about being artistic are exacerbated by physical complications, however, most patients need the encouragement and assistance of an art therapist.

The logistics of helping a bedridden patient in traction to create can be formidable. However, even when a person's faculties are greatly reduced, some kind of art expression is usually possible (Fig. 10–9), with creatively conceived adaptations and well-designed assistive devices (AT, 1997, p. 37). Even quadriplegics can be enabled to create images, by using **computers** (AT, 1985, p. 86). When a young man named Peter became so disabled that he could no longer hold a brush, art therapist Rita Simon supported his hand, sensitively following his instructions (AJAT, 1982, p. 13).

Group art therapy can be especially helpful, since people with the same disorder benefit from sharing feelings and frustrations, as in an art therapy support group for adolescents with **muscular dystrophy** (AJAT, 1994, p. 66). A group of young adults in a rehabilitation institute formed a production company named "**Wheelchair Accessibles.**" Together they created a videotape—a creative way to deal with the helplessness and anguish of their situation (Bejjani, p. 75).

People in rehabilitation do not always get better; in fact, some suffer from progressive disorders. Art therapy is especially helpful in coping with **chronic disease processes**, since it can fill long, tedious periods of time with creative activity. Milton M., a man in his mid-fifties, **homebound** for nine years with **multiple sclerosis**, "came alive" when a young art therapist was able to engage him in a playful drawing dialogue (Obernbreit and Robbins, in Robbins, 1980).

Art Therapy for Healing

The use of **mental imagery** to combat pain and disease is one of many interventions in the increasingly popular realm of **alternative** or **complementary medicine**. Some visualization techniques—like those used by Doctors Carl Simonton and Bernard Siegal—include **drawing** as well as mental imagery, as ways for those with cancer to mobilize their immune systems. Most approaches to the use of imagery in healing are focussed: the patient visualizes or draws his disease and his body's efforts to fight it.

Figure 10–9 A child with cerebral palsy creates on a tray.

In a study presented at an Imagery Conference some years ago, a researcher asked subjects to **visualize** their T-cells multiplying. He then asked them to **draw** what they had imagined. The slides he showed of their blood—drawn before and after the art activity—were so dramatically different, that even a skeptic could not deny that creating images had somehow helped to increase the number of "fighter" cells.

Many uses of art for healing are not so directive, but however it is employed, the idea is that making art can have a positive impact on the immune system—that creating affects not only the psyche, but the soma as well. The field of psychoneuroimmunology is in its infancy, but findings so far are encouraging. While I was revising this chapter, for example, a study reported on the evening news (December, 1997) demonstrated that music therapy measurably enhanced the immune system of children with cancer.

The new **Office of Alternative Medicine** in the National Institutes of Health (1991) recognized art therapy as an alternative or complementary therapy in 1993. Similarly, a new periodical, *Alternative Therapies in Health & Medicine* (1995) has explicitly invited papers in the creative arts therapies. There are other signs of the growing interest of medicine in the arts, like the **International Arts-Medicine Association**, formed in 1985 by a group of creative physicians, which publishes the *International Journal of Arts Medicine*; and a related group, the **Society for the Arts in Health Care**, organized in 1991.

Art therapists have been reporting for some time on the use of art for release, solace, and healing; like the 52-year-old paraplegic man who used mental imagery as well as art-making to deal with his cancer (AJAT, 1978, p. 59). "Fighting Cancer with Images" was a chapter in *Advances* (1989, p. 148), and Vija Lusebrink wrote about "Imagery & Emotions in Healing" in her book.

Art therapist Suzanne Lovell got better by fighting her illness through movement and art, telling her story in a video, and describing the method in a book chapter (CATT, p. 291). Another art therapist discovered for herself the critical value of making art while she was in a hospital and devastated by the potentially fatal disease of **lupus** (AT, 1993, p. 96). Art therapist Wendy Miller helped an artist to battle her **lymphoma**. The patient made drawings in intensive care after surgery—and during the long process of pain, fear, hope, and recovery (AP, 1997, p. 399).

In 1993, organ transplant recipients from all over the country were invited to submit art work done before and after their surgery to a competition called "**Art for Life.**" As a judge for the exhibit, I saw all of the work submitted, which was unbelievably powerful. Even more persuasive were the words of the artists which accompanied the slides. I came away convinced, like many of them, that making art had accelerated their recovery. Perhaps it was because the physiological transformation they had gone through—from dying to living—was so vividly reflected by similarly dramatic transformations in their art.

Art Therapy for Terminal Illness

A patient who is dying is usually dependent on his caregivers, so that taking charge of art materials and creating his own images can restore a sense of efficacy—at a time when he is otherwise helpless. We do not know to what extent art therapy can affect the progression of a terminal illness, but we do know that creating something new—when the world of the Self is shrinking—is beneficial. In clinics, hospitals, and **hospices**, even in their homes, people of all ages who are facing deterioration and death are being helped to cope by drawing, painting, and sculpting.

In addition to helping a dying patient to master his feelings through making art; the therapist plays a special role at a time *"When Art Is All There Is"* (AJAT, 1989, p. 45). By helping a person to cope with the illness while not being involved with the medical treatment; the art therapist participates in a uniquely *"Shared Journey"* (AJAT, 1989, p. 51) and bears witness as the patient comes to terms with his fate—with the help of art and her presence (Cf. also Pratt & Wood).

For youngsters with cancer, making art is a natural way of "helping normal children cope with abnormal circumstances" (AT, 1993, p. 78). Rachel, dying of leukemia, shared her spontaneous drawings and writings with her home/hospital teacher, Judi Bertoia.

Usually the creative activity is introduced by an art therapist, as in work with AIDS patients (Landgarten & Lubbers). Occasionally, art is provided by a physician, as in the **"painting therapy"** for cancer patients offered by Dr. Margarethe Hauschke in Germany. For a dying person, making art can be both soothing and painful. When it is watched over by a sensitive clinician, like art therapist Esther Dreifuss-Katan, even deeper healing can take place. In a book called *Cancer Stories*, she offers eloquent examples of her subtitle: *Creativity & Self-Repair.*

Although the body may not be curable, art is a wonderful way to repair the injured self. Art, after all, is an expression of the human spirit, and both have their own kind of immortality. In addition to work with patients, art therapy can also help the family—during the dying process as well as after their loss. Three generations of children and grandchildren were helped to deal with their feelings about a terminally ill grandparent through **family art therapy** (Landgarten, 1987). Esther Dreifuss-Katan's last chapter is about art therapy with the grieving family.

Both children and adults with life-threatening illnesses rarely give up hope of recovery, no matter how faint. One of the bravest women I have ever known was also one of the best art therapists I have had the privilege to train. In Susan Aach-Feldman's battle with ovarian cancer, she often turned to making her own art

Fighting Cancer with Art & Imagery: Sue

Susan Aach-Feldman was a young art therapist who did brilliant work with blind children (Fig. 10–10), and who died long before her time. Her fatal illness, ovarian cancer, was diagnosed two years before it finally conquered her body, perhaps delayed by the brave spirit she mustered to fight it.

While still in the hospital following her first operation, Sue asked for art materials, and we would talk about her drawings during my visits. Actively using imagery as a tool in her fight against the disease, she worked at visualizing the cancer cells and her immune system. Sue also drew bold and powerful pictures in her sketchbooks, trying to beat the

Figure 10–10 Susan Aach-Feldman working with a blind child.

challenge of cancer as creatively as she had met the challenge of helping multiply-handicapped children.

One year after her first operation, and a course of chemotherapy which brought a welcome period of comfort and energy, Sue was due to have a routine follow-up called "second-look" surgery. Just before she went into the hospital, she requested a meeting at my office. During an intense two-hour session, she drew and discussed a series of three chalk drawings, which, like her courageous spirit, were realistic, yet full of hope.

The first was a glowingly healthy portrait of her body, "What's Happening Inside: Visualizing the Best" The second was a representation of her T-Cells, entitled "My Fighters: the Swordsmen" (Fig. 10–11), and the third was a boat plowing its way through rough waters: "The Narrow Path: An Odds-Beater on a Sturdy Ship" (Fig. 10–12).

Sue did beat the medical odds in part, staying alive more than twice as long as the doctors had predicted before succumbing to the cancer. Though there is no way to prove it, I believe that Sue's passionate use of imagery and making of art helped to extend her life. As noted earlier, some studies support the power of mental and artistic imagery to strengthen the human immune system. And there is considerable evidence that such a spirit, a will to live so strong and vibrant—while it probably can't win—may well slow down the progress of even a terminal illness.

Art Therapy for Bereavement

When you lose a loved one you need to grieve, to deal with feelings like guilt about surviving, and anger at being abandoned. Making art allows for a visceral

Figure 10–11 "My Fighters: the Swordsmen" (T-cells).

expression of feelings too raw to put into words. I remember how badly I needed to paint after my friend Peter's sudden death, when I was about to turn seventeen . . .

Numbly, I went home to the funeral from the camp where I was working as an arts and crafts counselor. Numbly I returned, then succumbed to a high fever for several days and nights. When I awoke, I felt a strong need to go to the woods and paint. I did so on my first day off, and it felt good. The painting was not of Peter, but of someone playing the piano, making music in dark reds, purples, and blacks. It was a cry, a scream caught and tamed. It was a new object in the world, a mute, tangible testament. The doing of it afforded tremendous relief. It did not take away the hurt and the ache, but it did help in releasing some of the rage, and in giving form to some of the feelings which threatened to overwhelm me.

Years later, I was surprised that my mother—who was not an artist—became quite involved in work with clay after my father died, sculpting his head. She was able to discharge her feelings by squeezing, forming, and caressing the clay; while at the same time creating a concrete image of her lost spouse—a lasting

THE NARROW PATH — AN ODDSBEATER ON A STURDY SHIP!

Figure 10–12 "The Narrow Path: An Odds-Beater on a Sturdy Ship."

memorial (Fig. 10–13). Just a week after her death, I found that making a series of "free association" drawings was amazingly helpful to me in the work of mourning.

There is more sensitivity now to the need for "crisis intervention" for losses—giving help at the time of the trauma. If I had been offered art therapy after having a stillbirth—as one art therapist did for women following "**perinatal death**"—I might have been spared considerable psychological pain. That work was described in a special issue of *Art Therapy* (1992) on "**Art & Loss,**" which documented that the planned use of art therapy with the bereaved of all ages is growing.

Children who have lost parents have been helped to work on their grief through art therapy support groups in schools (*Advances*, CATT) and in hospices (*Advances*). Recently-widowed adults have been seen in groups led by an art therapist/psychiatrist team (AJAT, 1993, p. 91). And art therapist Marge Heegard has created *Drawing Workbooks* to help children who have suffered losses like separation, divorce, illness, and death. She has also written a *Guide* for professionals leading support groups.

Sandra (Kagin) Graves offered art therapy to mourners through churches and funeral homes. Individuals and families, who might not otherwise have sought help, could do so through the Grief Counseling Service she founded in

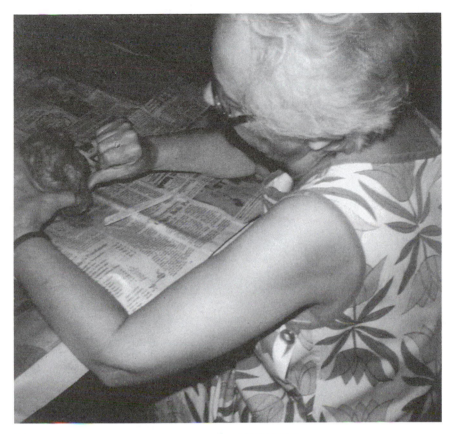

Figure 10–13   My mother sculpting my father after his death.

the early eighties. She later organized three other forms of art counseling intervention to deal with murder and suicide. And in 1994 she published *A Compassionate Workbook* for bereaved adults.

The loss of loved ones is a **normal crisis**, which, if not mastered, can lead to depression. Art activities can be a form of **prevention**, as vital in mental as in physical health. A young art therapist I know recently decided to use part of her dwindling savings for art supplies, saying that she knew that only creating her own art would help her to cope with an unanticipated series of dreadful losses. Seven-year-old Christopher knew that I helped children through art. After his mother had committed suicide, he requested a visit to my art room, and asked to come back a year later.

A Child Asks for Help After Mother Dies: **Chris** (7)

Since I was a friend of the family, Chris knew that I helped kids with their worries through art. In fact, after his mom's prior unsuccessful suicide

Figure 10–14   Christopher's "Save Me" flag and weapons.

attempt, he had proudly shown me his "magical" creation. Using cut paper and glue he had created a flag, writing "Save Me" on one side (Fig. 10–14) and "Trouble" on the other (Fig. 10–15). Inside, he had hidden a cardboard hatchet and knife. It was a poignant attempt to keep her from destroying herself.

Sadly, Chris's fears were all too well founded. His mother's melancholia won out, and she killed herself. After the funeral, Chris asked if he could come to my office. His father, concerned about the boy's silence

Figure 10–15   The other side of Christopher's flag: "Trouble."

Figure 10–16   The "Dog" Christopher saw in his scribble.

about the tragedy, brought him to the clinic where I worked. I, feeling sad and helpless about the death of a woman I had known for many years, was pleased to do what little I could to help.

Chris's visit to my art room was just a few weeks after his mother's death. He worried about getting messy with fingerpaint or chalk, because "my Mommy would yell at me." Projecting an image of "A Dog" onto his scribble, he said it must be the dog he had wanted so badly, but was not allowed to have because of his mother's illness (Fig. 10–16).

Chris then made a dark, messy fingerpainting, commenting anxiously on how angry his mother would be if she could see him. He wondered aloud as he painted whether she was angry at him, and if his being bad or naughty or wanting the wrong things (like the dog) had anything to do with her leaving him.

His story about the finger painting, as he drew lines in it with a stick, was that it was "A Road. But," he continued, "You'll never find your way out . . . No one can stop me . . . They'll never find their way out. They'll feel so sad . . . They'll be stuck there forever." I asked what "they" would do. Chris placed his hand in the black paint, lifted it up to show me, and then smashed it onto the paper, splattering the paint. He had certainly accomplished a lot in his single hour.

One year later, Chris asked to come in again. This time he symbolically represented his mother's suicide in his drawing: a pink person "falls" off a road, as she had "fallen" off a bridge. Later, he dramatized with clay and tools a crash, an emergency, and an operation in which he, as the doctor, magically but unsuccessfully tried to restore the injured patient. He accomplished a great deal in his second hour too.

Figure 10–17 A concentration camp execution.

Making art gave Chris a way to release his overwhelming anger and frustration. It also gave him an opportunity to clarify the event, and to cope with the painful reality he needed to accept. Bereavement is a particular kind of personal crisis, in which art can be therapeutic. Making art can also be therapeutic when there is a crisis in the community.

ART AS THERAPY IN TIMES OF CRISIS

War & Combat

Art as solace in times of anguish is older than the field of art therapy. Some events are so devastating that words fail, and images become the best way to say what presses for release. In a Nazi concentration camp, children made art to imaginatively escape (Volavkova), and adults drew pictures to record the truth of what was happening (Fig. 10–17; Green). Two Jewish adolescents in hiding before dying in the Holocaust left their journals for posterity. One is Anne Frank's famous *Diary*, a word portrait. The other is *A Diary of Pictures* by art student Charlotte Salomon, a series of paintings she made to deal with unthinkable events (Fig. 10–18).

Since the State of Israel was born in 1948, both Arabs and Jews have lived in a constant state of strife. Children in shelters drew pictures while bombs burst

Figure 10–18 "Nazi Take-Over in 1933," by Charlotte Salomon.

outside during the Six Day War (Fig. 10–19). And in 1995, art therapy helped Palestinians and Israelis on the West Bank and Gaza (AT, 1995).

During the First World War, the faces of many soldiers were badly disfigured by chemical warfare. I once heard a plastic surgeon tell the moving story of a woman **sculptor** who carefully made **masks** of the soldiers' pre-trauma faces from photographs. In an era before reconstructive surgery, wearing the masks allowed these maimed men to move in the world without excessive shame.

During the Second World War, the Red Cross sent **logbooks** to Americans in prisoner of war camps. The prisoners not only wrote in them, they also made drawings and paintings. Creating images—of the people and the places they

Figure 10–19 Soldiers in tanks by Israeli child.

missed—was a way to hold on to good memories, and to relieve months or years of tension and boredom.

The trauma of war does not disappear with the end of combat, but is often carried in the mind and body in the form of post-traumatic stress disorder (PTSD). Making art is one way to achieve some control over the intrusive imagery of flashbacks (Horowitz). Thirty years after an atomic bomb was dropped on Hiroshima, a Japanese TV station asked survivors of the attack to submit pictures of their memories. They were astonished by the response, as hundreds of adults welcomed the opportunity to deal with the still-painful trauma by creating images (Fig. 10–20). Vietnam veterans, who suffered massive culture

Figure 10–20 Painting by a survivor of Hiroshima (A-bomb).

shock as well as the trauma of combat, have been helped to heal through art therapy (AP, 1985, p. 285).

Natural Disaster & Violence

Art therapy is often part of public and private efforts to provide "crisis intervention." This is a particular form of "secondary prevention," offering help to those who are in the throes of responding to overwhelming events. Like medicating at the first sign of an infection, early clinical intervention can sometimes prevent more serious and prolonged emotional damage.

When a devastating **hurricane** hit the Miami area, art therapists were on the scene, offering their help to people in shelters. When a **tornado** decimated a Kansas town, a teacher helped her students to deal with the trauma by making art (AT, 1992, p. 42). In Armenia, children at a mental health clinic were encouraged to draw and paint pictures after an **earthquake**. The therapists were able to monitor the children's recovery by observing changes in their art and its "colors of disaster" (AP, 1996, p. 1).

When a **plane crash** in Pittsburgh left no survivors, an art therapist helped students to deal with their feelings through drawings (Kunkle-Miller, 1995 Conf.). When a **train collided with a school bus** in Israel, killing 22 and injuring 15, making art helped youngsters to cope with the trauma (AP, 1987, p. 153).

When a **nuclear reactor exploded** on Three Mile Island, children were invited to draw their fantasies about radiation.

Some children who had witnessed a **shootout** between the police and a radical political group were helped to deal with their fears and feelings through art therapy (Landgarten, 1981). A 1995 **terrorist bombing** in Oklahoma killed and injured many innocent people. The clinician in charge of helping the survivors to deal with their post-traumatic stress reported that **art therapy** was especially helpful to people of all ages (AT, 1997, p. 89).

Community Tensions

Sometimes these crises reflect racial tensions, like the **riots** in many cities after Martin Luther King's assassination in 1968. Children in one torn-up Washington neighborhood were helped to sort out what they had witnessed by writing and illustrating a booklet about it (Fig. 10–21). In Pittsburgh, a biracial group of artists and arts therapists got together and worked all summer at a joint volunteer creation—the "Martin Luther King Freedom School." Classes met in a church and a neighborhood center, where people from 2 to 82 came to dance, sing, act, paint and sculpt—finding hope and community in shared creative activities.

In 1992, a vivid image of police brutality in Los Angeles played repeatedly on TV screens across the country, fanning coals of resentment which burst into flaming riots following a court decision. When public and private groups moved in to try to contain psychological damage, art therapy was one of many modalities used to help (Riley & Malchiodi, p. 233; AT, 1992, p. 139). Because it was so effective, the local art therapy association was asked by the city to write a **Guide** for artists and teachers who volunteered their services (CATT, p. 429). Designed to help those offering art to do so safely, the guide is useful for any art therapist consulting to those with no clinical background who are providing art experiences to vulnerable individuals.

People & Families in Crisis

The inevitably disorganizing effects of family disruptions like **divorce, separation, custody battles, stepparents**, and "**blended families**" have brought many children and adults to clinicians for treatment. Art therapy has been helpful not only with individual clients, but also with families, since even when people are not speaking to each other they can still draw.

During the process of **divorce,** art therapy can help couples to communicate, and is also useful in **custody evaluation** (Landgarten, 1987). **Family art therapy**, (including **multiple family art therapy**) has helped **single-parent households** (Landgarten, 1981; Brook in Linesch); as well as the "**parentified grandparents**" who often bear the burden (Riley & Malchiodi).

Art therapy has also been used in the most recent attempt to stem the tide of family breakdown—"**family preservation**." One such program, "**Parents &**

Figure 10–21 Drawing by a child who witnessed riots.

Children Together,'' was an outgrowth of one of the most original efforts to bring the benefits of art therapy to a wider community: ''**Free Arts for Abused Children**.'' Started in 1977 by Los Angeles art therapist Elda Ungar, it was a program in which artist volunteers were taught by art therapists to offer art to vulnerable individuals. By 1993, over 750 volunteer artists were reaching 1,500 children weekly in 75 residential care facilities; and the program had expanded to Phoenix, AZ (CATT, p. 411).

When families fracture, some children end up in **foster homes**. Art therapy has been used to help these dislocated youngsters deal with their inevitable ambivalence (AJAT, 1978, p. 39), and the ''fragile attachments'' to which they cling (AP, 1992, p. 433). These "rejected" children, who have been neglected, deprived, and sometimes literally abandoned; can articulate the mixed-up feelings they can't put into words through art (WCAT, p. 131). Art therapy can also serve their practical needs; like the tasks one art therapist designed to teach life skills to adolescents in a youth shelter who were leaving the foster care system (AT, 1997, p. 44).

In 1990 Cathy Malchiodi published *Breaking the Silence: Art Therapy with Children from Violent Homes.* I once treated a child who had witnessed a terrible sight: watching her mother shoot and kill her younger brother.

Art Therapy Helps a Girl with PTSD: **Jackie** (7)

Jackie suffered from nightmares and intrusive waking imagery. She was also miserable when awake, because her grumpy behavior with both adults and peers left her feeling very lonely. She had gone for play therapy for almost a year, with no change in her symptoms. Her child care worker, who had attended an art therapy workshop, finally decided to drive a fairly long distance, in order to see if art therapy might help.

At age five, Jackie had watched her mother shoot and kill her younger brother. Like most children with abusive parents, Jackie could not safely know or acknowledge anger at her mother. She was afraid of losing what little good feeling she clung to on her infrequent visits to the jail. But she could safely direct her rage at me (as the mother in the transference) in "ugly" drawings of "Dr. Rubin's Face" (Fig. 10–22).

For several weeks, she put signs on my office door, warning other children not to believe what I said, and—projecting her own envy and neediness on to me—accusing me of being "a beggar." Thus, using art, she was able to work through her confused feelings about herself and others. Jackie eventually integrated good and bad images of both of us, and was able to leave therapy with a warm attachment.

Family art therapy can also be helpful to people of all ages suffering from "domestic violence" (Riley & Malchiodi, p. 179). Battered women, a long-silent group, are finally beginning to speak up and to be treated (*Advances*, p. 92). Sometimes they end up leaving abusive situations, and may be able to move "from entrapment to empowerment" through art therapy (CATT, p. 189).

When people flee trouble at home, they sometimes end up in shelters. Art therapy, so adaptable, portable, and allowing instant expression, is finding its way into many such new and challenging settings. For a person whose life is in chaos, art can provide order. For someone in a state of impermanence, art can supply something durable. So it is not surpising that people are receiving individual and group art therapy in places like soup kitchens (Liebmann, 1996), transitional "bridge" housing programs (AT, 1990, p. 55), and shelters for the homeless (AT, 1997, p. 118).

Some of the newer settings for clinical work with people in crisis, like halfway houses and homeless shelters, are the result of changes in the psychiatric hospitals where art therapy began. With the closing of many state hospitals and

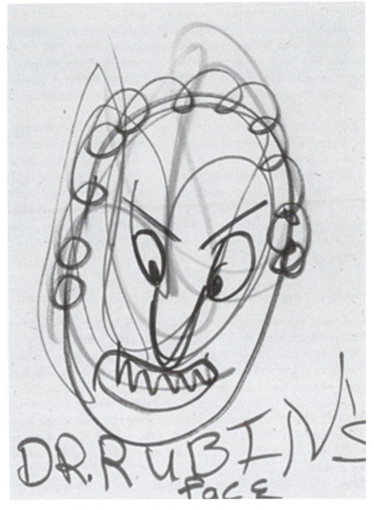

Figure 10–22 Ugly Drawing of "Dr. Rubin's Face" by Jackie.

shortened stays in others, patients with chronic mental illness and developmental disabilities have moved into the community, opening new doors for art therapists. Art therapists themselves have also created new doors, such as the **open studios** which have been developed in a number of urban neighborhoods (AT, 1995, 12(3)).

Displaced Persons

Like the runaway adolescents in one shelter who sorted out who they were by making masks (CATT, p. 27), people who are dislocated are confused about their identity. Being "a stranger in a strange land" is hard, even if the person has left a dangerous situation. The German children who fled to Czechoslovakia in the late thirties were fortunate to have been able to create with art therapist Edith Kramer. Five adult refugees were lucky to make art for two hours a week with Henry Schaeffer-Simmern (1939–1942). "The unfolding of [their] artistic activity" under his guidance probably increased their self-confidence, as they adjusted to life in a new country.

Art therapy itself has been used with many immigrants, because art is a truly universal language. For example, migrant women and their children worked together in art as a way to be closer (1979 Conf., p. 32). Art therapists have helped refugees with "acculturation problems" who were Hispanic (AT, 1986, p. 122), and those who had come from many different places, such as the West Indies (AT, 1995, p. 129; *Advances*, p. 43), Cambodia (*Advances*, p. 5), or Central America (Linesch, 1993, p. 128). And a British art therapist wrote a fine chapter on "art therapy in a multi-cultural school" (WCAT, p. 161) (Cf. also Dokter, 1998, 1999).

Economically Disadvantaged Individuals

Another group of people who are at risk for social and emotional disorder are those who are poor, whose stress is chronic. The artist's role as a social change agent is not really new. In 1931, a British artist named Jeannie McConnell Cannon volunteered to work with unemployed miners and steelworkers in the most depressed area she could find—South Wales. Her modest account in the *Bulletin* (1964, p. 43) is a delight to read, and a fine precursor for later efforts. As noted in Chapter 3, some artists taught in hospitals during the Depression under the Federal Arts Project of the WPA. Others worked on community arts projects; like painting wall murals in poor neighborhoods, or teaching art to unemployed youth.

The sixties and the seventies were another period of social activism in America. At the Pittsburgh Child Guidance Center, half of my job involved work in the community, with children and families who were at increased risk for psychological problems, i.e., "secondary prevention." In addition to developing art programs in schools for those with disabilities, we also worked in poor neighborhoods.

At PCGC, the head of Social Group Work in 1969 was a woman named Mattie Addis. A member of our expressive arts study group, Mattie invited Ellie Irwin and me to participate in her work in poor neighborhoods; so we conducted **art** and **drama therapy groups** with girls in their **schools** and in a summer **day camp**. For the next few summers, I coordinated creative arts programs in two "model cities" (i.e., poor) neighborhoods. The children and their parents who came and participated in the arts activities enhanced both self-image and neighborhood pride.

These programs were documented in *"Children and the Arts: A Film About Growing,"* designed to convey the mental health values of the arts for all children. Like an earlier film about the creative abilities of multiply-handicapped blind children—*"We'll Show You What We're Gonna Do!"*—it was a form of public education—another aspect of prevention (see Audio-Visual Materials section in Resources).

These brief but earnest efforts used art activities to allay social and psychological distress. Increasing unrest and crime in America are leading to a renewal of neighborhood arts projects. One art therapist used film, photography, and art with ghetto adolescents in diverse settings, which included not only schools, but also a gang clubhouse (Robbins, 1994). Like basketball, art is a healthy way to get kids off the streets, and away from the drugs and crime so rampant in poor neighborhoods. When offered by trained art therapists, it can lead to the kind of internal growth which fortifies people against such temptations.

ART THERAPY IN CORRECTIONAL INSTITUTIONS

Unfortunately, many of those who have suffered poverty or abuse do not get help. Some end up committing crimes for which they are usually not treated, but punished. Yet the only way to break what can become a vicious cycle is to make the period of incarceration one of rehabilitation. Art in prison is a constructive way to fill time. When it is provided by a clinically sophisticated art therapist, it is also a form of treatment. Most inmates will not cure themselves through creativity, like the man whose success with needlepoint pictures was described in Chapter 9. But some offenders can be helped to rebuild their lives through art therapy, which is becoming increasingly available in correctional institutions.

Delinquents and criminals, while often suspicious, are also troubled individuals who are hungry for interest and attention. I remember making visits to the Allegheny County Jail in the early seventies. I was pleasantly surprised by the inmates' enthusiastic response to the opportunity to paint, draw, and model with clay. A few years later I received a letter from a man in a N.Y. State prison, begging me to write his superintendent. He had discovered a love of oil painting, but was not being permitted to pursue it. I wrote, assuring the superintendent that, far from being a waste of time, making art could be highly therapeutic, and encouraged him to hire an art therapist. As in other areas, there were earlier precursors.

From 1940 to 1942, for example, Schaeffer-Simmern taught art to **delinquents** at the N.Y.C. **Reformatory** (Cf. also Grant, 1958); and in 1965 two **prison art programs** were described in the *Bulletin* (p. 21). From 1963 to 1965, Tarmo Pasto, a psychologist with an interest in art, had an NIMH grant to study the usefulness of art therapy in California institutions—including the Departments of **Corrections** and **Youth Authority**. Donald Uhlin, an art therapist who worked with Pasto, used **projective drawings to evaluate defendants** for the criminal justice system. Bette Levy published her work at a **women's correctional facility** (AP, 1978, p. 157). At the 1979 Conference, a number of presentations reflected the growing use of art therapy with such groups, like a panel on art therapy with **delinquent youth,** and a paper on art therapy with **prisoners in solitary confinement** (Cf. also AP, 1979, p. 95).

Although "**making art in a jail setting**" (*Advances*, p. 126) has been rare in the U.S., it is a growing area of service. There are all sorts of criminal art therapy clients—like the **abusive men** treated by Connie Naitove (AP, 1988, p. 151); or the **mother who killed her child,** treated by Rose Marano Geiser (AT, 1990, p. 86)—whose exploration of art therapy in prisons began when she was a graduate student (Wadeson, 1987, p. 211). Art therapy in a **probation camp** for **adolescent offenders** was also described in CATT (p. 51).

While we in the U.S. have been rather slow to penetrate the walls of correctional institutions, those in the U.K. seem to have been more effective. Joyce Laing did art therapy for years in an **experimental unit in a prison** (Dalley, 1984; Laing & Carrell). Marian Liebmann, who had contributed chapters on the topic to two earlier books, in 1994 edited *Art Therapy with Offenders*. Some of the chapters in her *Arts Approaches to Conflict* also describe work in correctional settings. The first American book devoted to the topic is *Drawing Time: Art Therapy in Prisons & Forensic Settings*, edited by David Gussak and Evelyn Virshup.

ART AS THERAPY FOR WELLNESS

Art as Therapy in Everyday Life

From the cave man to the Sunday painter, normal people in ordinary settings have been making art as a form of self-therapy. Sometimes it's to unwind or to relax, as a way of dealing with the stresses of everyday life. Sometimes it's to cope with a trauma—an event which is too much for the ego to assimilate. The very fact that creative activity is therapeutic is one reason for the existence and the effectiveness of art therapy.

Making art available to more people in a way that allows them to honestly express themselves is good medicine, like taking vitamins or getting regular checkups—a form of "primary prevention." When I was the "art lady" on "Mister Rogers' Neighborhood," a public television program for young children (1966–1969), my goal was to demonstrate the value of art expression for self-esteem, self-definition, and dealing with feelings. In Los Angeles, Evelyn Virshup hosted a regular TV program on art therapy.

Art as Therapy for Children & Families

Public and professional education can take many forms. For example, for many years I contributed a child's drawing for the cover of a journal for preschool educators, along with a written commentary. The goal was to teach these professionals about the therapeutic values of art in the classroom. Two of the chapters in *Child Art Therapy* are "Helping the Normal Child Through Art" and "Helping Parents Through Art and Play." When I worked at the Pittsburgh Child Guidance Center (PCGC) from 1969 to 1980, half of my job was in **Community Services**.

This involved not only work with children and families who were at risk, but also work with **normal teachers, parents, and children**. This included things like teaching **courses in the therapeutic value of art** to art and classroom teachers, other caregivers, and interested parents. We also trained professionals from different disciplines to run "**Art Awareness**" groups for **adolescents** and "**Parent Play**" groups for **adults,** offering follow-up consultation as well. The following vignette is from a preschool that was attuned to children's expression of feelings through art, due to mental health consultation.

Art as Therapy in a Preschool: **Sammy** (5)

Sammy's mother had just come home from the hospital with a new baby sister. She was the first girl in the family, and everybody was making a big fuss about her. Sammy did too . . . he helped with the diapers, kissed the baby, and told all the friends and relatives how much he loved his new sister. But Sammy was also jealous. His mom used to have much more time for him before the baby came, and now she was always busy or tired.

So one day at his preschool he drew a picture of a bird diving down toward a nest (Fig. 10–23). And he told his teacher the story: "That big

Figure 10–23 "A Bird's Gonna Knock Another One Off the Nest."

Figure 10–24   Endless Easel: Three Rivers Arts Festival.

boy bird's gonna knock that other one off the nest! There ain't no room for two!" Sammy could not get rid of his sister in reality, nor would he want to most of the time. But he could express that wish with symbolic disguise in a drawing, free of guilt or anxiety. Because his teacher had been taught that, if "scary mad wishes" are accepted with understanding, children are less likely to act them out; she could empathize with his drawing.

On a larger scale, Pittsburgh has an annual citywide arts festival where people of all ages come to look at art and watch performances. Since 1973, there has also been a place where children and families can create art themselves—the **Family Creative Arts Center**, started by Community Services of PCGC (Fig. 10–24). Being part of this department allowed me to spread the word about the therapeutic benefits of art to many settings, like preschools, community centers, and churches.

There were **art groups for parents**, where they created with media and, through their own experience and discussion, understood the value of art for their children. There were **mother-child** and **family art sessions**—where the activity with the children was followed by discussion groups for the adults, so they could reflect on and learn from the joint experience. There were a variety of **pilot programs in schools**; including art activities specifically designed to promote self-awareness (**"Art-Awareness"**); and the **making of animated films**—which tended to be about normal concerns and fears that kids don't often get to talk about.

Consultation to art and other teachers, as well as to school guidance counselors, was another avenue for getting more health-promoting art opportunities into the classroom. Just as medical art therapy serves the primary goal of physical healing; so **School Art Therapy** serves the primary goal of enhancing the child's ability to learn.

Sometimes such art therapy is done with individuals or small groups who are having difficulties. There have always been a few art therapists in schools who have worked with **normal children experiencing temporary stress**, a role pioneered by Edna Salant at the **National Child Research Center** in Washington, D.C. (ATV, p. 280). Janet Bush's program in the Dade County public schools has, since 1979, provided individual and group art therapy to troubled youngsters, as well as staff training for teachers. John Allan of Vancouver did art counseling in schools with individuals and groups, collaborating respectfully with teachers.

Sometimes therapeutic art activities occur in the classroom, like those in Carol Ross's book, *Something to Draw On* (Cf. also Singer; Furrer). There are several fine chapters in WCAT and in Liebmann's book on conflict resolution about art therapy in British schools. A 1997 issue of *Art Therapy* (Vol. 8, No. 2) was also devoted to "Art Therapy in the Schools," a growing trend in public and private settings.

Art as Therapy for Normal Adults

Art can be therapeutic for normal individuals of all ages, not just school children. Sunday painters from Winston Churchill to Judy Collins have found making art to be immensely helpful, especially during periods of stress—like the kind Churchill was under during WWII.

Art classes—taught by clinically sensitive teachers or art therapists—can also be therapeutic, like Schaefer-Simmern's work with "**persons in business and the professions**;" or that of Florence Cane, who released the creativity of many adults in her New York studios. Art therapist Elinor Ulman described the therapeutic value of **art classes** for the normal adults she taught at a museum (*AAUW Journal*, November 1972, p. 19). Art therapist Robert Ault opened an art school after 18 years at Menninger's. In "Art Therapy with the **Unidentified Patient**" (*Advances*, p. 222), he described the therapeutic benefits of learning art for students of all ages.

Creative art activities can also be therapeutic for normal adults when they are used in "**sensitivity**," "**encounter**," or "**human potential**" **groups**, as in Janie Rhyne's early work at Esalen (1973, 1995). "Growth centers," like Omega, offer many workshops using art for self-development.

Art therapists working in a variety of settings have sometimes used their understanding of art and group dynamics for **staff development**. Art exercises can be helpful in looking at both individual and interpersonal dynamics—as applicable to a staff group as to a family. Such workshops help employees to function more effectively in the work place, since art is a dramatic tool for clarifying interpersonal issues. Robert Ault, who did this kind of work through the Menninger Foundation, has continued it as a **business consultant** (AT, 1988, p. 12; 1983 & 1997 AATA Confs.).

Another possible role for an art therapist in the business world is in **Employee Assistance Programs** (**EAPs**) (AT, 1986, p. 21). As in other nonpsychiatric settings—like medical hospitals or schools—art therapy is an efficient tool for the "screening" which is a major part of the job of an EAP counselor.

CONCLUDING THOUGHTS

Art therapy, then, is extremely useful in both primary and secondary prevention—not only in treating people who have ended up in psychiatric settings. As mental hospitals close ("deinstitutionalization") and patients with chronic disorders go elsewhere—like group homes and recreation or rehabilitation programs—art therapy is often an available source of support and growth. If such people get lost in the shuffle, they may end up in shelters or even prisons, where they may also be helped by art therapy.

People in all kinds of crises—personal, medical, social, economic—can be helped to master them through art therapy. And normal people of all ages dealing with the ups and downs of everyday life, can be helped to cope and to grow through the therapeutic use of art. Making art provides practice in creative problem-solving, useful in all aspects of living. It also helps people to articulate a clearer sense of themselves, through their own unique creations. These preventive roles for art therapy have led to an expansion of the field, well beyond its original role in mental hospitals and clinics. Art therapists are therefore finding themselves in new places, sometimes with new people and purposes as well (Cf. Sandle).

Art therapists in different places work at different tempos, depending on the nature of the setting. Art therapists also enter people's lives at different points in the process of growing or coping with stress. Sometimes the art therapist's involvement with those she serves is brief, as in a shelter or an emergency room. Sometimes the art therapist's involvement is sustained, as in a prison or a school. Whether short or long, and whether the tempo is rapid or slow; art therapy can facilitate screening, coping, working through, healing, and even dying.

Chapter 11

Accountability

Standards
Evaluation
Research
Ethics

EVOLUTION OF STANDARDS

It may come as a surprise to some that the desirability of a national art therapy association in America was hotly debated before it was formed, and that the debates were due primarily to concerns about excellence. The pioneers whose writings had given birth to the profession in the U.S. were scholarly individuals with high standards. They feared that their devotion to quality might be weakened, and the worth of their creation cheapened. An organization in 1969 included people with widely varying backgrounds in art and therapy, and equally varied ideas about qualifications.

Nevertheless, art therapy has benefitted greatly from AATA's birth. Only a national professional association could define and enforce standards for individuals, for training programs, and for practice. As a result, art therapy has come of age as a responsible profession, respected by other disciplines and by the public. That would not have happened without defining excellence in all these areas, as well as creating mechanisms for measuring and certifying its presence.

Standards for Registration

There were heated disputes at the first meeting of AATA about the desirability of any codified standards. Pioneer art therapists, all of whom had creatively defined their own work, feared that specific requirements for practitioners might choke the growth of the new field. In a very close vote, the decision was made to define some people as "Registered," in order to begin to differentiate those who were qualified from from those who were not. "**Registered Art Therapist**" was and still is designated by the initials **ATR**. As is usual when a profession establishes a credential, a "**grandfather clause**" was adopted for those with five years of experience.

This passionate group of people had banded together, despite their individual and collective anxieties about organizing a field based on the creative process. One of their first and most difficult tasks, after agreeing to have credentialling, was to articulate standards for what they were doing. They eventually came up with an inventive solution to the problem of specifying **Criteria for Registration**. It was quite a challenge to define competence in a discipline with hardly any formal training and widely different kinds of preparation among practitioners. Then, the field of art therapy was composed of people who had wandered into its pastures on the way **from** or **to** somewhere else, like art, education, or mental health.

Although masters' level training or its equivalent is now the norm, that was not the case in 1970. The solution to the problem of setting fair and flexible standards was solved by Sandra (Kagin) Graves, a member of the first AATA Board, and Director of one of the earliest art therapy training programs. She came up with the notion of what she later fondly called "pukies" (**PQCs**) or "**Professional Quality Credits**." In this system, **points** could be earned for a wide **variety** of preparatory learning experiences, including apprenticeships, academic courses, even original contributions. A minimum of **1,000 hours of supervised work** was the only non-negotiable requirement. Each applicant had to demonstrate that her experiences qualified her for a total of 12 PQCs, which would enable her to be a Registered Art Therapist (ATR).

Over time, the **Criteria for Registration** have been modified, due to the increased availability of formal education in art therapy, and the decision that the masters' degree be the entry level for the profession. **Registration**, originally handled by the **Standards Committee** of AATA, is now administered by a separate entity, the **Art Therapy Credentials Board** (**ATCB**). A combination of masters' level education and supervised clinical experience is currently required to become an **ATR**, a credential held by more than half of AATA members.

Standards for Board Certification

In 1994, also after much debate, a written **Certification Examination** was developed, designed to identify a higher level of proficiency than the entry level of registration. Passing this exam entitles the art therapist to identify herself as **Board Certified** (**BC**). Since Registration is a prerequisite for taking the examination, art therapists at this level are identified as **ATR-BC**. In order to **maintain** Board Certification, each individual is required to accumulate 100 **Continuing Education Credits** (CECs) every five years.

Credentialling mechanisms in all human service professions—like psychology, psychiatry, social work, teaching, or nursing—exist primarily to protect the public from incompetent practitioners. Like **Licensing**, already available to art therapists in some states, both **Registration** and **Certification** are ways of identifying legitimacy—not for art therapists—but for those who pay for and receive their services.

Standards for Educational Programs

A quandary similar to the one about registration standards faced early AATA Boards as they tried to establish **criteria for educational programs**. Wishing to preserve the wide variety of orientations in art therapy, and wanting program standards to be at least as flexible as those for Registration, AATA published *Guidelines for Academic, Institute & Clinical Art Therapy Training*, revised as *Education Standards* in 1994.

The document includes requirements for academic, insititutional, and clinical training programs, and combines firmness with flexibility. This is true because it is clear about the fundamental courses and clinical work essential to learning art therapy, but allows for a wide variety of interpretations on the part of specific training programs. AATA also distributes "*Recommendations for Undergraduate Programs*," which provides guidance for programs at the bachelors' level.

The **Educational Program Approval Board (EPAB)**, developed by AATA in 1978, was originally called the **Education & Training Board (ETB)**. Its task is to assess the quality of educational programs, to designate those qualifying for "**Approval**," and to periodically review approved programs. As of November, 1996, over half of the eligible graduate programs on the AATA **Education List** met the criteria for Approval. Students graduating from an approved program are required to have 1,000 post-graduate hours of supervised clinical work in order to be eligible for registration. Those graduating from programs which have not been approved are required to accumulate 2,000 hours of supervised work.

Standards for Practice & Treatment Programs

Most professions establish standards for practitioners, including those already credentialled. In 1989 the Clinical Committee of AATA published the *General Standards of Practice*. This document articulates clear guidelines for providers and for programs. It spells out in considerable detail standards for conducting responsible art therapy at all steps of the process: referral, acceptance, assessment, program planning, documentation, and termination of services. It also outlines standards for accountability and for the working environment.

Health care settings are accredited by **JCAHO**, the **Joint Commision for Accreditation of Healthcare Organizations**. In order to help art therapists prepare for periodic site visits, AATA published a *Continuous Quality Improvement Manual* in 1994, edited by Paula Howie and Kathy Gutierrez. The manual includes many examples of ways to monitor and to assess art therapy programs. Contributed by art therapists from places around the country, they are relevant for many different settings.

In 1985 AATA published a "position paper" on *Art Therapy in the Schools*, following up in 1986 with a *Resource Packet* for school art therapists. The association is currently editing *Standards of Practice for School Art Therapists*, to further assist those working in this area. Janet Bush's *Handbook of School Art Therapy* (1997) also contains useful guidelines for setting goals, for planning, and for evaluating various art therapy interventions. In addition, she has included a number of forms developed for schools, which can be used or modified as needed.

Standards for Ethical Conduct

Although policing one another is an unpleasant duty, it is also a necessary one. AATA's **Committee on Ethics & Professional Practice** (originally the **Peer Standards Review Board**) revised its *Code of Ethics* in 1995, "*Ethical Standards for Art Therapists.*" Like assessing competence and reviewing the quality of training programs, maintaining ethical standards is the responsibility of a mature professional organization.

In human beings, the **Superego** or **Conscience** is the part of the personality that typically feels guilt. It is also the part that invokes or seeks punishment for thoughts or actions perceived as "bad." Happily, there is another part of the superego known as the **Ego Ideal**, which establishes goals, aspirations, and approval for thoughts or actions seen as "good." If the **Superego** is the part that spanks (punishes) people, the Ego Ideal would be the part that applauds (rewards) people.

In **AATA**, rewards are given by the **Honors Committee**, which awards the **Honorary Life Membership (HLM)** to art therapists who have made significant contributions to the profession. The **Distinguished Service Award (DSA)** is given to individuals who have done especially important work for the Association. The **Clinician Award** is given to those who have done outstanding clinical work in some specialty.

Awards carrying a modest stipend are given to the author of the best **Research** proposal and the winner of the "Elinor Ulman Prize for Excellence in Writing." There are also a number of **Scholarship** funds and a variety of **Special Awards**.

SELECTING ART THERAPY

When I was first invited to start a pilot program at the Pittsburgh Child Guidance Center, my supervisor, Dr. Shapiro, asked me to find out how to select patients for art therapy. In March of 1969, I went to New York with a list of questions for all of the experienced art therapists I interviewed. These included psychologist supporters of the field, like Ernest Harms and Ionel Rapaport, who promoted art for the retarded. They also included pioneer art therapists, like Edith Zierer, Edith Kramer, and Margaret Naumburg. All of them agreed that the question of the "treatment of choice" was a complicated one about which very little was known, especially in regard to the new discipline of art therapy.

One suggestion was to do an **art interview** as part of the intake for everyone, and see how they responded. Another suggestion was to ask clients whether or not they would like to have art therapy. Although **self-selection** was never tried, such an approach has worked well in a variety of settings. In that sense, we seem to have come full circle. The beginnings of art therapy stemmed in part from **spontaneous** art by the mentally ill, certainly a self-selection process. And in the early days of the field, some artist-therapists travelled the wards, offering art supplies and assistance to whoever was interested—like Adrian Hill in England or Prentiss Taylor at St. Elizabeth's Hospital in the United States.

Sometimes there was an "**open studio**" in a psychiatric hospital, where patients could come and use art materials on a **voluntary** basis, like Edward Adamson's at Netherne or Mary Huntoon's at Menninger's. Although contemporary art therapists work in settings where people are generally **referred** for treatment, it is also common to offer "**open groups**" as well, especially in long-term settings. People in private practice often get clients who have decided to come, specifically because they want to be treated by an art therapist.

But that reminds us of a larger question: Since resources of people and money are limited, why use art therapy as opposed to some other kind of intervention? And how can we evaluate whether or not our efforts to help through art have been effective?

EVALUATING ART THERAPY

All service professions are increasingly being asked to account for the effectiveness of what they do. When budgets need to be cut, whether in society, education, or health care; both **art** and **mental health** are often viewed as "frills" or "luxuries." As noted earlier, the consistent growth of the relatively new field of art therapy, despite the cutbacks of recent years, is an indirect index of its remarkable power.

Qualitative Evidence

Although quantifiable success in outcome studies would indeed be a strong argument for support, it appears that art therapy is funded as often because of qualitative effects at a more intimate human level. Reading the testimony offered at the Senate Hearings on the "**Older Americans Act**," I suspect it was the eloquent words and stunning pictures of Elizabeth "Grandma" Layton, who described drawing her way out of a lifelong depression at 68, that moved the lawmakers as much as any of the more rational arguments (Fig. 11–1; Cf. also Fig. 9–10). A genuine smile on the face of a previously withdrawn person can often be infinitely more persuasive than any statistics, no matter how stunning (Fig. 11–2).

Perhaps the most convincing evaluation of any therapy is whether or not people feel they were helped. If they do, they are likely to refer others, as well as to come back in the future for further assistance. Most of my own referrals during 25 years of private practice came from what might, for want of a better term, be called "**satisfied customers**."

Figure 11–1 Elizabeth "Grandma" Layton doing a drawing.

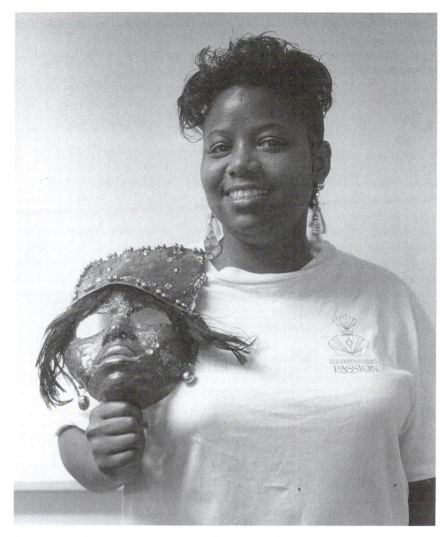

Figure 11–2 A woman is proud of her self-image mask.

In November of 1995 *Consumer Reports* published an article entitled "**Does Therapy Help?**" It confirmed what clinicians have known for a long time and have been unable to prove, since our assessment of our own effectiveness is naturally seen as biased. But those who come for help, and who complain as much as they applaud, told a clear and positive tale:

> "*The results of a candid, in-depth survey of 4,000 subscribers—the largest survey ever to query people on mental health care—provides convincing evidence that therapy can make an important difference.*" (p. 734)

Equally important, the survey found that *"the **longer** people stayed in therapy, the **more they improved**"* (p.734). In a professional periodical, Dr. Martin Seligman, consultant to the *Consumer Reports* study, argued that the findings were comparable to those of conventional outcome research.

Hopefully, by the time the next such large-scale survey is published, art therapy will be listed along with more established professions (psychiatry, psychology, social work, psychiatric nursing, and family therapy).

Quantitative Evidence

Demonstrating the effectiveness of art therapy through tightly constructed research designs, however, has not been easy to do. This problem has plagued all clinical outcome studies because of the huge number of critical, uncontrollable, and perhaps unquantifiable variables involved in measuring change in human beings. It has been argued that well-designed investigations, which would unequivocally demonstrate art therapy's ability to positively affect its recipients, are desperately needed in order to get those in power to pay its providers for their services. The few outcome studies available have shown positive results, but most have also had undeniable weaknesses (AP, 1997, p. 375), as is true in the following vignette of an early outcome study.

Assessing Change After Group Art Therapy

In an exploratory art program with thirteen multiply-handicapped youngsters at the Western Pennsylvania School for Blind Children in 1970, the children were first interviewed individually in order to be able to group them most effectively (Fig. 11–3). Because of their disabilities, they were offered a wide range of sensory stimuli (Fig. 11–4), as well as a choice of art materials.

Two **observers** using a **24–item, nine-point rating scale** were asked to note where each child was on each **behavioral dimension**. Some items were descriptive of overall behavior, such as passive/active, tense/relaxed, distractible/involved, and depressed/alert. Others referred to the children's interaction with the therapist, like dependent/independent, suspicious/trusting, and withdrawn/outgoing. Some related to their use of the art materials, such as awkward/coordinated, impulsive/deliberate, stereotyped/original; or to their attitude toward their work, like critical/pleased. Yet others were about the nature of their creative process, e.g., barren/fluent, rigid/flexible. An average of the two observers' ratings on each dimension was used. They agreed almost 90% of the time.

After seven weeks of group art sessions, we repeated the individual interviews with each child, again using the mean of two observers' ratings on each dimension (Fig. 11–5, p. 309). The differences between the pre- and post-program scores were all in the desired direction. They were **statistically significant** (beyond chance expectation) on the following five dimensions: **Relaxation, Involvement, Independence, Originality,**

Figure 11-3 A blind girl during a pre-program assessment.

and **Flexibility**. These objective assessments confirmed our subjective sense of individual and group gains. Jimmy, for example, who had been so shy and lacking in self-confidence that at first he declined art altogether, had become comfortable with drawing and—more important—proud of his work (Fig. 11–6, p. 310).

ART THERAPY RESEARCH

The idea of "research" has never been particularly congenial to artists, whether they are painters, teachers, or therapists. It seems antithetical to the intuitive, spontaneous nature of art itself. Nevertheless, art therapists interested in research continue to strive to evaluate their work as well as possible in this admittedly complicated area (Cf. AT, 1998, 15(1)).

Most early studies in art therapy were done by people who worked in settings where a lot of research was going on, like Hanna Kwiatkowska and Harriet Wadeson at NIMH, or myself at PCGC. Some were done by those trained in other disciplines to conduct objective investigations, like psychologists Bernard Levy, Mala Betensky, and Janie Rhyne; and art educators Rawley Silver, Donald Uhlin, and Frances Anderson.

Figure 11–4   A partially-sighted boy examining texture: Pre-program assessment.

The next generation of art therapy researchers seems to be much more sophisticated in their understanding of research methodology. I expect that people like Linda Gantt, Marcia Rosal, Anne Mills, Deborah Linesch, and Trudy Manning will be able to do a far better job of assessing the effectiveness of art therapy intervention. The few studies done so far tend to indicate art therapy's success, but also serve to remind us of the terrific complexity of measuring change (Cf. AT, 1997, pp. 23, 30).

Despite the discomfort of many art therapists with the idea of research—apparent in a survey of research approaches in various training programs (AT, 1992, p. 129)—in 1992 AATA published *A Guide to Conducting Art Therapy Research*, edited by Harriet Wadeson. With contributions by many, the book is a useful introduction to the area.

Significantly, the AATA book includes no fewer than six chapters on some **methodological challenges specific to art therapy**. Because of the limitations of experimental psychology's "scientific method" for this kind of work, art therapy researchers on both sides of the Atlantic have been attracted to **models of inquiry from other disciplines**. In addition to psychology and psychiatry, art therapists have been drawn to such diverse viewpoints as: philosophy, aesthetics, art history, archeology, linguistics, hermeneutics, anthropology, ethnography, sociology, and ethology. Shaun McNiff's new book, *Art-Based Research*, offers many stimulating ideas and proposals.

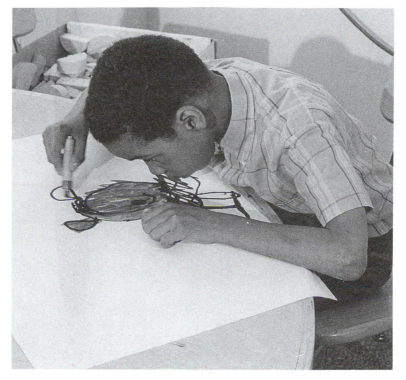

Figure 11–5 A partially-sighted boy: Post-program evaluation.

Our British colleagues, equally uncertain about quantifying the creative process, have recently published two edited collections of research. There are two chapters by art therapists in the *Handbook of Inquiry in the Arts Therapies* (Payne, 1994) and seven in *Art & Music: Therapy & Research* (Gilroy & Lee, 1995). Both books contain stimulating discussions of general issues, as well as some fascinating studies—like the one written by an art therapist with her patients: a "collaborative inquiry in process work, art therapy, and acute states" (Payne). Another, on "making sense of marking space" (Gilroy & Lee, p. 117), describes a unique approach to "researching art therapy with people who have severe learning disabilities."

In a chapter on "research in art therapy with people who have psychotic illnesses," the authors make the suggestion that such studies should lead to "a model for effective art therapy practice with psychotic patients" (Gilroy & Lee, p.101). In other words, research is most relevant when it helps us to be able to modify and improve what we do. From Donald Uhlin's studies of neurologically handicapped children (1972), for example, I learned that drawing with white chalk or crayon on black paper helps a child to work at a higher developmental level. From Claire Golomb's research (1974), a similarly useful finding: that

Figure 11–6   A Partially-Sighted Boy is Proud of his Art.

when the parts of a human figure are dictated aloud, a young child's drawing is
more integrated than when it is requested in a global fashion—i.e., when the
child is simply asked to "Draw a Person."

The Art Product in Evaluation

There are many ways of assessing the effectiveness of work in art therapy, both
directly and indirectly. One that is unique involves the art product—which is
available for reflection or measurement, like a taped or transcribed verbal interview. It is possible to evaluate single products, a sequence of work from a
session, art done during some period of time, or art produced over the entire
course of therapy.

The art can be evaluated by the therapist alone or with the patient. For more
objectivity, someone not involved in the process can assess the product(s). The
art can be looked at in a global, phenomenological way. It is also possible to
assess broadly descriptive areas like subject matter or style, using some sort of
rating manual and scale. Finally, the art can be assessed by measuring such

quantifiable variables as: details, placement, composition, color usage, or specific content items.

The Art Process in Evaluation

Unlike verbal psychotherapy, which is often studied through analyses of audiotapes or transcriptions of what is said; art therapy involves not only the product, but also the dynamically significant creative process. This can be studied "live" by having observers behind a one-way mirror or in the art therapy space, as in the pilot study at the School for Blind Children earlier in this chapter. It can also be viewed and re-viewed through videotaped recordings, which can capture the much greater amount of movement and action involved in art (vs. verbal) therapy.

Like analyses of the art, observational possibilities range from global judgments to the identification of specific behaviors. As with products, investigations which aim at quantification usually involve rating scales of some sort. Whether the researchers are measuring what they say they are (validity), and whether the scale is dependable (reliable), are questions of concern to anyone aiming at objectivity. Many art therapists, stimulated by the demand for accountability, are working creatively at developing reliable and valid modes of assessment, some of which are noted in Chapter 7.

ASSESSMENT IN PLANNING AND EVALUATION

Art therapists, like all responsible clinicians, routinely assess whether what they are doing is working. When the job demands evidence, which is becoming the rule rather than the exception, the art therapist needs to define specific goals and to evaluate progress—in a fashion that can be communicated to the others involved. For example, an art therapist working with disabled children in a school is able to articulate short-term **objectives**, long-term **goals**, ways of achieving them, and ways of measuring them. This is all part of a child's **I.E.P.**, or "**Individualized Education Plan**." Treatment planning, as well as periodic evaluation, is also required in mental health settings, whether they are inpatient, partial, or outpatient. Setting specifically defined objectives, and demonstrating that the art therapy intervention is working, are central to the most recent development in mental health—**managed care**.

Evaluators, who often have the power to approve further art therapy, are most comfortable with **behavioral objectives**, whether they are in developmental, cognitive, emotional, or social domains. Art therapists therefore look at behavior during the creative process, measuring changes in such areas as autonomy, organization, and interaction with others. They also look at indices external to art therapy, like behaviors at home, in school, or at work. Rating scales by self or others are sometimes used, as are objective measures like number of absences or level of performance.

Three of the AATA publications noted above can be especially helpful in this area: The *General Standards of Practice* document provides clear guidelines for assessment, treatment planning, documentation, and evaluation. The *Continuous Quality Improvement Manual* includes model forms and examples for record keeping and evaluation, as does Janet Bush's *Handbook of School Art Therapy*. The other useful resource is the *Guide to Conducting Art Therapy Research* (Wadeson, Ed.), which includes examples of and references to a wide variety of possible assessment tools.

The Ethics of Assessment

As a matter of professional ethics, responsible art therapists continually evaluate their work. Of course, the big question is not so much whether the **art** changed, but whether or not the **person(s)** changed in the way(s) the therapist and the artist(s) had hoped.

There are important issues about **societal norms** regarding **goals**, some of which are especially relevant to art therapists. As artists, we may be more rebellious than conforming, and more isolated than socialized. Yet as therapists who work with colleagues, we have had to find sufficient ways of adapting to survive. Therefore, art therapists may be especially able to help those who are atypical or deviant in finding ways to live with others, while preserving their individuality and authenticity.

Although art therapists may be more open-minded and flexible than some of our colleagues about areas like acceptable fantasy or appropriate behavior, some values about human mental health are common to all workers, regardless of theoretical orientation or technical persuasion.

These include being able to set achievable goals, and feeling good about oneself and one's relationships. Whether the person's disability is temporary or permanent, a generally acceptable objective is to be able to make the most of personal and societal resources. We all wish to free people to fulfill their potential, whatever that may be—to be able to live, love, work, and play to the fullest. All in the helping professions, including art therapists, share a wish that optimism will triumph over pessimism, and that hope will be victorious in the battle with despair.

ETHICS IN ART THERAPY

Being a human service professional, whether in private practice or under an institutional umbrella, requires strict adherence to such principles as maintaining the patient's privacy, and the clarity of both roles and boundaries. Artists, however, have few such concerns. In fact, since they exhibit their work publicly, they actively invite people into their worlds. Nevertheless, it should be possible to expand art therapy's horizons—as in an ''open studio''—without abandoning our responsibility to those we serve.

The fundamental underpinning of any system of ethical conduct is **respect** for those involved. If there is sincere respect for the other, then ethical guidelines flow naturally. This is true whether we are talking about respecting an individual's **artwork, imagery,** or **personal boundaries**. Respect also means not taking advantage in any way of the **power** of the special relationship a clinician has with patients in therapy. This is true for all who are in a position of power over others, including supervisors, teachers, doctors, clergy, friends, and parents.

Responsible art therapists are knowledgeable about **legal** and **ethical issues,** especially when they are in **private practice**. A primary concern of those who protect the public through **licensure** is assuring that the professional is accurately representing her qualifications. Even though I, for example, have been licensed to practice as a psychologist in the state of Pennsylvania since 1979, I would not dream of doing things for which I am not trained, like pychological testing, marital therapy, or hypnosis. Admitting that one is floundering is also a matter of ethical responsibility, as is seeking more experienced and objective consultation.

ETHICS AND THE ART CREATED IN ART THERAPY

Provocative Images

There are some ethical concerns which are peculiar to art therapy, such as the issue of what to do about **violent or provocative images** in **group** situations. This has been discussed by Martha Haeseler, who frequently encountered this problem in her work with hospitalized adolescents. In ''Censorship or Intervention: 'But You Said we Could Draw Whatever we Wanted!''' (AJAT, 1987, p. 11), she described a range of possible interventions based on the meaning of the imagery for that particular milieu, as well as the probable impact of its display. Several years later, she offered an equally thoughtful discussion of the particular ethical concerns of the **art groups** which are part of most graduate training programs (AJAT, 1992, p. 21).

Ownership and Storage

Although **institutions** sometimes view patient art as a part of the clinical or educational ''**record,**'' most art therapists feel that the art ultimately **belongs to the artist**. Many of us encourage patients to **store** art work in the therapy space if at all possible during treatment, since it offers a marvellous opportunity to reflect on the progress of the therapy. While potentially useful at any point in time, such a visual review is especially worthwhile as part of the termination process.

Confidentiality

Because patient art can not only be displayed in its original state, but can also be reproduced as photographs or slides, guidelines have been developed for this delicate area of confidentiality. In addition to **model consent and release forms** regarding the art, **AATA** has a section in its code of ethics dealing specifically with the "**public use and reproduction of patient art expression and therapy sessions.**" This has been an area of concern to many art therapists over the years, and was the subject of a thoughtful paper by Laurie Wilson (AJAT, 1987, p. 75).

Exhibitions

Martha Haeseler has pointed out the possibility of exploiting patients, especially with the current popularity of "**outsider art**" (AJAT, 1988, p. 83). In an article on "exhibiting art by those with mental illness," Susan Spaniol reviewed the subject (AT, 1990, p. 70). Concerned about the possible use of artwork without explicit consent, she proposed a new **agreement form** as a more respectful way of writing about and displaying client art (AJAT, 1994, p. 69). Spaniol also published a **Manual** on organizing such shows, which was favorably reviewed by Mickie McGraw, who has organized more than 150 in the 27–year history of "The Art Studio."

Over the years, I have participated in a variety of public activities involving art by patients with mental illness. These events have been in connection with many types of settings, from inpatient units to partial hospitals to museums, and have included competitions and exhibitions for which I have served as a judge. It seems to me that, as with our overall stance in relation to our clients, the notion of **respect** offers an appropriate guiding principle for assessing what is best in each instance.

When it is possible to bring admiration and sometimes income to individuals through their art, exhibiting their products can be a wonderful experience, as long as the artists are in full agreement (Fig. 11–7). It is a bonus beyond the intrinsic pleasures and therapeutic benefit of involvement in creative activity. When we are also able to use such expressions of the human spirit to educate the public and to demystify the myths about mental illness, that seems to me to be a marvellous message for our medium. The key to doing it ethically is respecting the artists whose work is involved.

ETHICS AND CLIENT/THERAPIST DIFFERENCES

Disability Issues

Although respect is essential when doing art therapy with anyone in any setting, it may be more difficult to achieve when the client is radically different in some way that might not be fully grasped by the therapist. The difference might be the particular disease or disability from which the person suffers. David Henley has pointed out ethical considerations, for example, in the use of art for **assessment with those who are physically or mentally handicapped** (AT, 1987, p. 57).

Figure 11-7 Mary Barnes working on a painting.

The **otherness** of the handicapped person's experience is difficult but vital for any therapist to comprehend. It can affect how the individual experiences the world and art as well, both when responding and while creating with materials. Just as it is vital for art therapists to know developmental issues when working with people at different stages of growth; so it is necessary to try to apprehend, as much as possible, the person's different way of being-in-the-world.

For example, Viktor Lowenfeld noticed that some partially-sighted and blind children used their sense of touch and kinesthesis more to "see" the world, whereas others relied more on their limited vision. He named these two types of perception "**haptic**" and "**visual**." In experiments with sighted individuals, he concluded that the two perceptual types were also present in those with vision, to varying degrees. These differences would affect how the worker would motivate and guide the person's art-making. I made a similar discovery while working with blind children, of what I called a "**tactile aesthetic**," which turned out to be different from a visual one . . .

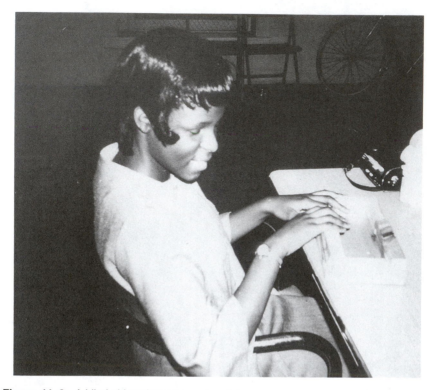

Figure 11–8 A blind girl explores a wood sculpture.

Phenomenological Study of a Tactile Aesthetic

Judges who were blind, partially-sighted, and sighted were asked to choose their most favorite and least-liked object from a group of wood-scrap sculptures—with equal numbers of sculptures made by all three populations. Our **hypothesis** was that the children would **prefer art work done by someone like themselves**; whether they had useful vision (sighted and partially-sighted), or were blind.

We found that art work preferred by visually-impaired (Fig. 11–8) or blindfolded (Fig. 11–9) youngsters differed significantly from what was preferred by children using whatever sight was available to them (Fig. 11–10), and it was confirmed at a **statistically significant** level.

We also found **qualitative** similarities and differences in the judges' verbal and tactile responses to the sculptures, unrelated to their choices. Most of the youngsters liked sculptures with some variety and a sense of order. The visually-impaired tended to label objects as representational, while the sighted were able to be interested in abstract work. The blind children also reacted more strongly to certain structural features—particularly projections, which they disliked; and holes or enclosures, which they liked.

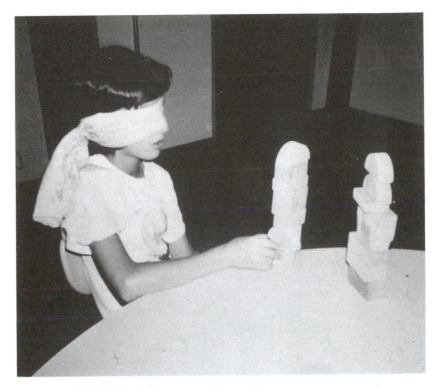

Figure 11-9 A blindfolded girl compares two sculptures.

While the sighted judges tended to be fairly objective in their responses, the blind youngsters were more subjective, often relating things
to themselves, reacting with anxiety to anything perceived as dangerous
or unstable. A girl preferred one sculpture to another, for example, "because it won't get knocked over as easy as this one. Things make me
nervous that can fall over easily." Our work with these blind artists was
enhanced by a better understanding of how their aesthetic responses were
different from our own.

Sometimes the person being helped by the art therapist is not only different
in regard to disability, but in regard to culture as well. The art therapist who
worked with a Native American woman with schizophrenia needed to be aware
of her feelings about both ways in which her patient was unlike her (AJAT,
1981, p. 25). Similarly, the clinicans who used art and storytelling with deaf
Indian men, had to be knowledgeable about both their clients' disability and
their culture (AP, 1992, p. 29).

Multicultural Issues

Just as art therapists monitor their preconceptions about the disabled, so they
are attuned to their attitudes toward the different cultures from which their clients

Figure 11–10 A partially-sighted boy explores a sculpture.

come. Respect for the values and traditions of the other is the key to multicultural sensitivity, including the culture's aesthetic.

Some years ago, a study demonstrated that Hispanic subjects had patterns of emotional response to color that were similar to those of non-Hispanics, but different in that they were consistently more intense (AJAT, 1986, p. 119). A Brazilian art therapist discussed issues specific to working in art with Latino women (AP, 1983, p. 63). And a number of art therapists have described and reflected upon their work with Native Americans (AP, 1993, p. 143; AT, 1994, p. 191; AT, 1995, p. 220). Such considerations are essential when we serve clients whose backgrounds are radically different from our own.

This issue has been of particular concern in the United States, because of the many ethnic backgrounds of the people who live and work here who are sometimes referred for art therapy—and the very small number of mental health professionals who come from the same cultural milieu. While the number of minority art therapists is steadily increasing, there is a tremendous need to raise the consciousness of those art therapists who daily serve Black, Hispanic, Asian, and Native American clients.

Figure 11–11 Georgette Powell teaching in the community.

America, like many societies, has a long history of deep-seated **racial tensions**. One aspect of President Johnson's "Great Society" programs—implicit in Model Cities, Head Start, and Arts for the Poor—was an effort to improve the self-image of Black children. Viktor Lowenfeld, who had escaped Nazi persecution by leaving Austria, taught art for a few years at a Negro college, Hampton Institute. He believed strongly in helping his students to create paintings and sculptures that were **true to their cultural soul**. Their work was so honest and passionate that it was widely exhibited and praised in art journals. Robert Saunders, one of Lowenfeld's students, used his post as Art Consultant for Connecticut to raise consciousness about cultural issues with pamphlets on planning *"An Afro-American Art Program"* (1969) and a *"Curriculum on Puerto Rican Culture"* (1971).

In the beginning, the **American Art Therapy Association** had very few minority members, despite the presence of individuals like Christine Wang (Cf. Fig. 5–3) and Lucille Venture, whose doctoral dissertation was entitled *"The Black Beat in Art Therapy Experiences"* (1977). In 1974 Cliff Joseph (Cf. Fig. 6–10) convened a panel on *"Art Therapy and the Third World,"* which included pioneers like Lemuel Joyner from New York, and Georgette Powell from Washington, founder of one of the first community-based art therapy programs, "Tomorrow's World" (Fig. 11–11).

Figure 11–12 Charles Anderson with an intern at Menninger's.

For many years, Charles Anderson of The Menninger Foundation led what was then known as the **Third World Committee** (Fig. 11–12). The committee sponsored a number of consciousness-raising events, such as a panel on "Cultural Awareness & the Creative Process" at the 1981 Conference, chaired by Sarah McGee. The group has recently been revitalized by the presence of a new generation, like Gwendolyn Short and Anna Hiscox (CATT, p. 117; AT, 1995, p. 129). First renamed the **Mosaic Committee**, it is now called the **Multicultural Committee**. In 1996, the committee further sensitized those at the AATA Conference, whose theme was "**Many Paths: Multicultural Perspectives in Art Therapy.**"

Many art therapists, especially those who have taught in different parts of the world, have discussed cross-cultural considerations (AT, 1984, p. 125; AJAT, 1991, p. 34). A special section of *Art Therapy* on "Art Therapy & Multicultural Issues" had several fine papers on the topic, including addressing it in training (AT, 1994, p. 184). Helen Landgarten's *Magazine Photo Collage* is subtitled *A **Multicultural** Assessment & Treatment Technique*. Like the "Primers" for beginning readers that finally included pictures of people of color as well as whites, the technique allows the minority patient to find images with which he can identify. The book also has case material on assessment and therapy with **Asian**, **Black**, and **Hispanic** clients, filling a previously unmet need (Cf. also Coleman & Farris-Dufrene, 1996).

The 1996 AATA Conference, as noted above, focussed on multicultural issues, with many presentations which helped to sensitize the largely white, female, middle-class members of the organization. Even though artists as a group tend to be "color-blind," there is always the danger that an individual art therapist might be equally blind to her own unconscious socioeconomic and racial biases. These are so much a part of the dominant culture that even those who consider themselves to be open-minded may harbor prejudices of which they are completely unaware.

It would seem therefore that the ethics of respectful treatment require as much soul-searching about one's internalized attitudes regarding race and class, as about those regarding mental illness and other disabilities. Just as I was about to send off the final draft of this text, a new book appeared, edited by the multicultural team of Anna Hiscox and Abby Calisch: a *Tapestry of Cultural Issues in Art Therapy* (Cf. also Dokter, 1999).

Although the emphasis here has been on people of color, I was recently reminded of the need to respect the sensitivities of all cultural groups. A Jewish student in a graduate art therapy course became greatly distressed because another member had drawn a swastika on a group mural. The artist, explaining that her swastika was a Greek symbol which had nothing to do with the Nazis, was supported by others in the class. As it happened, the offended student received a telephone call the next day telling that the house of a Jewish community leader—a few doors from her uncle's home—had been vandalized. Windows had been smashed and swastikas had been painted all over the outside. The coincidence of the two events underscored the multicultural insensitivity in the otherwise-excellent class.

The standards for training, practice, and ethics outlined in this chapter are central to responsible art therapy. They provide the necessary context, within which the art therapist can then use the tremendous power of the creative art experience to **help—without doing harm**.

Chapter 12

What Next?

*What if imagination and art are not the **frosting** at all,*
*but the **fountainhead** of human experience?*

ROLLO MAY

Now that you have read something about art therapy, you might be wondering where to go from here. Whatever your level of interest, this book can offer no more than an overview of the discipline. Like an aerial map of the territory, it has hopefully given you a broad view of "the lay of the land," historically and currently. In order to further explore the area, you would need to deepen your knowledge, and you can do that in a number of possible ways.

FINDING OUT MORE ABOUT ART THERAPY

Since many readers of this book may already have made their decision to study the field of art therapy, and may, in fact, be at a fairly advanced level of development, my apologies for the following "tips," which are mainly for those who are newcomers to the discipline. Since I hope that this book will be utilized by people who want more information but do not have other avenues, I felt such details needed to be included. These are the kinds of things I have told people over the years who have called for information and advice about art therapy. While perhaps not identical to the counsel of my colleagues, it is probably similar.

Contact Professional Associations

You can contact the **American Art Therapy Association (AATA)** for free informational materials about the field. You might consider joining that organization as a Student or Associate Member, or the Chapter in your region; since you would receive newsletters and a journal, as well as reduced rates on other periodicals and on meetings. Another excellent way to get a feeling for art therapy is to attend an Annual Conference, where experiencing the workshops and hearing the presentations can give you a condensed introduction to the discipline.

If you are not from the United States, you can contact the **International Networking Group (ING/AT)**, in order to identify the closest national art therapy association, and some members or institutions you can visit. The **International Society for Psychopathology of Expression (I.S.P.E.)** is another potential resource, as is the **International Expressive Arts Therapy Association**. There are also regional groups overseas, some of which are noted in Chapter 3.

Take an Introductory Course

Prospective students who are interested in finding out what is available can request **AATA's Education List,** and write to institutions that interest them for more detailed information about specific programs. If you have access to an Introductory Course on Art Therapy, that is a wise thing to do prior to investing in masters' level training. In addition to classes that may be available where you live, there are also special summer courses and institutes sponsored by many of the training programs, from weekend workshops to more elaborate courses. Information about these may be obtained from schools offering such opportunities. If choosing a school is a priority, attending an AATA conference and talking to students from different places is a quick way to get an overview of the strengths and weaknesses of different programs. Some information about training is also available on the computer, via the Internet.

Interview, Observe, Volunteer

Another excellent way to find out more is to **meet** with one or more art therapists, if that is at all possible. The *Membership Directory* of AATA lists individuals by states and cities, as well as alphabetically. You can probably find someone via that route, and possibly through the closest local association. Most art therapists are pleased to be of assistance, and may allow you to observe, too.

You may also want to **volunteer** your services, which will give you a more intimate acquaintance with what it feels like to do this kind of work. Because of the wide diversity in populations and settings served by art therapists, you need to realize that any particular volunteer experience you may have, while it will be invaluable in your decision-making process, cannot possibly be broadly representative.

Watch Videotapes

Another way to get an idea of what art therapy can look like in practice is to watch the videotape which is being prepared along with this text—and others, as they become available (Cf. AT, 1997, p. 238). Like the book, it will offer an **overview of the field**, from glimpses of the pioneers, to examples of different people doing and discussing art therapy with individuals, families, and groups. It will contain segments from art therapists with diverse orientations, working in a variety of settings and with different populations. If any generalization can be made about art therapy, it is that it is like a multifaceted mosaic, made with many more materials than one could possibly count.

Read More Widely

Before deciding whether or not you want to make art therapy your life's work, there are other ways to find out more about it. The book that is being prepared in conjunction with this text, *Classic Readings in Art Therapy*, should be a helpful adjunct. It will contain some of the classic early work in art therapy and related fields. An effort will be made to include material which is out of print and hard to locate. Case studies will be featured, as the best way to get an intimate sense of the growth that can be accomplished through the therapy of art. Each selection will also be described in its particular historical context.

Growing Art Therapy Literature

There is an extensive and rapidly-growing literature which can either be skimmed or read in depth. I remember smiling inwardly and somewhat condescendingly when Bernie Levy stressed the importance of requiring art therapy students to be familiar with what he termed **"the literature in the field."** At the time those words were first printed in *Guidelines for Art Therapy Training* it seemed to me to be a rather bad joke, though being young and shy and new on the Board, I never said so out loud.

Much to my skeptical surprise, however, it is now only twenty years later and, in fact, the literature is growing like the discipline itself, so rapidly that it is hard to keep up with it. A brief overview of its history and present state will orient the reader to what may be found on library shelves about art therapy. Although some of the early books are now out of print, libraries of universities with training programs usually have copies which may be borrowed through interlibrary loan. The same is true of the journals in the field, which are probably not available everywhere, but are likely to be on the shelves of schools which offer training.

You may also come across some of the early **Illustrated Pamphlets**, usually funded by drug companies or foundations, which were extremely useful for public relations as well as the education of others; such as the description of an art therapy group with adolescents by Dunn and Semple at the Devereux Foundation, *"But Still it Grows"* (1956), Felice Cohen's case study, *"Mark and the Paint Brush"* (1971), or Harriet Wadeson's NIMH research report, *"Portraits of Suicide"* (1972).

Bibliographies

There have been several useful Bibliographies. The first one was in a book by Norman Kiell, *Psychiatry and Psychology in the Visual Arts & Aesthetics*

(1965), which included **278** listings under "Art Therapy," as well as many related items in other categories. The second, from Great Britain, compiled in 1972 by Philip Pacey of St. Albans School of Art and based on the work of the Department of Remedial Art, was entitled *Remedial Art: A Bibliography*. The third, *Art Therapy: A Bibliography*, compiled by Linda Gantt and Marilyn Schmal in 1974 for the National Institutes of Mental Health, was an annotated bibliography of **1175** items published between 1940 and 1973. Also funded by NIMH, *Art Therapy in Mental Health* was an annotated listing of **392** items covering the period between 1973 and 1981, and was compiled by Rosanna Moore. In 1982, Kathleen Hanes published an annotated bibliography, *Art Therapy & Group Work*.

In addition, Frances Anderson and her colleagues reviewed the *"Research Literature on the Arts for Persons with Disabilities"* between 1971 and 1992 (AT, 1983, p. 26; 1994, p. 96). From its inception in 1961 until February, 1989, the *Bulletin of Art Therapy* (later the *American Journal of Art Therapy*) printed a regular listing (biannually until 1983, then annually) of "Recent Periodical Literature & Other Brief Publications." *Psychoanalytic Abstracts* now lists articles on *"Art & Dance Therapy;"* and computerized databases, like **ERIC** and **PsycInfo**, are starting to include art therapy journals as well as those in older disciplines.

Journals

Although the **Bulletin of Art Therapy** (later the **American Journal of Art Therapy**) was the first periodical in the field, founded in 1961; articles on art therapy and reports of related meetings were also published in **Confinia Psychiatrica**. This was the official organ of the International Society of Art and Psychopathology (also known as I.S.P.E.—the International Society of Psychopathology of Expression) which began, as did the organization, in the late fifties. In 1973, Dr. Ernest Harms founded *Art Psychotherapy* which later changed its name and scope to *The Arts in Psychotherapy*. Like *Confinia Psychiatrica* which was multilingual, it is also international, but all the articles are written in English.

In 1983 the **American Art Therapy Association**, which was officially "affiliated" with the *American Journal of Art Therapy* from 1974 to 1983, began the publication of its own journal, *Art Therapy*. Most of these periodicals are quarterly, and all are still published regularly, except for *Confinia Psychiatrica*, which ended in 1980. Having served on the Editorial Boards of all of them, I can attest to a slow but steady increase in the quality of submitted manuscripts.

There are also art therapy journals in English in Canada, in Great Britain, and in other countries (20 on the latest **ING** list). The **World Wide Web**—the computer information pool accessible through the **Internet**—has begun to carry information about art therapy, which will no doubt increase significantly in the future. The "information super-highway" will hopefully carry the vehicle of art therapy further and faster into the next century.

Books on Art Therapy by Art Therapists

All three art therapy journals in this country include regular book and video-tape review sections. The number of items on the AATA list of books authored by members has grown rapidly over a fairly short period of time. In December of **1974**, when I had to make a case for writing a book on art therapy as my dissertation, there were only **12** books by art therapists on art therapy. There were two by Adrian Hill, four by Margaret Naumburg, two by Edith Kramer, one by E. M. Lyddiatt, one by Janie Rhyne, one by Mala Betensky, and one by Cliff Joseph (with psychiatrist Jay Harris). It wasn't hard to convince my committee of the need for more literature in this still-small discipline.

By the time I published *The Art of Art Therapy* in **1984**, there were **19** more books by art therapists: Two each by Frances Anderson, Arthur Robbins and colleagues, Judith A. Rubin, and Elinor Ulman and colleagues (selected articles from *AJAT*); one each by Lucia Cappacchione, Margaret Frings Keyes, Hanna Kwiatkowska, Helen Landgarten, Xenia Lucas, Shaun McNiff, Rawley Silver, Evelyn Virshup, Harriet Wadeson, and Geraldine Williams and Mary Wood; and a third volume by Edith Kramer. As you will see in the Reference List, over 100 additional books on art therapy have been published by art therapists since then, and there are a great many more in process.

Conference Proceedings

Beginning with its seventh meeting in **1976**, **AATA** has published an annual ***Proceedings***, the title of each being the theme of the particular Conference. Until 1982, they contained many of the papers and panels in full, and these are listed in the References, along with the titles for each year. Since 1983, one-page abstracts of Conference presentations have been published annually, a list of which is available from the AATA office. Although no longer published by S. Karger as *Psychiatry & Art*, editor Irene Jakab continued to print the *Proceedings* of **A.S.P.E.** and **I.S.P.E.** Congresses when they have been held. Like the AATA *Proceedings*, the title of each one is the theme of the meeting.

List of Resources

Despite the fact that I had noticed my shelves gradually filling up and spilling over, I had not realized how extensively the literature in art therapy had grown until I began reviewing it for this text. Books by art therapists themselves have continued to proliferate; as well as more and more from our peers in **Great Britain**, where the first book in the field since Hill and Lyddiatt was published in 1984–*Art as Therapy*, edited by Tessa Dalley. Because there are so many recent publications of note by art therapists on both sides of the Atlantic, an alphabetical list is available in the **References.** Selected books by individuals in related fields are also included, as well as addresses and telephone numbers for some of the professional associations based in the United States.

ART THERAPY AS A CAREER

Reality Check: Jobs and Salaries

Perhaps you have already read, observed, volunteered, and gone to conferences, and you are becoming more and more convinced that art therapy is right for you. In fact, you may even be enrolled in a program of study. However, because art therapy is still so new and still relatively unknown, you should be aware that jobs are not easy to find. And while the salaries are much better than they used to be, they are still not as high as in many other fields requiring comparable training.

It is therefore critical that those deciding to study art therapy be absolutely certain that it is right for them. If it is, the rewards are immense, and the potential for personal growth and satisfaction is tremendous. But if income and job security are vital, you will want to be very sure as well as pragmatic about your career choice. Although some of my art therapy colleagues might consider this advice heretical, I think it is only fair and honest to describe the situation, at least as it is in 1998.

For a full-time job as an art therapist, following what is usually two years of full-time training, you may be able to find a job in your community or you may need to relocate. If you cannot move, you may have to work hard to create or modify an employment situation where you can have the pleasure of using what you have learned. In areas which have had training programs for many years, however, and where students have interned in various settings, there is a much greater awareness of art therapy and its benefits, and therefore more jobs.

Credentialling in Other Areas

You might also want to consider the practical advantages of obtaining training—and perhaps certification or licensure—in a related field which is better established, and can therefore open more doors. If you plan to work with handicapped children, for example, you might want to become credentialled in special education or rehabilitation. Or, if you want to do psychotherapy in a clinical setting, you might consider a masters' degree in social work or marriage and family counseling. And if you desire further study, a doctorate in clinical psychology—either a Ph.D. or the newer and more clinically-oriented Psy.D.—might be a practical choice.

Some training programs offer combined degrees, such as those in California, where marriage and family counseling is taught along with art therapy. If art therapists continue to become eligible for licensure in more and more states, it will not be necessary to obtain other credentials. The movement for "umbrella" licensing bills for masters' level disciplines is growing, and art therapists are benefitting because of the much larger numbers of "counselors" who are promoting such legislation. It is equally important to be recognized by insurance companies, HMOs, and managed care organizations, which currently hold many of the purse strings in health care in this country.

New Employment and Funding Sources

As noted in Chapter 10, employment for art therapists is rapidly becoming available in a wider range of settings, in some of which there is less need for the kind of credential required in the past. Prisons and shelters, for example, do not necessarily require a license or certification, like schools or clinics. Job openings in such places may even enhance earning power.

It is also possible to obtain funding from other sources for programs in art therapy. Funding for the arts is increasingly less available through the government, and will probably have to be sought and secured privately even more often in the future than in the past. In the rapidly growing area of **Arts Medicine**, state arts councils and private foundations have often supported art programs in places like shelters, hospitals, and hospices.

"**Free Arts for Abused Children**," a program in which art therapists help artists to deliver services, seems to have been highly effective; not only in serving many youngsters, but also in raising money and recruiting volunteers. Described by founder Elda Ungar in CATT (p. 411), this program may point the way to some of the vast and undeveloped potential in the field of art therapy . . . in other words, towards the future.

THE FUTURE OF ART THERAPY

Art Therapist Predictions: Past and Present

By now you may be wondering, not so much where art therapy came from or even where it is right now, but rather where it seems to be going. The present health care situation is characterized by its volatility and unpredictability. Nevertheless, it is worth trying to identify probable and possible directions for this still-youthful and evolving discipline.

During the **AATA**'s 25th Anniversary Year (1994), the editor of *Art Therapy* invited all those who had been honored by the association to answer the following questions: "How will the profession of art therapy change in the next 25 years? In other words, what is your vision of the 21st century art therapist?"

While reviewing the responses, I was reminded of a **panel** organized by Arthur Robbins at the **1979** Conference entitled "**The Future of Art Therapy: Fantasy vs. Reality**." As a panel member, I had both wishful dreams and fearful nightmares about the field, and—like many—I found myself vacillating between great optimism and equally strong pessimism.

By **1994**, despite the insecure and unpredictable quality of the times, I found myself much more squarely in the camp of those who saw the future as holding mostly promise for the therapeutic use of art, especially in non-traditional set-tings. It seemed to me that we had become remarkably well-established for a profession that was still practically brand-new. We were even listed as one of the "**top 40 niche specialties**" in mental health, in a 1995 *Newsletter* for practitioners.

Some of my colleagues were more pessimistic. Both Myra Levick and Janie Rhyne warned that the degree of diversity we were encompassing within the definition of art therapy might be less enlivening than we would like to think, and might even be hazardous to effective communication. Many were concerned that art therapy would have a difficult time surviving the massive budget-cutting of human services in the nineties.

Worries about the instability of the system prompted a good deal of advice, like an injunction to conduct more rigorous outcome studies. Some recom-mended that art therapists form alliances with much larger groups with greater political power, such as the American Counseling Association with its 60,000 members.

Some exhorted us to hold fast to our roots, and to the central vision of the healing power of art. Others urged us to let go of outmoded theories and ways of working, and to embrace and explore new concepts. Despite differences in the details, almost everyone remarked on the need to go beyond the past, to work with others in a more mature and collaborative fashion, and to embrace the incredible challenges of our times by offering creative solutions. All sug-gested being active rather than passive. And, in one way or other, almost every-one had something to say about the risks and hazards of the previous trend toward "clinification" in the field, at the possible expense of the unique thing we have to offer: **Art**.

Some spoke of **soul** and some spoke of **systems**, and many spoke of the **sickness** of our times, of the crisis in our world, and of the desperate hunger for the kind of order and meaning and sense of effectiveness potentially available through the making of art.

In a subsequent issue of *Art Therapy* there was a follow-up piece by Jim Young of Santa Fe, New Mexico—with its rich indigenous tradition of a cul-ture in which art is not only alive, but central. He reflected on what leaders of both past and present generations had written, reminding us about where art therapy comes from. He offered the delightfully wishful vision that: *"Art thera-pists of the future will play a major role in bringing art back to the communities as a healing force."* Young called his article, "**The Re-enchantment of Art Therapy**" (1995, p. 193). My only quarrel with him is that, for many of us, art therapy never lost its enchantment.

The Future Panel of 1979 was in the **Student Section** of the Conference, addressed to those who really do hold the future of any field in their hands. When I recently reread what I had written then, I was certain that we had come a long way, since my nightmares of 1979 no longer apply. In the area of art therapy theory, they consisted of "half digested hodgepodges, built on poorly-understood and inadequately-integrated ideas from various sources," much less common now than they were then. In the practice of art therapy, my reactions ranged "from deep admiration to horrified dismay." I am pleased to be able to say that there is considerably less sloppy thinking and careless work these days, though a little knowledge can still be a very dangerous thing in untrained hands.

Also in 1979 I had written: "If we can somehow make the clinical skills of those who practice more synchronous with the power of their modality, I predict that we will not only be extremely successful, but also highly respected. There will then be no need to acquire credentials in other fields, nor any economic or political pressure to do so, for the sophistication and effectiveness of a qualified art therapist will be quite sufficient."

Even though the training of art therapists in 1998 is superior to what was available almost 20 years ago, recognition in the marketplace has taken more time than I had imagined. Yet, while it is clear that we're not quite there, we are nowhere near as far from achieving that goal as we were then. Excellent training and a flexible registration procedure were not sufficient to open enough doors. So it has been necessary to create a national **Certification Exam**. And it seems likely that having a form of credentialling objective enough to be relevant for licensure or insurance coverage may well lead to greater official recognition.

Art Therapy Has Much to Share

Art therapists have a great deal to contribute beyond direct work with "identified patients." In addition to being helpful in many alternative settings, especially "normal" ones, art therapists have much to offer to our colleagues in related fields. My psychoanalytic training, for example, has been immensely helpful in all of my work. I have wanted to share these understandings with art therapists, as I did in my chapter for *Approaches*. But I also look forward to writing a book for psychoanalysts some day about the power of art and imagery in analytically-informed therapy. Shirley Riley made a similar observation about the relevance of art therapy to systemic family therapy, how each enhances the other. Cathy Malchiodi has recently completed a book, on *Understanding Children Through Their Drawings*, for social workers, counselors, and other child therapists. There is a great deal that art therapists can usefully share with workers in other disciplines, as well as with members of the general public.

As noted in Chapter 2, art therapists do not own art, any more than we own therapy. It is my hope that we will be able to expand the reach of our modality by reaching out to both professionals and interested lay people. The experience and skill of a trained art therapist in the use of materials with others is not literally transferable. But a little help can sometimes go a long way. I was reminded of this just recently, while consulting to a group of advanced residents in Child Psychiatry.

These eager young physicians already had some minimal drawing supplies in their offices, and were curious about the pictures the children had done. Because they did not know how to ''read'' what had been communicated, they did not realize how very much their patients were actually telling them through their art. And, because they also did not know how to talk with the youngsters about their drawings, they had been unable to find out more about the messages being conveyed.

With just a little support, they were able to improve the quality of the art materials they made available to the children, greatly increasing their appeal and usage. And, as these young child psychiatrists began to appreciate the richness of what was being expressed and worked through in the drawings, they began to see them as possibly equivalent in value to the verbalizations they used to view as the only ''real'' therapy. As they learned how to talk with the youngsters about their pictures, they were able to extend and expand their symbolic meaning, as well as the therapeutic effectiveness of the art activity.

This was demonstrated so vividly in the art they brought in each week, that this group of residents was easily ''sold'' on the value of art in child therapy. I suspect they will be more likely to hire and to consult with art therapists in their future work. They are also more likely to value art as an outlet for their own children, and maybe even for themselves.

Art Therapy in the Age of Virtual Reality

A decade ago, I was invited to speak at the ''International Conference on Mental Health and Technology'' in Vancouver, B.C., Canada. Even though I was expected to tell the participants everything they ever wanted to know about art therapy in only 15 minutes, it was not that hard to articulate the importance of art therapy for an industrialized society. The ensuing ''post-modern'' years have seen the dominance of the computer chip and the emergence of new ways to know the world, like ''cyberspace'' and ''virtual reality.'' Such developments, it seems to me, make the words I wrote in 1986 even more meaningful today . . .

''Although the technological revolution has wrought wondrous extensions of human perception, enabling us to see the otherwise invisible with instruments like the CAT-Scan or the Electron Microscope; it can never replace direct sensory experience as a mode of being alive, of coping, and of psychotherapy. Through art, human beings can **make visible the invisible**—which cannot be seen by any physical means. Through art, people can be literally **in touch** with their environments, in a fashion which is concrete and real, yet also imaginative and creative.

For those whose inner worlds are confused and chaotic, who are unable to connect comfortably with life; art can be a vital avenue for finding and knowing themselves, others, and the world around them. For those who are out of control, art offers order. For those who are empty, art provides richness. For those who are lost, art gives meaning. For those whose resources are not fully available because of the psychological chains which bind their energies, art therapy can be the road to liberation, recovery, and renewal.''

As we honor art as the core of who we are and what we do, we also honor a deep respect for the creative potential and integrity of each and every individual we serve. We have great power in art therapy to help and to heal and to restore hope. If anything, the pressures of the nineties have accentuated the unique values of art as an enlivening form of healing and of therapy, despite the field's continuing—and perhaps inevitable—confusion about its identity.

Artist or Therapist?

During the summer of 1994, a freelance writer named Beth Baker took a good long look at our field, read a great deal, and interviewed a lot of people. On the basis of this research, she wrote an article for a magazine called *Common Boundary* entitled ''**Art Therapy's Growing Pains**'' (July/August). The subtext indicated how far we have come, yet how we still struggle with the identity issue which has concerned us from the first (Cf. Chapter 4): ''*With certification looming, a burgeoning mental-health specialty finds itself at a crossroads. Should practitioners be artists or clinicians? The answer could change the role of creativity in the healing process*'' (p. 42).

Many of us believe that we are **both** artists and therapists, in which case there is little meaning to the question, and little anguish about the response. To ask if we are artists **or** therapists seems, therefore, to be a meaningless question, embodying a **false dichotomy**. That is also how I and many of my colleagues have viewed the heated disagreements between proponents of ''art *as* therapy'' and ''art *psychotherapy*. Since helping the person(s) being served is the prime concern, a responsible art therapist moves flexibly along the continuum of interventions, according to the needs of the moment. As in the skating and sailing metaphors noted in Chapter 8, it is impossible to move along without also being able to shift the emphasis between art and therapy—as needed.

I have often found myself quoting lyrics by the smart and compassionate creator of ''Mister Rogers' Neighborhood,'' to patients of all ages, like: ''*What do you do with the mad inside when you feel so mad you could bite?*'' Among the many possible ways Fred Rogers cites to express anger without doing harm is ''*You could pound some clay or some dough,*'' one of the ways in which art therapy helps.

One of my favorites is ''*I like you as you are, exactly and precisely. I think you turned out nicely, and I like you as you are.*'' Another is, ''*You are special. You are the only one like you. I like you.*'' Both lyrics, it seems to me, are about the kind of respect for the uniqueness and creativity of each human being, which is the foundation of art therapy.

I'm not even sure that the name of the discipline is so important. I like ''**art therapy**'' myself because it contains a reference to each of our parents. Like all siblings, art therapists have varied configurations of appearance, talents, and personality. So of course we are different, but each in his or her own way is true to our common genetic background. The name of the field is not as vital as being true to our faith in the therapy of art, i.e., the integrity of what we do and how we do it.

Need for Art in Times of Change

Thirty years ago, a Jungian analyst named H. Irene Champernowne spoke to a meeting of the British Association of Art Therapists. In 1968 she said: *"Perhaps even more today when the intellect and cerebral activity is too highly valued to the exclusion of feeling, **man is turning for very life to the means of expression in the arts**."*

The current state of disequilibrium and of radical change in social structures is at least as great as it was then, and is both symptomatic and scary. But, like a crisis in an individual or a family, it can also be an opportunity for change, for bold exploration, for freely and creatively addressing the question of how to make the healing power of art more accessible to more people. People in large numbers nowadays are turning to the arts as consumers. How much more therapeutic it would be if we could help them to become creators as well.

ART + THERAPY = ART FOR LIFE

Several years ago I was asked to participate as a judge in an art show competition for those who had undergone transplant surgery. The project was called "**Art for Life**," a most fitting way to think, not only about this particular group of artists who were indeed fighting life-threatening illness; but also about art therapy. For it is, in a very profound and powerful way, "art for life" . . . for life lived as well, as freely, and as fully as possible.

I hope that the benefits of art therapy will continue to be extended to ever new people in ever new places, and in ever new ways. Like the many movements of our time which reflect a search for basic meaning, art therapy may indeed help in the effort to save our world from the mess we have made of it. My own wishful image of the future of art therapy is that the swords of human aggression will be beaten not only into plowshares, but also into poems, paintings, or pottery.

One of my mentors, Marvin Shapiro, used to point out that the oil from a gusher can be destructive; it can kill defenseless animals or ignite a fire. But that same energy, when channeled into a pipeline, can be a powerful and constructive force. Frank Barron was a psychologist interested in the creative process, who contributed a good deal through his writings (and who worked with art therapist Janie Rhyne in her doctoral studies). He reminded us that the Latin root for **violence** and **vitality** is the same—**vis**. In other words, the energy can be expressed either way. And creating art has, for centuries, been a wonderful way to tame raging passions into forms of beauty.

Art is **sensual**, enabling you to feel your impact on the physical world—an increasingly rare experience in these technologically sophisticated but humanly impersonal times. And if you look at the world with **artist-eyes**, you can see more loveliness in ordinary things. Shaun McNiff's *Earth Angels* is subtitled *Engaging the Sacred in Everyday Things*.

Talk therapists work to **listen**, as well as to **hear**; **art therapists** seek to **see**, as well as to **look**. To **see** and to **feel** the **beauty in the Self** as well as **in the World** can be the gift of the kind of truly transformative therapy, which may be uniquely possible through art.

Appendix

The Process of Art Therapy

The clinical vignettes in this book offer only brief glimpses of the lively and dynamic process of art therapy. This appendix has been added to give the reader a more in-depth look—first, at a single creative process, then at a therapeutic process over time. In both instances, the description of what happened is followed by reflections on its meaning for art therapy.

Most people enter this field because their own work in art has been helpful to them in coping with issues in their lives. Many years ago, shortly after becoming an art therapist, I found myself reflecting on an unusually intense painting experience. Because I was so moved by it at the time, I tried to put the event into words, in an effort to clarify and to understand it for myself. Here is some of what I wrote, three weeks after it happened . . .

AN EXPERIENCE OF THE CREATIVE PROCESS

I would like to try to give words and form to an essentially nonverbal and formless experience, an experience of such power and intensity that it demands clarification, and invites sharing. I wonder to myself, how universal or how personal was this happening? And I wonder, too, what it can tell me about the meaning of art in therapy.

I was painting this past summer, with a strange awareness of functioning on several levels simultaneously. I was the mother who responded to the child who called from his bed for a drink of water. I was also the technician who periodically changed brushes and added colors to my acrylic palette in order to achieve the desired effects. Yet further, I was the artist, deeply and actively engaged in the creative process, which simultaneously involved every layer of my psyche.

The painting had begun as a group portrait of my children, full of conscious loving of their exterior and interior selves. I strove intently to draw them as they sat painting around a table, concerned with reproducing both their features and the warm, proud feelings they evoked. This first stage of the picture seemed to be conscious, careful, with sincere and very deliberate attempts at naturalistic representation.

Then they went to bed, and I continued with the painting, having temporarily interrupted the process to play my maternal bedtime role. I was aware of my resentment at having to stop work in order to bed them, but even more powerfully conflicted feelings rose to the surface, as I continued to apply the paint. An onrush of diffuse and intense destructive impulses impelled me to work more rapidly. I found the activity gathering a momentum which did not seem to be under my voluntary control.

Before I had worked slowly, deliberately, and carefully to make them beautiful. Now I worked with a somatic sensation of pressure, as if the intensity and perhaps guilt of the propelling feelings required such speed. With quick, short strokes I modified—and partially obliterated—their forms.

My husband remarked sadly that I was destroying what had recently been so attractive, but his criticism was acknowledged only intellectually as reasonable. On another level, I resented the intrusion, and went on at an accelerated tempo, doing what at that moment had to be done. The sense of both compulsion and excitement was almost too great to bear. Yet it was thrilling as well as painful, as the tension quickly mounted. Coexisting were love and hate, creation and destruction, joy and pain.

And yet the figures remained, less clear but perhaps more intense for their ambiguity. I found them more beautiful now, as they reflected the full complexity and ambivalence of my emotions. And I was aware of another kind of tension—between the need to modify and the desire not to destroy, but to enhance. Though executed at a quick pace, each stroke felt crucial.

While working so intensely, I felt simultaneously a high level of ego control, and an equally high level of communication with the unconscious forces which threatened the very control I prized so dearly. At the end of the painting process, my working pace slowed down. With deliberate calm and rather cool control, I found myself standing back and looking, modifying, and completing the portrait (Fig. A-1).

Discussion

And now, weeks later, I reflect upon the event. Perhaps it was that very experience of teetering at the brink, of allowing such a powerful upsurge of unconscious and irrational feeling—while maintaining a tight control over it—that is the essence of at least one aspect of the "therapy" in art. For without the experience of near-loss of control, it must be feared as catastrophic. It is only by "letting go" as fully as possible that one learns that the fantasied fear is a somewhat myth. If one always holds tight the reins of conscious control, there is no danger—yet the danger still exists by implication. The more unknown and unfelt, the more it is feared.

Indeed, one might question whether it is ever possible to learn self-control in the deepest, most secure sense, without allowing oneself at times to loosen the bonds of control as well. What is vital is that this was felt as a "peak experience," both thrilling and frightening, both soaring and plunging. It was aesthetic as well as personal, as was the resultant painting.

The implications for the use of art in therapy are manifold—as multileveled as the experience itself. The tension-producing and tension-reducing inherent in an involved creative experience are somatically therapeutic, the interaction of the artist with the work of art not unlike that with a human

Figure A–1 My painting of my three children.

partner in a similarly orgastic experience. To experience in any sphere "letting go," yet remaining simultaneously aware and ultimately in charge, is a profound lesson. Whether or not the content of the art work is affectively toned, the dynamics of the creative process itself provide an essential learning experience.

One might also argue that limiting, or in any way protecting the client from "letting go," might serve to reinforce already-crippling fears of loss of control. The art therapist who prematurely limits the client's activity in the name of safety or security may actually be saying, "Yes, you are right. Loss of control is disastrous in its consequences, so I will set limits and help you to keep a brake on your dangerously strong and destructive feelings and impulses." Yet learning to be in charge of the self may only be possible, when one has allowed conscious controls to relax sufficiently to explore the consequences of strong expression of affect, then to find that one may still be master of one's fate.

What is emerging is not a position which suggests no limits at all. Rather, the creation of a work of art has its own built-in limits, which provide sufficient safety, along with the opportunity for constructive abreaction and channeling of strong feelings. Indeed, the expressive arts are vital both to healthy personality growth and to therapy precisely because they allow for a channeled, controlled "letting go." The very nature of each art form sets the limits which, when broken, negate the art. Throwing paint on the wall is not the same as making a vibrant picture by slashing with the brush; and random body movements are not the same as those which are "in tune" with the music.

Nevertheless, it has been my experience that many disturbed youngsters, whether their superficial behavior is inhibited or hyperactive, need initially to release in a cathartic and often formless fashion, at first unfocussed and heretofore repressed feelings. Only when this has been safely experienced, can the child then give a genuinely artistic form to such feelings. Perhaps it is only then that he feels in control of himself and in charge of the process, not in a compulsively tight, but a relaxedly free way.

Surely my painting process involved regression with control, and while form was given to feeling, feeling was also "given" to form. They intermingled in an inseparable fashion, each one evoking the other, neither one the chronological precursor of the other. My painting was not meant primarily as a communication to others, but rather as a kind of self-communication, a rhythmic dialogue between picture and creator which gradually rose and finally fell in intensity. I think the process was neither primarily cathartic nor primarily integrative, but was both simultaneously, and was meaningful just because of the tension and interplay between constructive and destructive forces. It was both an aesthetic and an intellectual experience, producing art as well as insight.

While the above was written almost 30 years ago and was first published 20 years ago, the ideas still seem valid—even if the writing is a bit windy.

I originally planned to write this book with my friend and colleague, Laurie Wilson. Although she was unable to collaborate on the writing when the time came, she has agreed to the inclusion of an unpublished case study of her work with an anxious girl—in which she first describes and then analyzes what happened in nine months of art therapy with Francine. Here is a somewhat condensed version of what she wrote . . .

ART THERAPY WITH AN ANXIOUS 12-YEAR-OLD GIRL

Francine, a twelve-year-old girl, was referred for art therapy at a suburban clinic in New Jersey by a psychologist, because treatment had reached an impasse. The oldest of two, she lived at home with her recently divorced mother and younger sister. At her sister's birth, when Francine was three, both parents turned their attention away from the previously adored only child, to whom the mother had a particularly close attachment. Since then, Francine had a hard time with new experiences, manifested in a long history of nightmares, tics, and various somatic symptoms.

Recent problems had taken the form of phobic concerns, excessive dependency, and reactions to separation from mother. These included dreams in which both she and mother died; a late night episode during which she insisted someone was following her and coercing her to do something—like kill her mother; and repeated claims that she feared growing up, because her maturing would make her mother age and die, and she could not imagine life without mother. Those concerns propelled her into action when mother attempted to date after the parents' divorce. Upon the arrival of a visitor, Francine would retreat to her bedroom, screaming and crying for hours, and throwing her shoes at the door.

Unaware of any hostile feelings toward her mother, Francine had become increasingly silent in treatment with a psychologist, who had almost reached the point of abandoning the idea of further therapy for the time being. **As a last recourse, she was referred for art therapy with the hope that it would open avenues of expression and communication**. Aware of the anger and disappointment toward mother experienced by the girl, the psychologist reported that Francine had never been able to acknowledge such feelings—but to do so was presented only as a long-term goal.

Francine was seen once a week for art therapy beginning in March, with the understanding that treatment would continue at least through June. In her first session Francine was offered a range of drawing materials, several sizes and types of paper, clay, and paint, and was invited to make anything she wished with them. She produced seven defensive and stereotypical pieces, which nevertheless revealed some of her concerns as well as some of her strengths.

Starting with her preferred theme, she drew an abundance of hearts, most of which were joined together. She then drew a rather immature figure, explaining that she had learned this technique when she was four. When I commented that she had stayed with this method a long time, and asked if she wanted to learn other ways to draw people; she responded that she was not very creative with people, but could be with hearts.

Figure A–2   Francine's drawing in her first art session.

She then rejected paint, a medium that encourages the expression of feelings, and instead made a sensitive decorative design on a flat clay plaque. This was followed by two extremely defensive pieces: a pair of clay dice, and a crayon drawing of almost the entire repertoire of typical preadolescent girls' stereotypes—a rainbow, a butterfly, a smiling sun, flowers, and balloons (Fig. A-2). Finally, she drew Cabbage Patch Doll faces, which led to a brief discussion of her not having what she wants but not minding it. (She did not have her own doll at this time, but a four-year-old cousin of hers did.) Her last piece was a list of pets and hobbies.

Thus, already in the first session, a pattern of expression was evident, albeit inhibited and defensive. Francine's fear of learning to draw people differently than she had at four, her heightened capacity for expression with the most regressive material—clay—her own emphatic use of stereotyped hopeful images, all fit with the picture of a girl struggling mightily against unacknowledged feelings.

In the next session this struggle came closer to surfacing. She began with pastels, experimenting with relative freedom and obviously enjoying the messiness of the medium. After smearing all the colors together, she reacted to her picture with sharp disappointment and displeasure, left the room to wash her hands, and returned to do another "heart" picture. She explained that the hearts represented, respectively—friends, enemies, mother, father, a group, or being lonely. She agreed when I commented that a person would have different feelings in each one of these situations.

After several more pictures in this almost totally silent session she did a quick sketch of a stick figure representing Michael Jackson, the rock music star. Guessing that the flame-like marks on the figure's head referred to a recent incident when Jackson's hair was accidentally set on fire during the filming of a commercial; I commented that it must have been pretty scary, and asked her what she had thought of it. This unleashed a remarkable expression of angry feelings about the film producer's callous and unfair exploitation of Jackson, which she characterized as "snobby." When I asked her if something like that had happened to her too, she said, "Yes, but I'm also snobby with some people." With this last remark she vigorously crossed out the entire picture and threw it away.

In the course of the treatment, which lasted nine months, many themes emerged in the artwork. Occasionally, work appeared which seemed to convey the play of defense and drive via abstract formal qualities. One such example was a crayon drawing, done after Francine had looked through a photographic encyclopedia of animal life. In the course of perusing this book, she had exclaimed with revulsion at any images which appeared either sexual or aggressive. Her drawing commenced with a black grid done with a ruler. After counting the 160 squares produced, she began to fill them in, working from the two sides toward the center. The final result of this obsessively structured method was an amazingly delicate and dynamic work of sublimation. Francine's defenses had provided a temporary structure, sufficient to contain her feelings. The balance was harmonious and the result, at least to my eye, looked hopeful.

Several months later, after it was decided that I should continue to see her through the summer at the clinic, she began to openly depict and discuss her fears and concerns. At this time her sessions with the psychologist were curtailed because of scheduling difficulties. The drawing which introduced this new phase, Francine entitled "A Road Waiting". She was able to connect the woman in the picture with her mother, and her fears that mother would die. We began to look for patterns in the content and timing of these fears, and she eventually came to see connections between her sleep difficulties and her wish to be close to mother.

She brought in poetry and her diary and, during sessions, her drawings were more like doodles, which tracked in an offhand way the feelings she was beginning to explore. Francine spoke of her confusion, and questioned the relationship of love to hate, as well as her desires and fears about understanding her own feelings. She described ways in which she frightened herself, and was persuaded by me to try drawing her "Panic" (Fig. A-3). Francine was then able, for the first time, to relate some angry feelings toward her mother. We ended the session with my suggestion that she try to think about what kinds of thoughts or feelings she had just before she felt scared or panicky.

Three days later, she had an anxiety attack at home in the evening. Afterward, her mother labeled it for her and suggested that it was due to Francine's anger toward mother. In the session immediately following the anxiety attack, Francine described her experience and showed me a written description she had made for her diary. She then asked me to explain

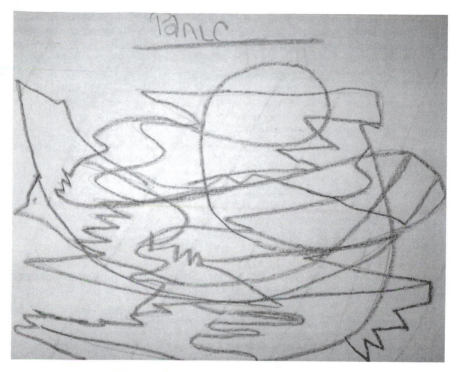

Figure A–3 "Panic," by Francine.

what an anxiety attack is, and why it had happened to her. She was as tense, confused, and upset about her mother's explanation of it as she was about its actual occurrence.

In the next session we reconstructed the events of the day of the attack. She had learned that day of the fatal heart attack, two days before, of the father of Sam, one of her campmates. She spoke with praise of Sam, who looked like "nothing had happened and didn't want people to feel sorry for him." After a discussion of the different ways people express feelings—including through their bodies in the form of anxiety attacks—I suggested that she make a drawing of how her anxiety attack had felt.

She was reluctant to draw, but very willing to accept the alternative of an abstract colored-paper collage (Fig. A-4). Depicting herself as a large yellow heart, Francine used jagged black and purple shapes to portray the shooting pains she had felt, and wavy orange lines to represent her "shaking." She titled the picture, said no more about it, and then asked me to play jacks with her, explaining that she plays jacks all the time now because it helps her forget how upset she is. During the course of a companionable game, she was able to calmly explore the relationship of her feelings about Sam's experience, her dislike of unhappy endings, and her anxiety attack.

Figure A–4 "Anxiety Attack," by Francine (collage).

In the next session, Francine entered listlessly, told me of having been sick with a fever the night before, and said that she now felt dizzy. She then showed me a poem, written at home two days after the previous session, entitled "Growing Pains." Its content alluded to her fears of separation from her mother and it ended with the lines "I want to know what it [growing] is and I want to know very quickly: I wish I knew now."

I suggested that she might make a picture about her many different feelings, and that it might help her discover what she wanted to know. After some initial hesitation she began to draw, and as she drew she cried. She drew a very schematic set of images, which detailed with words and images her feelings associated with growing: pain, loneliness, emptiness, panic, hate, and anger—"Growing Pains" (Fig. A-5). When she had finished drawing, Francine poured out her fears and feelings in a stream of words. As she cried and talked about the pictures and the feelings, she seemed to discover an unexpected capacity to distance herself from them, and gradually to accept her own ambivalence.

In the following session there was a similar pattern of discussion combined with artwork, with a focus on her angry feelings toward her mother, and her fear that the feelings themselves might cause harm. She spoke openly about her guilt at discovering her mother's imperfection, and wondered whether she might have been adopted.

At the last session before my summer vacation, she spoke with enthusiasm of her plans for the future, with calmness of her relationship to her mother, and of the concurrent separation from me and from the psychologist, who was also taking a vacation at this time. She then drew a picture she entitled "The Sun is Starting to Shine Again," saying that she now felt better and that **making pictures and talking about things made her feel better**.

Upon my return a month later, the psychologist reported a dramatic improvement in Francine. Her mother felt that she was behaving normally, and was delighted with her progress. Though she came for a few more art therapy sessions, it was soon evident that—since she was asymptomatic—neither Francine nor her mother saw a need for continued treatment at this time. Follow-up contacts eight months and then two years later revealed that Francine was doing well in school, had an active social life, and was no longer troubled by anxiety symptoms or depression.

Discussion

The apparent success of art therapy for Francine could be attributed to several factors . . . The art materials allowed her an avenue of expression at a time when she could not use words. In addition, we could theorize that the symbolic expression of her unconscious conflicts and feelings through making art led to some catharsis, as well as to a renewed capacity to work on those feelings and conflicts, but now with words. Francine herself experienced the visible concrete representations of her problems as integrating and clarifying experiences.

The production of artwork, both in the context of a therapeutic relationship and outside of it, can be an internalized integrative experience. Francine's picture of her "Panic" (Fig. A-3) is a powerful evocation of the

Figure A–5   "Growing Pains," by Francine.

feelings, conscious and unconscious, associated with her actual experience of panic. Once depicted, her experience could become accessible for communication and interpretation through language . . .

It seems that making a visual image of a recalled memory or experience makes it "more real" for the patient, especially if this is followed by naming or discussing the experience. Even if the image produced is several levels removed symbolically from the unconscious memory, feeling, or experience—like Michael Jackson standing for Francine, or the unseen exploiter representing father and/or mother—it still seems to serve a function.

I would speculate that the displaced representation allows some degree of feeling to be expressed and connected, and starts an upward shifting of the repressed material from an unconscious level toward a preconscious one. This seems to me to be the basis for working "within the metaphor" in psychotherapy. In the course of time, the metaphor often becomes more transparent, as it did with Francine, who chose by the 11th session to begin to speak directly about her feelings toward her mother.

The art productions of patients, along with associations and comments, can give the art therapist sufficient information to determine something of the status and nature of current defenses, drives and conflicts. Thus, with Francine, I could guess—from the highly defended stereotypical imagery of hearts, flowers, rainbows, and so on which appeared in her early sessions—that she was struggling to contain some painful feelings.

It could be argued that the stereotypical images that Francine used are the common coin of preadolescent and early adolescent girls' art. As with any form of defense, it was the exaggerated quality and sense of excess that suggested problems that went beyond the usual developmental issues. There were too many hearts and flowers. And, they were too quickly followed by hints at underlying aggressive feelings.

By the second session, some of these feelings surfaced, not only in the imagery and its associations—when she drew the stick figure of Michael Jackson and told of her angry feelings toward his exploiter—but also in the way she forcefully covered over the image and threw it out. The symbolic displacement of her anger at both parents could be expressed at this early stage, as long as its unconscious meaning was not brought home to her.

Let us examine closely two different instances during the treatment of this girl when the production of artwork seemed to have a significant effect on the course of the session as well as the treatment. The first is the collage, "Anxiety Attack" (Fig. A-4), and the second is the set of pencil drawings depicting Francine's fears about losing mother, "Growing Pains" (Fig. A-5). Both sessions occurred relatively late in the course of this short-term treatment, but not until a solid therapeutic alliance had been forged.

Francine had been assured that she would be able to continue in art therapy as long as she would need it, and she had had the repeated experience of setting her own pace during sessions, with regard to the amount of verbal expression (talking) vs. art production. She had also, by this time, become comfortable speaking directly with me about her feelings, and was no longer using only metaphor to convey her confusion.

In the session following the anxiety attack, it seemed evident that Francine was having difficulty accepting or using verbal means to grasp or deal with her recently upsetting experience and the feelings it had brought to the surface. Her mother's supportive efforts the night of the attack and my discussion with her had not clarified the experience for her. However, once she had made a visual depiction of her experience (Fig. A-4), she was once again able to use words to calmly comprehend and accept it.

On the one hand, we might see this as the art therapist serving as an auxiliary ego—supplying knowledge of a mental phenomenon, and helping to clarify and personalize that knowledge through the combination of image-making and discussion. On the other hand, we might equally well understand this vignette as a nonverbal sensorimotor experience, with unconscious content in derivative fantasies being translated first and more easily into another nonverbal symbolic mode—via art expression—before it can reach consciousness and be fully integrated through language.

The shift which occurred with Francine's visual depiction of her anxiety attack seems to be an example of a controlled regression, which led to a new integration of unconscious, preconscious, and conscious material. The two-step sequence seems to have functioned to consolidate the experience for the patient in a way that had not occurred earlier. It led to a new capacity and willingness to master her inner fears, as she proceeded in the subsequent sessions to approach even more directly her long-repressed ambivalent feelings toward her mother.

The second vignette, with Francine tearfully discussing her schematic picture, "Growing Pains" (Fig. A-5), might be seen as a cathartic or abreactive experience. Her readiness to shift from images to words without a return to an excessively defensive posture came after a relatively brief, but sufficiently long period in which she had been allowed and encouraged to sublimate her intense feelings, and to translate them into what Susanne Langer calls "presentational" or emotion-arousing symbols through art.

In art therapy this period may vary in length, depending on the psychological needs of the patient; and it is assumed that valuable growth occurs during its course. For many patients that growth takes the form of the development of stronger and healthier ego functioning, particularly the development of sublimatory capacities, increased autonomous functioning, and greater tolerance for the delay of immediate discharge.

Francine was readier than many art therapy patients for insight-oriented treatment, and the cathartic experience of this vignette allowed her to make an affective connection with the repressed content which was evident in her drawing. We might understand this as not only bridging the barriers between preconscious and conscious, but also as binding affects (feelings) which had hitherto been too intense to be rendered consciously, much less to be accepted.

Again it seems to me that the two-step process—of first depicting the painful affects in images, followed by rendering them in language—was especially effective in this case. The affects, having been seen and spoken, could become a piece of recognizable external reality, allowing a shift from repetitive symptomatic behavior to thought and insight.

In addition, several of the ways in which the art therapist behaved probably helped Francine to move in positive directions. By virtue of being an artist and encouraging the production of artwork, the art therapist was a model of an individual comfortable with controlled regression. In addition, regressive materials were offered in a permissive environment, thus metaphorically encouraging the expression of regressive feelings and wishes. Nevertheless, autonomy was also encouraged in all aspects of the artwork, implicitly giving support to her progression toward adolescence. Finally, a product was sometimes expected, which was experienced either as a demand beyond her capacities, or a belief in her potential strength.

The case of Francine demonstrates how the production of significant visual images by the patient can lead to catharsis, as well as to the capacity for talking about previously unapproachable conflicts. Displacement onto visual representations allows both the expression and binding of affect. The visual depiction of unconscious feelings, thoughts and fantasies seems to promote an upward shift towards preconscious or conscious states . . .

Thus, when Francine had reached the point of being able to talk about her problems, the artwork could be used to help her to clarify and integrate her feelings and discoveries—at moments when words did not suffice, either because they had lost their meaning through repetition, or because they were too overwhelming to be accepted.

The concrete representations that she made of her own feeling-states allowed her to accept and to take responsibility for those feelings. Once having accepted the reality of her artwork and her part in its production, she could also begin to accept the feelings behind it.

CONCLUSION

My painting experience and Francine's treatment have several things in common. In both, making art helped to relieve internal pressures, and to express affective states of which the artist had not been aware. Francine was able to express previously-repressed feelings, first in a displaced, and then a more direct fashion. She was also able to achieve freedom from her disabling symptoms, through understanding and then accepting her ambivalence toward her mother. Similarly, my unconscious ambivalence toward my children energized my experience of painting their portraits, which became both cathartic and integrative.

Art therapy does not always involve a creative process as intense and compelling as my painting experience. Nor does treatment through art therapy always look like the story of Francine. But if it is successful, it embodies some elements of the processes described in both situations.

As noted throughout this book, art therapy has many different faces. Thus, no single example of the creative or the treatment process can possibly represent everything that might happen in the effort to help people to overcome pain and to grow through art—known as **art therapy**.

Resources

ASSOCIATIONS

American Art Therapy Association (AATA).
1202 Allanson Road, Mundelein, IL 60060. (847) 949–6064.
National Coalition of Arts Therapy Associations (NCATA).
2000 Century Plaza, Suite 108, Columbia, MD 21044. (410) 997–4040.
American Society of Psychopathology of Expression (ASPE).
Also **ISPE** (International). Dr. Irene Jakab, 74 Lawson St., Brookline, MA 02146. (617) 738–9821.
International Networking Group of Art Therapists (ING/AT).
Bobbi Stoll, ATR-BC. 8020 Briar Summit Drive, Los Angeles, CA 90046. (213) 650–5934.
International Expressive Arts Therapy Association (IEATA).
P. O. Box 641264, San Francisco, CA 94164. (415) 522 8959.

JOURNALS

American Journal of Art Therapy (formerly *Bulletin of Art Therapy*).
　1961–Present (Vermont College of Norwich University, Montpelier, VT).
The Arts in Psychotherapy (formerly *Art Psychotherapy*).
　1973–Present (Ankho International, New York).
Art Therapy.
　1983–Present (American Art Therapy Association, Mundelein, IL).
Confinia Psychiatrica.
　1958–1980 (S. Karger, Switzerland). International Society of Psychopathology of Expression.
International Journal of Arts Medicine.
　1994–Present (MMB Music, Inc., St. Louis, MO). International Arts Medicine Association.

CONFERENCE PROCEEDINGS
American Art Therapy Association

1976–1982: Full Papers (Various Editors)
1976: *Creativity & the Art Therapist's Identity* (Shoemaker & Gonick-Barris)
1977: *The Dynamics of Creativity* (Mandel, Shoemaker & Hays)
1978: *Art Therapy: Expanding Horizons* (Gantt, Forrest, Silverman, Shoemaker)
1979: *Focus on the Future: The Next Ten Years* (Gantt & Evans)
1980: *The Fine Art of Therapy* (Gantt & Whitman)
1981: *Art Therapy: A Bridge Between Worlds (Di Maria, Kramer & Rosner)*
1982: Art Therapy: Still Growing (DiMaria, Kramer & Roth)
1983–Present *Proceedings* (1 page abstracts) List available from AATA.

Society of Psychopathology of Expression

Jakab, I. (Ed.). (ISPE, 1966/1968). *Psychiatry & art, Vol. I*. New York: S. Karger.
Jakab, I. (Ed.). (ISPE, 1968/1970). *Art Interpretation and Art Therapy, Vol. II*. New York: S. Karger.

Jakab, I. (Ed.). (ASPE, 1969/1971). *Conscious and Unconscious Expressive Art, Vol. III*. New York: S. Karger.
Jakab, I. (Ed.). (ASPE, 1973/1975). *Transcultural Aspects of Psychiatric Art, Vol. IV*. New York: S. Karger.
Jakab, I., & Miller, L. (Eds.). (1976/1978). *Creativity & Psychotherapy*. New York: S. Karger.
Jakab, I. (1981). *The Personality of the Therapist*. Pittsburgh, PA: ASPE.
Jakab, I. (Ed.). (ISPE, 1984/1986). *The Role of the Imagination in the Healing Process*. Pittsburgh, PA: ASPE.
Jakab, I. (Ed.). (ISPE, 1988/1990). *Stress Management Through Art*. Boston, MA: ASPE.
Jakab, I. (1990). *Art Media as a Vehicle of Communication*. Brookline, MA: ISPE.

Psychoanalytic Perspectives on Art

Gedo, M. M. (Ed.) (1985). *Psychoanalytic perspectives on art, Vol. 1*. Hillsdale, NJ: Analytic Press.
Gedo, M. M. (Ed.) (1987). *Psychoanalytic perspectives on art, Vol. 2*. Hillsdale, NJ: Analytic Press.
Gedo, M. M. (Ed.) (1988). *Psychoanalytic perspectives on art, Vol. 3*. Hillsdale, NJ: Analytic Press.

American Association for the Study of Mental Imagery

Shorr, J. E., Sobel, G. E., Robin, P., & Cannella, J. (Eds.) (1979/1980). *Imagery: Its many dimensions & applications* (Vol 1). New York: Plenum.
Klinger, E. (Ed.) (1980/1982). *Imagery: Concepts, results & applications* (Vol. 2). New York: Plenum.
Shorr, J. E., Sobel-Whittington, G. E., Robin, P., & Cannella, J. (Eds.) (1981/1983). *Imagery: Theoretical & clinical applications* (Vol. 3). New York: Plenum.

AUDIO-VISUAL MATERIALS (by the author)

Rubin, J. A. (1972). *We'll Show You What We're Gonna Do! Art for Multiply Handicapped Blind Children*. Pittsburgh, PA: Expressive Media, Inc.
Rubin, J. A. (1973). *Children & the Arts: A Film About Growing*. Pittsburgh, PA: Expressive Media, Inc.
Rubin, J. A., & Irwin, E. C. (1979). *The Green Creature Within: Art & Drama in Group Psychotherapy*. Pittsburgh, PA: Expressive Media, Inc.
(Videos available from Expressive Media, Inc., 128 No. Craig St., Pittsburgh, PA, 15213.)

BOOKS ON ART THERAPY & RELATED SUBJECTS

Adamson, E. (1990). *Art as healing*. London: Coventure.
Adler, G. (1961). *The living symbol*. New York: Bollingen.
Akeret, R. U. (1973). *Photoanalysis*. New York: Peter H. Wyden.
Allan, J. (1988). *Inscapes of the child's world*. Dallas, TX: Spring.
Allan, J., & Bertoia, J. (1992). *Written paths to healing*. Dallas, TX: Spring.
Allen, P. B. (1995). *Art is a way of knowing*. Boston: Shambhala.
Alschuler, R., & Hattwick, L. W. (1947). *Painting & personality* (2 Vols.). Chicago: U. of Chicago Press. (Revised, 1969.)
Amman, R. (1991). *Healing & transformation in sandplay*. La Salle, IL: Open Court Pub. Co.
Anderson, F. E. (1978). *Art for all the children* (1st ed.). Springfield, IL: Charles C. Thomas. (2nd Ed., 1992)
Anderson, F. E. (1994). *Art-centered education & therapy for children with disabilities*. Springfield, IL: Charles C. Thomas.
Anderson, W. (Ed.). (1977). *Therapy & the arts*. New York: Harper & Row.

Arieti, S. (1976). *Creativity: The magic synthesis*. New York: Basic Books.

Arnheim, R. (1954). *Art & visual perception*. Berkeley, CA: U. of California Press.

Arnheim, R. (1967). *Towards a psychology of art*. Berkeley, CA: U. of California Press.

Arnheim, R. (1969). *Visual thinking*. Berkeley, CA: U. of California Press.

Arnheim, R. (1992). *To the rescue of art*. Berkeley, CA: U. of California Press.

Ault, R. E. (In Preparation). *Drawing on the contours of the mind*.

Bach, S. (1990). *Life paints its own span*. Zurich: Daimon.

Barnes, M., & Berke, J. (1971). *Mary Barnes: Two accounts of a journey through madness*. New York: Ballantine Books.

Baynes, H. G. (1961). *Mythology of the soul*. Princeton, NJ: Bollingen.

Bejjani, F. J. (Ed.). (1993). *Current research in arts medicine*. Pennington, NJ: Cappella Books.

Bender, L. (Ed.). (1952). *Child psychiatric techniques*. Springfield, IL: Charles C. Thomas.

Bertman, S. L. (1991). *Facing death*. Bristol, PA: Washington, DC: Taylor & Francis.

Bertoia, J. (1993). *Drawings from a dying child*. New York: Routledge.

Betensky, M. G. (1973). *Self-discovery through self-expression*. Springfield, IL: Charles C. Thomas.

Betensky, M. G. (1995). *What do you see?* London: Jessica Kingsley.

Birkhauser, P. (1980). *Light from the darkness*. Boston: Birkhauser-Verlag.

Bradway, K., & McCoard, B. (1997). *Sandplay*. New York: Routledge.

Brooke, S. (1996). *A Therapist's guide to art therapy assessments*. Springfield, IL: Charles C. Thomas.

Brooke, S. (1997). *Art therapy with sexual abuse survivors*. Springfield, IL: Charles C. Thomas.

Brown, A. (1997). *And don't tell anyone*. St. Cloud. MN: North Star Press.

Brown, D. (1997). *Principles of art therapies*. London: Thorsons.

Brown, W. (1967). *Introduction to psycho-iconography*. New York: Schering.

Burns, R. C., & Kaufman, S. H. (1970). *Kinetic family drawings*. New York: Brunner/Mazel.

Burns, R. C., & Kaufman, S. H. (1972). *Action, styles, & symbols in kinetic family drawings*. New York: Brunner/Mazel.

Burns, R. C. (1982). *Self-growth in families*. New York: Brunner/Mazel.

Burns, R. C. (1987). *Kinetic house-tree-person drawings*. New York: Brunner/Mazel.

Burns, R. C. (1990). *A guide to family-centered circle drawings*. New York: Brunner/Mazel.

Bush, J. (1997). *The handbook of school art therapy*. Springfield, IL: Charles C. Thomas.

Caligor, L. (1957). *A new approach to figure drawing*. Springfield, IL: Charles C. Thomas.

Campbell, J. (1993). *Creative art in groupwork*. Bicester, UK: Winslow.

Cane, F. (1951/1983). *The artist in each of us*. Craftsbury Common, VT: Art Therapy Publications/ Chicago: Magnolia St. Pubs.

Capacchione, L. (1979). *The creative journal* (and six subsequent Creative Workbooks, 1988–1992). Chicago: Swallow Press.

Caprio-Orsini, C. (1996). *A thousand words*. Quebec, CAN: Diverse City Press.

Cardinal, R. (1972). *Outsider art*. New York: Praeger.

Case, C., & Dalley, T. (1990). *Working with children in art therapy*. London: Tavistock.

Case, C., & Dalley, T. (1992). *The handbook of art therapy*. New York: Routledge.

Chickerneo, N. B. (1993). *Portraits of spirituality in recovery*. Springfield, IL: Charles C. Thomas.

Cohen, B. M., & Cox, C. T. (1995). *Telling without talking: Art as a window into the world of multiple personality*. New York: W. W. Norton.

Cohen, B. M., Barnes, M-M., & Rankin, A. (1995). *Managing traumatic stress through art*. Lutherville, MD: Sidran Press.

Cohen, F. (1971). *Mark & the paintbrush*. Houston, TX: Hogg Foundation.

Coleman, V. D., & Farris-Dufrene, P. B. (1996). *Art therapy & psychotherapy*. Washington, DC: Taylor & Francis.

Coles, R. (1992). *Their eyes meeting the world: The drawings & paintings of children*. New York: Houghton Mifflin.

Collot d'Herbois, L. (1993). *Light, darkness & colour in painting-therapy*. Hamburg, GER: Goetheanum Press.

Cox, M. V. (1992). *Children's drawings*. London: Penguin Books.

Cox, M. V. (1993). *Children's drawings of the human figure*. Hillsdale, N.J.: Lawrence Erlbaum.

Cox, M. V. (1997). *Drawings of people by the under-5's*. London: Folmer Press.

Crowley, R., & Mills, J. (1989). *Cartoon magic*. New York: Brunner/Mazel.

Dalley, T. (Ed.). (1984). *Art as therapy*. London: Routledge.

Dalley, T., Case, C., Schaverien, J., Weir, F., Halliday, D., Hall, P. N., & Waller, D. (1987). *Images of art therapy*. London: Routledge.

Dalley, T., Rifkind, G., & Terry, K. (1993). *Three voices of art therapy: Image, client, therapist*. London: Routledge.

Dax, E. C. (1953). *Experimental studies in psychiatric art*. London: Faber & Faber.

Dennis, W. (1966) *Group values through children's drawings*. New York: Wiley.

Dewey, J. (1934). *Art as experience*. New York: Capricorn Books.

DiLeo, J. H. (1970). *Young children & their drawings*. New York: Brunner/Mazel.

DiLeo, J. H. (1974). *Children's drawings as diagnostic aids*. New York: Brunner/Mazel.

DiLeo, J. H. (1983). *Interpreting children's drawings*. New York: Brunner/Mazel.

Dokter, D. (Ed.) (1994). *Arts therapies & clients with eating disorders*. London: Jessica Kingsley.

Dokter, D. (Ed.) (1998). *Arts therapists, refugees, & migrants*. London: Jessica Kingsley.

Dokter, D. (Ed.) (1999). *Art therapy, race, & culture*. London: Jessica Kingsley.

Drachnik, C. (1995). *Interpreting metaphors in children's drawings: A manual*. Burlingame, CA: Abbeygate Press.

Dreifuss-Kattan, E. (1990). *Cancer stories*. Hillsdale, NJ: The Analytic Press.

Dreikurs, S. E. (1986). *Cows can be purple: My life & art therapy*. Chicago: Adler School of Professional Psychology.

Dunn, M. B., & Semple, R. A. (1956). *But still it grows*. Devon, PA: Devereux Foundation.

Edinger, E. F. (1990). *The living psyche*. Wilmette, IL: Chiron.

Edwards, B. (1979). *Drawing on the right side of the brain*. Los Angeles: Jeremy Tarcher.

Edwards, B. (1986). *Drawing on the artist within*. New York: Simon & Schuster.

Erikson, E. H. (1950). *Childhood & society*. New York: W. W. Norton & Co.

Erikson, E. H. (1977). *Toys & reasons*. New York: W. W. Norton & Co.

Erikson, E. H., Erikson, J., & Kivnick, H. (1986). *Vital involvement in old age*. New York: W. W. Norton & Co.

Erikson, J. M. (1976). *Activity, recovery & growth*. New York: W. W. Norton & Co.

Erikson, J. M. (1988). *Wisdom & the senses*. New York: W. W. Norton & Co.

Fausek, D. (1997). *A Practical guide to art therapy groups*. New York: Haworth.

Feder, E., & Feder, B. (1981). *The expressive arts therapies*. Englewood Cliffs, NJ: Prentice-Hall.

Fein, S. (1976). *Heidi's horse*. Pleasant Hill, CA: Exelrod Press.

Fincher, S. F. (1991). *Creating mandalas*. Boston: Shambhala.

Fleshman, B., & Fryrear, J. L. (1981). *The arts in therapy*. Chicago: Nelson-Hall.

Fordham, M. (1944). *The life of childhood*. London: Kegan Paul.

Fryrear, J. L., & Corbit, I. E. (1992). *Photo art therapy: A Jungian perspective*. Springfield, IL: Charles C. Thomas.

Fryrear, J. L., & Corbit, I. E. (1992). *Instant images: A guide to using photography in therapy*. Dubuque, IA: Kendall/Hunt.

Fryrear, J. L., & Fleshman, B. (Eds.) (1981). *Videotherapy in mental health*. Springfield, IL: Charles C. Thomas.

Fugaro, R. A. L. (1985). *A manual of sequential art activities for classified children & adolescents*. Springfield, IL: Charles C. Thomas.

Fukurai, S. (1974). *How can I make what I cannot see?*. New York: Van Nostrand Reinhold.

Furrer, P. J. (1982). *Art therapy activities & lesson plans for individuals & groups*. Springfield, IL: Charles C. Thomas.

Furth, G. M. (1988). *The secret world of drawings*. Boston: Sigo.

Gaitskell, C. (1953). *Art education for slow learners*. Toronto: Ryerson.

Gantt, L., & Schmal, M. S. (1974). *Art therapy: A bibliography*. (1/40–6/73). Washington, D.C.: National Institutes of Mental Health.

Gantt, L., & Tabone, C. (1997). *Rating manual for the Formal Elements Art Therapy Scale*. Morgantown, WV: Gargoyle Press.

Gardner, H. (1973). *The arts & human development*. New York: John Wiley & Sons.

Gardner, H. (1980). *Artful scribbles*. New York: Basic Books.

Gardner, H. (1982). *Art, mind & brain*. New York: Basic Books.

Gedo, J. E. (1983). *Portraits of the artist*. New York: The Guilford Press.

Gillespie, J. (1994). *The projective use of mother-and-child drawings*. New York: Brunner/Mazel.

Gilroy, A., & Dalley, T. (Eds.) (1989). *Pictures at an exhibition*. London: Routledge.

Gilroy, A., & Lee, C. (Eds.) (1995). *Art & music: Therapy & research*. London: Routledge.

Gladding, S. T. (1992). *Counseling as an art: The creative arts in counseling*. Alexandria, VA: American Counseling Association.

Gold, A., & Oumano, E. (1998). *Painting from the source*. New York: Harper/Collins.

Golomb, C. (1974). *Young children's sculpture & drawing*. Cambridge, MA: Harvard University Press.

Golomb, C. (1992). *The child's creation of a pictorial world*. Berkeley, CA: University of California Press.

Gondor, E. I. (1954). *Art and play therapy*. New York: Doubleday.

Goodnow, J. (1977). *Children Drawing*. Cambridge: Harvard University Press.

Grant, N. (1958). *Art & the delinquent*. New York: Exposition Press.

Graves, S. (1994). *Expressions of healing*. Van Nuys, CA: Newcastle.

Green, G. (1969). *The artists of Terezin*. New York: The Hawthorn Press.

Greenberg, P. (1987). *Visual arts & older people*. Springfield, IL: Charles C. Thomas.

Gussak, D., & Virshup, E. (Eds.). (1997). *Drawing time: Art therapy in prisons & forensic settings*. Chicago: Magnolia Street Publishers.

Hall, M. D., & Metcalf, E. W. (Eds.). (1994). *The artist outsider*. Washington. D.C.: Smithsonian Institution Press.

Hammer, E. F. (Ed.). (1958). *The clinical application of projective drawings*. Springfield, IL: Charles C. Thomas.

Hammer, E. F. (Ed.) (1997). *Advances in projective drawing interpretation*. Springfield, Il: Charles C. Thomas.

Hanes, K. M. (1982). *Art therapy and group work: An annotated bibliograpy*. Westport, CT: Greenwood Press.

Hanes, M. J. (1997). *Roads to the unconscious*. Oklahoma City, OK: Wood'n'Barnes.

Harding, M. E. (1965). *The parental image: A study in analytical psychology*. New York: Putnam Press.

Harris, D. B. (1963). *Children's drawings as measures of intellectual maturity*. New York: Harcourt Brace & World.

Harris, J., & Joseph, C. (1973). *Murals of the mind: Image of a psychiatric community*. New York: International Universities Press.

Harris, P. (1993). *A Child's story: Recovering through creativity*. St. Louis, MO: Cracom Corporation.

Hauschka, M. (1985). *Fundamentals of artistic therapy*. London: Rudolf Steiner Press. (English translation of 1978 book)

Heegaard, M. E. (1992). *Facilitator guide for drawing out feelings* (for her six Workbooks for Children). Minneapolis, MN: Woodland Press.

Henley, D. R. (1992). *Exceptional children: Exceptional art*. Worcester, MA: Davis Publications.

Herrera, H. (1983). *Frida: A biography of Frida Kahlo*. New York: Harper & Row.

Hill, A. (1945). *Art versus illness*. London: George Allen & Unwin.

Hill, A. (1951). *Painting out illness*. London: Williams & Northgate.

Hiscox, A., & Calisch, A. (Eds.). (1997). *Tapestry of Cultural issues in art therapy*. London: Jessica Kingsley.

Hoffman, D., Greenberg, P., & Fitzner, D. (1980). *Lifelong learning & the visual arts*. Reston, VA: NAEA.

Hogan, S. (Ed.) (1997). *Feminist approaches to art therapy*. New York: Routledge.

Hornyak, L. M., & Baker, E. K. (Eds.). (1989). *Experiential therapies for eating disorders*. New York: Guilford Press.

Horovitz-Darby, E. G. (1994). *Spiritual art therapy*. Springfield, IL: Charles C. Thomas.

Horowitz, M. J. (1983). *Image formation & psychotherapy* (originally *Imagery & cognition*, 1970). New York: Jason Aronson.

Jakab, I. (1998). *Pictorial Expression in Psychiatry*. Budapest, Hungary: Akademiai Kiado.

Jamison, K. R. (1993). *Touched with fire: Manic-depressive illness & the artistic termperament*. New York: Free Press.

Jeffrey, C. (1996). *That why child*. New York: Free Association Books.

Jennings, S., & Minde, A. (1993). *Art therapy & dramatherapy*. London: Jessica Kingsley.

Jung, C. G. (1964). *Man & his symbols*. New York: Doubleday.

Jung, C. G. (1972). *Mandala symbolism*. Princeton, NJ: Princeton Univ. Press.

Jung, C. G., Institute of San Francisco (1981/1990). *Sandplay studies*. Boston: Sigo Press.

Junge, M. B., & Asawa, P. P. (1994). *A history of art therapy in the United States*. Mundelein, IL: American Art Therapy Association.

Jungels, G. (1982). *To be remembered: Art & the older adult in therapeutic settings*. Buffalo, NY: Potentials Development.

Kalff, D. M. (1980). *Sandplay*. Boston: Sigo Press.

Katz, F. L., & Katz, E. (1977). *Creative art of the developmentally disabled*. Oakland, CA: Creative Growth.

Katz, F. L., & Katz, E. (1990). *Art & disabilities* (Rev. ed.). Cambridge, MA: Brookline Books.

Kaufman, B., & Wohl, A. (1992). *Casualties of childhood*. New York: Brunner/Mazel.

Kaye, C., & Blee, T. (Eds.). (1996). *The arts in health care: A palette of possibilities*. London: Jessica Kingsley.

Kellogg, J. (1978). *Mandala: Path of beauty*. Clearwater, FL: ATMA.

Kellogg, J. (1980). *MARI card test*. Clearwater, FL: Mandala Research Institute.

Kellogg, R. (1959). *What children scribble & why*. Palo Alto, CA: NP Pubs.

Kellogg, R., & O'Dell, S. (1967). *Psychology of children's art*. New York: Random House.

Kellogg, R. (1969). *Analyzing children's art*. Palo Alto, CA: NP Pubs.

Keyes, M. F. (1974). *The inward journey: Art as therapy* (Rev. ed. 1992). La Salle, IL: Open Court.

Kiell, N. (1965). *Psychiatry and psychology in the visual arts & aesthetics*. Madison, WI: University of Wisconsin Press.

Killick, K. & Schaverien, J. (Eds.) (1997). *Art, psychotherapy, and psychosis*. London: Routledge.

Kinget, G. M. (1952). *The drawing completion test*. New York: Grune & Stratton.

Kirchner, L. (1977). *Dynamic drawing: Its therapeutic aspect*. Spring Valley, NY: Mercury Press.

Klepsch, M., & Logie, L. (1982). *Children draw & tell: An introduction to the projective use of children's human figure drawings*. New York: Brunner/Mazel.

Kluft, E. (Ed.). (1993). *Expressive & functional therapies in the treatment of multiple personality disorder*. Springfield, IL: Charles C. Thomas.

Knill, P. J., Barba, H. N., & Fuchs, M. N. (1995). *Minstrels of soul: Intermodal expressive therapy*. Toronto: Palmerston Press.

Koppitz, E. M. (1968). *Psychological evaluation of children's human figure drawings*. New York: Grune & Stratton.

Koppitz, E. M. (1984). *Psychological evaluation of HFD's by middle-school pupils*. New York: Grune & Stratton.

Kramer, E. (1958). *Art therapy in a children's community*. Springfield, IL: Charles C. Thomas.

Kramer, E. (1971/1993). *Art as therapy with children*. New York: Schocken Books. (reprinted 1993, Chicago: Magnolia St.).

Kramer, E. (1979/1998). *Childhood & art therapy*. New York: Schocken Press (reprinted 1998, Chicago: Magnolia St.).

Krauss, D. A., & Fryrear, J. L. (1983). *Phototherapy in mental health*. Springfield, IL: Charles C. Thomas.

Kreitler, H., & Kreitler, S. (1972). *Psychology of the arts*. Durham, NC: Duke Univ. Press.

Kris, E. (1952). *Psychoanalytic explorations in art*. New York: International Universities Press.

Kubie, L. S. (1958). *Neurotic distortion of the creative process*. Lawrence, KS: Univ. Kansas Press.

Kunkle-Miller, C. (1985). *Competencies for art therapists whose clients have physical, cognitive or sensory disabilities*. Unpub. Ph.D. Diss., Univ. Pittsburgh.

Kwiatkowska, H. Y. (1978). *Family therapy & evaluation through art*. Springfield, IL: Charles C. Thomas.

Lachman-Chapin, M. (1994). *Reverberations: Mothers & daughters*. Evanston, IL: Evanston Publishing Co.

Laing, J., & Carrell, C. (Eds.). (1982). *The special unit, Barlinnie Prison: Its evolution through its art*. Glasgow: Third Eye Center.

Lambert, D. (1995). *The life & art of Elizabeth "Grandma" Layton*. Waco, TX: WRS Publishing.

Landgarten, H. B. (1981). *Clinical art therapy*. New York: Brunner/Mazel.

Landgarten, H. B. (1987). *Family art psychotherapy*. New York: Brunner/Mazel.

Landgarten, H. B. (1993). *Magazine photo collage: A multicultural assessment & treatment technique*. New York: Brunner/Mazel.

Landgarten, H. B., & Lubbers, D. (Eds.). (1991). *Adult art psychotherapy*. New York: Brunner/Mazel.

Langer, S. K. (1942). *Philosophy in a new key*. Cambridge, MA: Harvard University Press.

Langer, S. K. (1953). *Feeling & form*. New York: Scribner's.

Levens, M. (1995). *Eating disorders & magical control of the body: Treatment through art therapy*. New York: Routledge.

Levick, M. F. (1983). *They could not talk and so they drew*. Springfield, IL: Charles C. Thomas.

Levick, M. F. (1986). *Mommy, daddy, look what I'm saying*. New York: M. Evans & Co.

Levick, M. F. (1997). *See what I'm saying*. Dubuque, IA: Islewest.

Levine, E. (1995). *Tending the fire*. Toronto: Palmerston Press.

Levine, S. K. (1992). *Poesis*. Toronto: Palmerston Press.

Levine, S. K., & Levine, E. (Eds.) (1998). *Foundations of expressive art therapy*. London: Jessica Kingsley.

Levy, F. J., Fried, J. P., & Leventhal, F. (Eds.) (1995). *Dance & other expressive art therapies: When words are not enough*. New York: Routledge.

Lewis, P. B. (1993). *Creative transformation: The healing power of the arts*. Wilmette, IL: Chiron Pubs.

Liebmann, M. (1986). *Art therapy for groups*. Brookline, MA: Brookline Books.

Liebmann, M. (Ed.). (1990). *Art therapy in practice*. London: Jessica Kingsley.

Liebmann, M. (Ed.). (1994). *Art therapy with offenders*. London: Jessica Kingsley.

Liebmann, M. (Ed.). (1996). *Arts approaches to conflict*. London: Jessica Kingsley.

Lindsay, Z. (1968). *Art is for all*. New York: Taplinger Pub. Co.

Lindsay, Z. (1972). *Art & the handicapped child*. New York: Van Nostrand Reinhold.

Linesch, D. (1988). *Adolescent art therapy*. New York: Brunner/Mazel.

Linesch, D. (Ed.). (1993). *Art therapy with families in crisis*. New York: Brunner/Mazel.

Lisenco, Y. L. (1971). *Art not by eye*. New York: American Foundation for the Blind.

Lowenfeld, M. (1971). *Play in childhood*. New York: John Wiley & Sons.

Lowenfeld, M. (1979). *The world technique*. London: Allen & Unwin.

Lowenfeld, V. (1939). *The nature of creative activity*. London: Routledge.

Lowenfeld, V. (1957). *Creative & mental growth* (3rd ed.). New York: Macmillan.

Lowenfeld, V. (1982). *The Lowenfeld lectures* (John A. Michael, Ed.). University Park, PA: Pennsylvania State University Press.

Lucas, X. (1980). *Artists in group psychotherapy*. Athens: Litsas.

Luscher, M. (1969). *The Luscher Color Test*. New York: Random House.

Lusebrink, V. (1990). *Imagery & visual expression in therapy*. New York: Plenum Press.

Luthe, W. (1976). *Creativity mobilization technique*. New York: Grune & Stratton.

Lyddiatt, E.M. (1971). *Spontaneous painting & modelling*. London: Constable.

Machover, K. (1949). *Personality projection in the drawing of the human figure*. Springfield, IL: Charles C. Thomas.

MacGregor, J. M. (1989). *The discovery of the art of the insane*. Princeton, NJ: Princeton University Press.

MacGregor, J. M. (1992). *Dwight Mackintosh: The boy who time forgot*. Oakland, CA: Creative Growth.

Makin, S. (1994). *A consumer's guide to art therapy*. Springfield, IL: Charles C. Thomas.

Malchiodi, C. A. (1990). *Breaking the silence:Art therapy with children from violent homes*. (2nd ed. 1997). New York: Brunner/Mazel.

Malchiodi, C. A. (1998a). *Understanding children through their drawings*. New York: Guilford Press.

Malchiodi, C. A. (1998b). *The art therapy sourcebook*. Los Angeles, CA: Lowell House.

Malchiodi, C. A. (Ed.). (1998c, 1999). *Medical art therapy, Vol. 1: Children, Vol. 2: Adults*. London: Jessica Kingsley.

Malchiodi, C. A., & Riley, S. (1996). *Supervision & related issues*. Chicago: Magnolia Street Publishers.

May, R. (1975). *The courage to create*. New York: W. W. Norton.

May, R. (1985). *My quest for beauty*. Dallas, TX: Saybrook Publishing.

McElhaney, M. (1969). *Clinical psychological assessment of the human figure drawing*. Springfield, IL: Charles C. Thomas.

McNiff, S. (1977). *Art therapy at Danvers*. Danvers, MA: Danvers State Hospital.

McNiff, S. (1981). *The arts & psychotherapy*. Springfield, IL: Charles C. Thomas.

McNiff, S. (1986). *Educating the creative arts therapist*. Springfield, IL: Charles C. Thomas.

McNiff, S. (1988). *Fundamentals of art therapy*. Springfield, IL: Charles C. Thomas.

McNiff, S. (1989). *Depth psychology of art*. Springfield, IL: Charles C. Thomas.

McNiff, S. (1994). *Art as medicine*. Boston: Shambhala.

McNiff, S. (1995). *Earth angels*. Boston: Shambhala.

McNiff, S. (1998a). *Art-based research*. London: Jessica Kingsley.

McNiff, S. (1998b). *Trust the process*. Boston: Shambala.

Meares, A. (1957). *Hypnography*. Springfield, IL: Charles C. Thomas.

Meares, A. (1958). *The door of serenity*. London: Faber & Faber.

Meares, A. (1960). *Shapes of sanity*. Springfield, IL: Charles C. Thomas.

Miller, A. (1986). *Pictures of a childhood*. New York: Farrar, Straus & Giroux.

Mills, J. C., & Crowley, R. (1986). *Therapeutic metaphors for children and the child within*. New York: Brunner/Mazel.

Milner, M. (1957). *On not being able to paint*. New York: International Universities Press.

Milner, M. (1969). *The hands of the living god*. New York: International Universities Press.

Milner, M. (1987). *The suppressed madness of sane men*. New York: Tavistock.

Mitchell, R. R., & Friedman, H. S. (1994). *Sandplay: Past, present & future*. New York: Routledge.

Moon, B. L. (1990). *Existential art therapy*. (2nd ed., 1995) Springfield, IL: Charles C. Thomas.

Moon, B. L. (1992). *Essentials of art therapy training & practice*. Springfield, IL: Charles C. Thomas.

Moon, B. L. (1994). *Introduction to art therapy*. Springfield, IL: Charles C. Thomas.

Moon, B. L. (1997). *Art and soul*. Springfield, IL: Charles C. Thomas.

Moore, R. W. (1981). *Art therapy in mental health*. Washington: NIMH.

Morgenthaler, W. (1921/1992). *Madness & art*. Lincoln, NB: Univ. Nebraska Press.

Morris, D. (1962). *The biology of art*. New York: Alfred A. Knopf.

Moustakas, C. (1959). *Psychotherapy with children*. New York: Harper.

Naevestad, M. (1979). *The colors of rage & love*. London: Whitefriars Press.

Naumburg, M. (1928). *The child & the world*. New York: Harcourt, Brace.

Naumburg, M. (1947/1973). Studies of the free art expression of behavior problem children & adolescents as a means of diagnosis and therapy. *Nerv. & Ment. Dis. Monog*. No. 71, 1947 (reprinted as *Introduction to art therapy,* 1973, New York: College Press).

Naumburg, M. (1950). *Schizophrenic art*. New York: Grune & Stratton.

Naumburg, M. (1953). *Psychoneurotic art*. New York: Grune & Stratton.

Naumburg, M. (1966/1987). *Dynamically oriented art therapy*. New York: Grune & Stratton (reprinted by Magnolia Street Publishers, Chicago).

Nichols, J., & Garrett, A. (1995). *Drawing & coloring for your life*. Overland Park, KS: Gingerbread Castle Publications.

Nucho, A. (1987). *Psychocybernetic model of art therapy*. Springfield, IL: Charles C. Thomas.

Nucho, A. (1995). *Spontaneous creative imagery*. Springfield, IL: Charles C. Thomas.

Oaklander, V. (1969). *Windows to our children*. Utah: Real People Press.

Orleman, J. (1998). *Telling secrets*. Washington, DC: Child Welfare League of America.

Oster, G. D., & Gould, P. (1987). *Using drawings in assessment & therapy*. New York: Brunner/Mazel.

Oster, G. D., & Montgomery, S. S. (1996). *Clinical uses of drawings*. Northvale, NJ: Jason Aronson.

Pacey, P. (1972). *Remedial art: A bibliography*. Hatfield: Hertis.

Palmer, J., & Nash, F. (1991). *The hospital arts handbook*. Durham, NC: Duke University Medical Center.

Panter, M., Panter, L., Virshup, E., & Virshup, B. (Eds.) (1995). *Creativity and madness: Psychological studies of art & artists*. Burbank, CA: AIMED Press.

Paraskevas, C. B. (1979). *A structural approach to art therapy methods*. Elmsford, NY: Collegium Publishers.

Pasto, T. (1964). *The space-frame experience in art*. New York: Barnes.

Payne, H. (Ed.) (1994). *Handbook of inquiry in the arts therapies: One river, many currents*. London: Jessica Kingsley.

Peterson, L. W., & Hardin, M. E. (1997). *Children in distress: A guide for screening children's art*. New York: W. W. Norton & Sons.

Petrie, M. (1946). *Art & regeneration*. London: Paul Elek.

Pickford, R. W. (1967). *Studies in psychiatric art*. Springfield, IL: Charles C. Thomas.

Plokker, J. H. (1965). *Art from the mentally disturbed*. Boston: Little, Brown.

Pratt, A., & Wood, M. J. M. (Eds.) (1998). *Art therapy in palliative care*. London: Routledge.

President's Commision on Mental Health, Task Panel Report. (1978). *Role of the arts in therapy & environment*. Washington, DC: NCAH.

Prinzhorn. H. (1922/1971). *Artistry of the mentally ill*. New York: Springer.

Rambert, M. (1949). *Children in conflict* New York: Int. Univ .Press.

Read, H. (1958). *Education through art*. New York: Pantheon Books.

Rees, M. *Drawing or difference: Art therapy with people who have learning difficulties*. London: Routledge.

Rhyne, J. (1973). *The gestalt art experience*. Monterey, CA: Brooks/Cole Publishing (2nd ed., 1995, Chicago: Magnolia St.).

Rhyne, J. (1995). *The gestalt art experience*. (2nd ed.). Chicago: Magnolia Street Publishers.

Richards, M. C. (1962). *Centering*. Middletown, CT: Wesleyan Univ. Press.

Richards, M. C. (1966/1973). *The crossing point*. Middletown, CT: Wesleyan Univ. Press.

Ridker, C., & Savage, P. (1996). *Railing against the rush of years*. Pittsburgh: Unfinished Monument Press.

Riley, S., & Malchiodi, C. (1994). *Integrative approaches to family art psychotherapy*. Chicago: Magnolia Street Publishers.

Robbins, A., & Sibley, L. (1976). *Creative art therapy*. New York: Brunner/Mazel.

Robbins, A. (1980). *Expressive therapy*. New York: Human Sciences Press.

Robbins, A. (1987). *The artist as therapist*. New York: Human Sciences Press.

Robbins, A. (1988). *Between therapists*. New York: Human Sciences.

Robbins, A. (1989). *The psychoaesthetic experience*. New York: Human Sciences Press.

Robbins, A. (1994). *A multi-modal approach to creative art therapy*. Bristol, PA: Jessica Kingsley.

Robbins, A. (Ed.) (1998). *Therapeutic presence*. London: Jessica Kingsley.

Robertson, S. (1963). *Rosegarden & labyrinth*. London: Routledge.

Rogers, N. (1993). *The creative connection: Expressive arts as healing*. Palo Alto, CA: Science & Behavior Books.

Rosal, M. (1996). *Approaches to art therapy with children*. Burlingame, CA: Abbeygate Press.

Ross, C. (1996). *Something to draw on*. London: Jessica Kingsley.

Rubin, J. A. (1978). *Child art therapy: Understanding & Helping Children Through Art*. (Rev. ed., 1984). New York: Van Nostrand Reinhold/Wiley.

Rubin, J. A. (1984). *The art of art therapy*. New York: Brunner/Mazel.

Rubin, J. A. (Ed.) (1987). *Approaches to art therapy*. New York: Brunner/Mazel.

Rugh, M. M., & Ringold, F. (1989). *Making your own mark: A drawing & writing guide for senior citizens*. Tulsa, OK: Council Oak Books.

Ryce-Menuhin, J. (1992). *Jungian sandplay*. London: Routledge.

Salomon, C. (1963). *A diary in pictures*. New York: Harcourt, Brace & World.

Sandle, D. (Ed.) (1998). *Development and diversity: New applications in art therapy*. London: Free Association Books.

Sarason, S. B. (1990). *The challenge of art to psychology*. New Haven, CT: Yale University Press.

Schaeffer, C., & Carey, L. J. (Eds.) (1994). *Family play therapy*. Northvale, NJ: Jason Aronson.

Schaeffer-Simmern, H. (1948). *The unfolding of artistic activity*. Berkeley, CA: University of California Press.

Schaverien, J. (1992). *The revealing image: Analytical art psychotherapy in theory & practice*. London: Routledge.

Schaverien, J. (1995). *Desire & the female therapist: Engendered gazes in psychotherapy & art therapy*. London: Routledge.

Schaverien, J., & Killick, K. (Eds.). (1997). *Art, psychotherapy & psychosis*. New York: Routledge.

Schilder, P. (1950). *The image & appearance of the human body*. New York: John Wiley & Sons.

Schildkrout, M. S., Schenker, I. R. & Sonnenblick, M. (1972). *Human figure drawings in adolescence*. New York: Brunner/Mazel.

Schreiber, F. R. (1974). *Sybil*. New York: Warner Books.

Sechehaye, M. (1951). *Symbolic realization*. New York: International Universities Press.

Selfe, L. (1978). *Nadia: A case of extraordinary drawing ability in an autistic child*. New York: Academic Press.

Senior, P., & Croall, J. (1993). *Helping to heal: The arts in health care*. London: Calouste Gulbenkian Foundation.

Shaw, R. F. (1934). *Finger painting*. Boston: Little, Brown.

Sherman, J. T. (1994). *Dreams & memories*. Madison, NH: Heart's Desire.

Shoemaker, R. J. (1983). *The rainbow booklet*. Wisconsin: Renewing Visions Press.

Silver, R. A. (1978/1986). *Developing cognitive & creative skills through art*. Baltimore, MD: University Park Press.

Silver, R. A. (1983). *Silver drawing test of cognition and emotion* (3rd ed., 1996). Sarasota, FL: Ablin Press.

Silver, R. A. (1989). *Stimulus drawings & techniques*. Sarasota, FL: Ablin Press.

Silver, R. A. (1993). *Draw a story* (Rev. ed.). Sarasota, FL: Ablin Press.

Silverstone, L. (1997). *Art therapy—the person-centred way* (2nd ed.). London: Jessica Kingsley.

Simon, R. (1992). *The symbolism of style*. London: Routledge.

Simon, R. (1997). *Symbolic images in art as therapy*. London: Routledge.

Simonds, S. L. (1994). *Bridging the silence*. New York: W. W. Norton & Sons.

Singer, F. (1980). *Structuring child behavior through visual art*. Springfield, IL: Charles C. Thomas.

Skaife, S., & Huet, V. (Eds.) (1998). *Art psychotherapy groups*. London: Routledge.

Smith, S. L. (1979). *No easy answers*. Cambridge, MA: Winthrop.

Spaniol, S. E. (1990). *Organizing exhibitions of art by people with mental illness: A step-by-step manual*. Boston: Boston Univ. Center for Psychiatric Rehabilitation.

Spencer, L. B. (1997). *Heal abuse & trauma through art*. Springfield, IL: Charles C. Thomas.

Spring, D. (1993). *Shattered images*. Chicago: Magnolia Street Publishers.

Stevens, A. (1986). *Withymead*. London: Coventure.

Thevoz, M. (1976). *Art brut*. New York: Skira.

Thomas, G. V., & Silk, M. J. (1990). *An introduction to the psychology of children's drawings*. New York: New York University Press.

Thomson, M. (1989). *On art & therapy*. London: Virago.

Trechsel, G. A. (Ed.) (1995). *Pictured in my mind: Contemporary American self-taught art*. Birmingham, AL: Birmingham Museum of Art.

Ude-Pestel, A. (1977). *Betty: History & art of a child in therapy*. Palo Alto, CA: Science & Behavior Books.

Uhlin, D. M. (1972). *Art for exceptional children* (3rd ed. 1984, with Edith De Chiara). Dubuque, IA: Wm. C. Brown Co.

Ulanov, A. B. (1994). *The wizard's gate: Picturing consciousness*. Einsiedeln, Switzerland: Daimon Verlag.

Ulman, E., & Dachinger, P. (Eds.) (1975/1996). *Art therapy in theory & practice* New York: Schocken Press. (reprinted 1996, Chicago: Magnolia Street Publishers).

Ulman, E., Kramer, E., & Kwiatkowska, H. Y. (1977). *Art therapy in the United States*. Craftsbury Common, VT: Art Therapy Publications.

Ulman, E., & Levy, C. (Eds.) (1981). *Art therapy viewpoints*. New York: Schocken Press.

Viola, W. (1942). *Child art & Franz Cizek*. London: Univ. London Press.

Virshup, E. (1978). *Right brain people in a left brain world*. Los Angeles, CA: Art Therapy West.

Virshup, E. (Ed.). (1993). *California art therapy trends*. Chicago: Magnolia Street Publishers.

Volavkova, H. (Ed.) (1962). *I never saw another butterfly: Children's drawings from Terezin concentration camp*. New York: McGraw-Hill.

Wadeson, H. (1980). *Art psychotherapy*. New York: John Wiley & Sons.

Wadeson, H. (1987). *The dynamics of art psychotherapy*. New York: John Wiley & Sons.

Wadeson, H., Durkin, J., & Perach, D. (Eds.). (1989). *Advances in art therapy*. New York: John Wiley & Sons.

Wadeson, H. (1992). (Ed.) *A guide to conducting art therapy research*. Mundelein, IL: American Art Therapy Association.

Wallace, E. (1990). *A queen's quest*. Santa Fe, NM: Moon Bear.

Waller, D. (1991). *Becoming a profession: The history of art therapy in Britain, 1940–1982*. London: Tavistock.

Waller, D. (1993). *Group interactive art therapy*. New York: Routledge.

Waller, D. (1998). *Towards a European art therapy*. Buckingham, UK: Open University Press.

Waller, D., & Gilroy, A. (Eds.). (1992). *Art therapy: A handbook*. Buckingham, UK: Open University Press.

Waller, D., & Mahoney, J. (Eds.). (1998). *Treatment of addiction: Current issues for art therapists*. London: Routledge.

Warren, B. (Ed.). (1984). *Using the creative arts in therapy* (2nd ed. 1993). New York: Routledge.

Watkins, J. G. (1992). *Hypnoanalytic techniques*. New York: Irvington.

Watkins, M. M. (1976). *Waking dreams*. New York: Gordon & Breach.

Weaver, R. (1973). *The old wise woman*. New York: Putnam's.

Weiser, J. (1993). *Phototherapy techniques*. San Francisco, CA: Jossey-Bass.

Weiss, J. (1984). *Expressive therapy with elders & the disabled*. New York: The Haworth Press.

Wilkinson, V. C., & Heater, S. L. (1979). *Therapeutic media & techniques of application*. New York: Van Nostrand Reinhold.

Williams, G. H., & Wood, M. M. (1977). *Developmental art therapy*. Baltimore, MD: University Park Press.

Winner, E. (1982). *Invented worlds: The psychology of the arts*. Cambridge, MA.: Harvard University Press.

Winnicott, D. W. (1971). *Therapeutic consultations in child psychiatry*. New York: Basic Books.

Winnicott, D. W. (1972). *Playing & reality*. New York: Basic Books.

Wohl, A., & Kaufman, B. (1985). *Silent screams & hidden cries*. New York: Brunner/Mazel.

Wysuph, C. L. (1970). *Jackson Pollock: Psychoanalytic drawings*. New York: Horizon.

Zinker, J. (1977). *Creative process in gestalt therapy*. New York: Brunner/Mazel.

Index

SUBJECT INDEX

NAME INDEX